PRAISE FOR *WASTED TALENT*

"All of us who love our country but are looking for solutions to the compelling problem of how we must train, develop, and treat our workers need to put *Wasted Talent* on a must-read list. Sam Caucci has written a book that is not an academic argument—it's a battle cry for a better future of work. This book is both bracing and hopeful."

—Senator Bob Kerrey, former U.S. senator, governor, and U.S. Navy SEAL

"Sam gets it. Identifying talent is only the first step. A person's potential can only be fulfilled if they are put in the right environment for their unique blend of talents. There is no one-size-fits-all model. *Wasted Talent* is essential for those looking for a twenty-first-century approach to managing our most important resource—us!"

—Joe Baker, PhD, author, *The Tyranny of Talent*, and professor, University of Toronto

"In his new book *Wasted Talent*, Sam Caucci lays out a compelling plan for transforming the working life. Work is, in fact, a scam, and we must build something better to replace the current system. With humor, candor, and personality, Caucci's polemical style will both captivate readers and inspire change."

—Jamie McCallum, author, *Essential: How the Pandemic Transformed the Long Fight for Worker Justice*

"Sam writes with the clarity and compassion that this moment demands. *Wasted Talent* offers both a mirror and a map for leaders ready to do better by their people."

—Julie Lythcott-Haims, *New York Times* bestselling author of *How to Raise an Adult* and former dean of freshmen and undergraduate advising at Stanford University

"Great teams aren't built on talent alone—they're built on systems that nurture that talent every day. This isn't just a book—it's a challenge to every coach, manager, and executive: are you developing your people, or just managing them?"

—Kirk Everist, two-time U.S. Olympian, five-time national champion, and head men's water polo coach, University of California, Berkeley

"*Wasted Talent* is a great fountain of new ideas for any leader claiming to care about their people. Caucci explains outdated systems that hold employees back and offers new, alternative ideas born of his research, lived experiences, and expert input. Find out what's not working, why, and what to do instead."

—Jamie Madigan, gamer and expert on the psychology of video games, contributor to *Washington Post*, *The Guardian*, *BBC*, *CNET*, and more.

"Who is in front of me, and how do we balance what they want and what they need in order to develop? That is the question we teach coaches to ask about developing athletes, and it is exactly how companies need to start thinking about their people. Get to know them, give them both the soft and hard skills to succeed, challenge them, and create an environment and time for them to thrive. That is the best way to not only identify and develop the talent that shouts, but the talent that whispers. This book will show you how it's done."

—John O'Sullivan, author, *Every Moment Matters: How the World's Best Coaches Inspire Their Athletes and Build Championship Teams*, and founder, Changing the Game Project

"Work clearly isn't working. In his new book *Wasted Talent*, Sam Caucci presents a clear, practical pathway to revolutionize work for everyone—employers and employees. Caucci draws on unparalleled experience and insight to reveal a refreshing win-win strategy for anyone who wants to succeed in modern business and leadership."

—Fergus Connolly, author, *59 Lessons: Working with the World's Elite Coaches, Athletes, and Special Forces*

"Opportunity should be a gateway, not a barrier. In *Wasted Talent*, Sam Caucci charts a clear path forward through practical insights and innovative solutions, showing us how to build a future where talent can truly flourish—regardless of background. A vital blueprint for creating meaningful and developmental opportunities in today's workplace."

—Shadae McDaniel, SVP of Programs and Strategic Initiatives, All Stars Project

"*Wasted Talent* by Sam Caucci should be de rigueur reading for any management team. It is full of ideas, tips, and helpful comments that are revealing and enlightening."

—Chef Ken Hom, internationally renowned chef, author, television show presenter for the *BBC*, and pioneer of modern Asian cuisine

"Sam Caucci reminds us what it means to be seen. He uplifts the workers who are too often invisible—those returning from prison, those in recovery, and those juggling multiple jobs to provide for themselves and their families. *Wasted Talent* gives voice to those voices and demands we do better as a community. I am proud to stand with Sam in that call."

—Jim McGreevey, chairman of the board and executive director, New Jersey Reentry Corporation

"This book hits home. Talent alone doesn't win championships in football, business, or life. *Wasted Talent* reveals how building the right systems and support structures unlocks real potential. It's a playbook for developing people that's been long overdue."

—Glenn Cook, assistant general manager and vice president of player personnel, Cleveland Browns

"The current work environment is toxic and extremely inefficient at best. If you are looking for an authentic, common-sense solution that can and should be implemented right now, Sam Caucci in his book *Wasted Talent* has done the grunt work. It deserves a serious look."

—Tom Sterner, author, *The Practicing Mind, Fully Engaged,* and *It's Just a Thought*

"In the world of elite sports, the difference between good and great often comes down to coaching. After working with 160-plus championship teams, the best teams rise when leaders choose to coach—not control. Sam Caucci's *Wasted Talent* delivers that same message to every workplace in America. If you care about building a team that performs at its highest level, this book is your playbook. It is a call to lead differently, to develop people fully, and to win with heart. Every CEO should read this."

—Dr. Jerry Lynch, bestselling author and performance consultant to more than 160 NCAA and professional championship teams

"Champions aren't born; they're built. *Wasted Talent* is Sam Caucci's game plan to stop wasting potential and start creating champions in the workforce."

—Martin Rooney, internationally recognized trainer, speaker, author, and pioneer of strength and conditioning

"*Wasted Talent* is a must-read for every educator and executive shaping the future of work. As someone who prepares students for careers in sport and entertainment, I see firsthand how our systems overlook potential. This book is a powerful reminder—and road map—for building a world where every worker gets a real shot."

—Michelle Harrolle, PhD, director, University of South Florida MBA in Sport and Entertainment Management— Vinik Sport & Entertainment Program

"Drawing from research into the science of learning, Sam Caucci is a leader in frontline training. Lean into this book."

—Peter C. Brown, coauthor of *Make It Stick: The Science of Successful Learning*

"Whether you are in the classroom, boardroom, assembly line, in the office, or working from home, 'one-and-done' learning is often inefficient. In order to truly commit items to memory and to retrieve this information on command, you need to put in the work. As stated in the book *Make It Stick*, 'Learning that is easy is like writing in the sand, here today and gone tomorrow.' Sam Caucci in *Wasted Talent* shows how better learning and development can unlock talent and create real opportunities for every worker."

—Patrice M. Bain, Ed.S., educator and author, *Powerful Teaching*

"Work is done by people. Sam exposes the short-term mindsets that have led us to underinvest in humanity's most critical resource—people—and shows the path forward to create jobs that work for everyone."

—Scott Young, *Wall Street Journal* bestselling author, *Ultralearning: Master Hard Skills, Outsmart the Competition, and Accelerate Your Career*

amplify
an imprint of Amplify Publishing Group

www.amplifypublishinggroup.com

Wasted Talent: How Greed, Exploitation, and the Promise of the Future of Work Has Failed the Front Line, and a Plan to Fix It

For more information, please contact:
Amplify Publishing, an imprint of Amplify Publishing Group
620 Herndon Parkway, Suite 220
Herndon, VA 20170
info@amplifypublishing.com

Library of Congress Control Number: 2025902324

CPSIA Code: PRV0725A

ISBN-13: 979-8-89138-017-2

Printed in the United States

To my mom, for teaching me how to show up.

WASTED
TALENT

How Greed, Exploitation, *and*
the **Promise** *of the* **Future** *of*
Work *has* **Failed** *the* **Front Line,**
and a **Plan** *to* **Fix It**

SAM CAUCCI

amplify
an imprint of Amplify Publishing Group

CONTENTS

Introduction

Why do we love work but hate on workers?

This is a story about work. Now, before you put this book down and head for the door, let me explain.

I've spent time with hundreds of thousands of workers over the years, and our conversations have impacted how I look at work and the people who make work happen. I appreciate their trust and willingness to share while being in a position that is vulnerable to attack. For this reason, I have chosen not to identify the individuals by name and, in some instances, have changed some background details to avoid blowback from any bad bosses out there.

I will share my point of view. This is the fun part for me and clearly the best part of writing a book. I get to say what I want. And, of course, you get to come to your own conclusions.

I will share numbers. Some are mine, but many have been taken from elsewhere to tell the story. I will do my best to source data appropriately, but this is not an academic book and shouldn't be judged as such. Know that the numbers are well researched, fact-checked, and from trusted sources.

And finally, I will speak to multiple audiences. This is a book for anyone who cares about our future—CEOs, senior leadership, human resources, frontline managers, parents, teachers, government officials, and, of course, employees.

Let's begin.

0.44 SECONDS

The future of work.

Something about that phrase is catchy. Like a good political slogan, it's both sticky and intriguing. Everybody has an interest in what the future holds. And given how much we work, we can't help but have some kind of emotional reaction when we consider the word that consumes most of our waking minutes.

The future of work is everywhere. Literally and figuratively. The term shows up in everything from news articles to political debates to conference programs. I took to Google to really wrap my head around all the different definitions and points of viewaround this popular buzz phrase. It took Google only 0.44 seconds to come back with 3.89 billion results.

Books, news articles, magazine pieces, TV shows, documentaries, and podcasts cover the topic. If you're looking for information on the future of work, stop reading and head to Google. I'm not going to talk about the future of work.

Still here? Let's continue.

60 SECONDS ABOUT ME

Allow me to introduce myself.

I won't get into too much detail. After all, this book isn't about me. But a little personal background is par for the course when you write a book. And I always find understanding a bit about the experiences or background of an author is helpful.

I guess everybody sees their family as being a little different; I'm no exception. My mom is from Philadelphia and grew up in a family that decided to pay for the boy to go to school and not the girl. She ended up dropping out of high school to enroll in secretarial school. She would go on to spend the next fifty-four years as a legal secretary. My dad graduated high school and went into construction. He was in that up to the end. My experiences watching my parents work stick with me to this day.

They both moved to Miami in the 1960s, the place I would go on to call home. My parents divorced when I was six. My mom remarried. After graduating from high school, I decided to pass on an opportunity to play college football. I needed to get right to work to help out my family. My mother's second husband had unexpectedly passed away, and my dad had just returned from prison. I felt a responsibility to help out.

I enrolled in college with an eighteen-credit course load while working full time. I was hired to be the first salesperson for a new sports training facility for professional athletes. It was an awesome job. Like any new hire, I wasn't really sure what I was doing—but I was doing it. Over the years I would go on to work with thousands of the most elite professional athletes in the world, as well as their respective coaches and sports agents.

In 2008 I went on to coach and manage sales teams for Life Time Fitness, an upscale chain of fitness clubs. I grand-opened their brand new 165,000-square-foot fitness facility in New Jersey. This move brought me into a corporate environment, where I began to get a real understanding of how large companies work and how they think about workers.

Then I spent a couple years leading franchise sales and sales training for the Parisi Speed School, a sports performance fitness concept with forty-six locations in the United States. I helped grow the brand to more than seventy locations and our first international franchisees.

After these experiences, I had an idea. (OK, every entrepreneur says that.) In my experience to this point, every company I worked with struggled with training. It was a common complaint: They either can't find the right workers, or the workers don't do what's right. My idea was to create a technology company that better prepared workers for work but wasn't built on boring e-learning videos you were forced to watch or manuals you would rarely read. It would be different.

I wanted to make training for a job more engaging and even more effective. The idea was to create a mobile app where a company could transform any new employee onboarding, training, or communication into a competitive game. So, in 2015 I started 1Huddle.

As I look back, I didn't really know what I was doing. But I got to work. I hired a software development team, came up with a logo, created a pitch deck, and started selling. We got invited into the 500 Startups (now called 500 Global) tech accelerator program and moved to Silicon Valley, where we spent the next year building out the product, and I even joined the ranks of tech founders that did the sleep on couches thing. After pitching hundreds of venture capital investors from New York to Silicon Valley, we raised a few rounds of funding. Then we met a new venture capital firm in Newark, New Jersey that didn't just invest in us, but invited us to move to Newark to build the business. I moved to Newark in 2017. I still remember walking down Broad Street for the first time, looking around at a city that had been written off by so many yet was still fighting. My experiences in Newark would go on to directly contribute to the workforce development platform we created. These experiences gave me the opportunity to have countless conversations with frontline workers, managers, and leaders across dozens of industries.

Over the next few years, I engaged with the community. I felt the responsibility to get more involved, given my line of work. I slept outside to end youth homelessness with Covenant House, and I volunteered with the New Jersey Reentry Corporation to assist court-involved people with employment and career development. I was then invited to serve on the Newark Workforce Development Board by Mayor Ras Baraka, where I currently chair the city's Tech Taskforce. I also was invited to join the Biden–Harris 2020 policy committee, where I got to work writing policy that would be a part of President Biden's Day 1 executive actions and workforce innovation policy platform. And since 2018, I've been an adjunct professor for the Global Sports Business graduate school program at Rutgers University.

I enjoy the work. These experiences have taught me that while I can only do so much, I can do something. It's the limits that make the work we do so important.

I have hired, trained, and developed employees. I have had to be the one executing the layoff. I have fundraised from venture capital. I have run dozens of board meetings in defense of a business plan. I have taught at the university level. I have slept outside to end youth homelessness. I have written policy for a presidential campaign. I have keynoted at conferences across the globe.

I couldn't fit it all neatly on this book jacket but felt it was important to share.

Now, let's talk about the more important stuff.

WHY I WROTE THIS BOOK

Writing this book has been a challenge.

It has brought top of mind all I know and have experienced about work. From the construction workers I grew up working with, to my mother answering phones at the law office, to writing letters to my father in prison, to my wife working in soul-crushing big law as a Black woman, to the hundreds of thousands of frontline workers in everything from retail to restaurants I met onboarding on 1Huddle, to the adjuncts in higher education, to my niece working her summer job at the ice cream stand with a fear-mongering owner, to the many others I have read or heard about—they have all filled me with anger, sadness, and a call to act.

I wrote this book for one reason. To encourage all leaders to better see their people.

It is discouraging and disappointing to see what is focused on today—and the many fraudulent "leaders" who run rampant. It feels like every week a new documentary is released glamorizing the life of some scam artist who made it big by making most of it up.

Billy McFarland with Fyre Festival, Adam Neuner with WeWork, Anna Delvey with whatever it is she was, Elizabeth Holmes with Theranos, Sam Bankman-Fried the fraudulent crypto guy whose parents teach legal ethics at Stanford Law, and don't forget Bernie Madoff.

All scams. But what about the scam most people experience every day?

Work is also a scam. So many spend most of their lives selling their time, and usually aren't paid anywhere near what their true impact is to the organization that signs their check. Data will support my argument in the coming pages. Over the years, as the cost of living has gone up and wages have stagnated, these workers have had to spend more of their time on someone else's clock just to barely survive. And in many cases real wages have even declined. They're paying the most while being paid the least. Our frontline workers today are the driving force behind our economy. They aren't just the backbone; they're the foundation by which any business success happens. And this foundation is cracking.

We give up so much of our lives so a few selfish assholes can be rich. This reality divides us: one part for work, whatever is left over for everything else that is life.

Is this the way work is supposed to be?

I'M TALKING TO YOU

This book is for every worker. Not just managers. Not just owners. It's written to be a call to action.

And if you're on the front line, as over 80 percent of the U.S. workforce is, and you're reading this, know that I'm talking to you.

IT IS TIME FOR CHANGE.

DISCLAIMER

Fair warning. What I'm about to write may offend you. Please know that I'm not attacking your job, your role, your work, your passions—but I do intend to interrogate work.

I want to talk about work from the front line, from the daily life of the people who do the work.

You won't hear me saying, "I have the answer" or "This is the only way." Instead, I just want to lay out some facts and some data about working today, along with some of my own opinions, of course. And then you can decide for yourself.

I've spent my career on the front lines. I've watched my mom work 9 to 5 in a job where the only reason she was typing the memos instead of defending them in court was because of a lack of opportunity. I've watched my dad sit in prison, receive no job training opportunities, and then struggle to find work after his release. I've talked to workers across the globe about their work experience. I've talked to great leaders—and my fair share of bad ones. The bad ones may be to blame for my tone of voice at times. I'll try to maintain my composure. But just know, I may come off a bit angry.

You'll get used to me.

PART I

WHY DO WE WORK?

Blessed and rich is he who's wise in
all these things—and who works.

—HESIOD, *WORKS AND DAYS (700 BC)*

CHAPTER 1

A Brief History of Work: From Zeus to Gen Z

Who doesn't like a history lesson?

If we really want to talk about where work started, we must go back to the beginning. But as I've learned, when you start to look at the origins of things like work, you immediately find yourself wrapped up not just in science and religion, but in mythology.

And as the story goes, the creation of work goes back to the boss of all bosses, the Greek god Zeus.

MYTHOLOGY x WORK

In one of the earliest training manuals ever written, dating back to around 700 BC, the Greek poet Hesiod was instructing his brother on the fundamentals of farming when he shared a bit of the origins of work:

> For the gods keep hidden from men the means of life.
> Else you would easily do work enough in a day to supply
> you for a full year even without working; soon would
> you put away your rudder over the smoke, and the fields

worked by ox and sturdy mule would run to waste. But Zeus in the anger of his heart hid it, because Prometheus the crafty deceived him; therefore he planned sorrow and mischief against men. He hid fire.

So we have Zeus to blame. He was tricked by a mortal and took out his anger by punishing all humankind with "work." Hesiod went on to say that Zeus concealed from humans the knowledge of how to sustain themselves on the basis of only a day's labor.

It's good to be a god.

4.5 BILLION YEARS AGO

The earth was formed around 4.5 billion years ago. Animal life began to form around 540 million years ago, and to really put this whole show in perspective, human life formed just 300,000 years ago.[1]

Time really does fly.

Nearly fifty thousand years ago, humans began their migration out of Africa by traveling in small nomadic groups, kind of the original labor union. They then spent the next thirty thousand years as hunter-gatherers. Around twelve thousand years ago, humans began to abandon the hunter-gatherer model and settled down to be cultivators. (As a point of artistic note, some researchers believe the discovery of alcohol in the form of beer and wine played a part in the decision to stop moving around so much. More on that must be reserved for another book.)

The hunters and gatherers were gradually displaced by permanent settlements of farmers. As humans began to crowd into smaller spaces, about eight thousand years ago, a lot changed in their lives. In addition to a big change to personal hygiene and diet, the birthrate spiked, and the global population began to grow. States and societies with social classes with different kinds of work began to emerge.[2]

As time has gone on, it's become clear that working is a part of what we do and how we survive. Society has exploited our eagerness to create, build, explore, and trade by organizing itself in a way that work is required to survive.[3]

Work has been something we have worked really hard at for the last few centuries.

THE LAST FEW CENTURIES

In the fourteenth century, the creation of the clock tower enabled the breaking up of time into hourly units. This contributed to the eventual creation of the time clock and the common phrases "clocking in" and "clocking out."

In the sixteenth century, work came to be seen as not just important but as the "essence of life." It wasn't all about working to live; it was more that we were being conditioned to the concept that we live to work. In the 1840s, the essayist Thomas Carlyle proved the success of this campaign by saying, "A man perfects himself by working."[4]

The philosophy on workers in the time before the Industrial Revolution, which started around 1750, was beginning to develop structure and shape. That structure didn't really have a history that cared that much about the worker. Bethany Moreton, a professor of history at Dartmouth University, said the approach to building a workforce before the Industrial Revolution was, "You could capture one, enslave one, marry one, adopt one or give birth to one."[5]

It was also at this time that we began to see a shift in the way we valued labor. Prior to this era, work was based on "producerism," where work was a value and the only real producer of value. However, it was now time for a new approach, "consumerism." Now capital, not labor, creates wealth.

This shift away from the worker being the source of value in the market created an environment for the wealthy and corporations to suppress wages, reduce the bargaining power of workers, and attack the poor. Andrew Carnegie, an early founder of the steel industry and one of the richest Americans in history, along with some of his ultra-rich industrial buddies launched a cultural campaign in churches, schools, and universities to change the point of view of workers. He would argue that capital, not labor, is the primary source of wealth and prosperity. Carnegie would be quoted as saying, "Coddling the poor with high wages was not good for the race."[6]

In the twentieth century, it was time to put some permanent structure around the shifts in how capitalists control labor. Enter a guy you may have never heard of, but you should. You have him to thank for the origin of a term that you can't go a day at work without hearing and a department you try to constantly avoid.

THE FIRST HR REP

Frederick Winslow Taylor, a mechanical engineer and efficiency expert, wrote *The Principles of Scientific Management* in 1911. If you read it today, it most likely will bore you to death, but you have him and his book to thank for the creation of the concept of management and the death of an economy centered on the worker. This book laid the foundation for "human resources management" and the design of the business unit centered on keeping "humans" under control.

So, you can think of Fredo as the first HR executive. (Fredo is my preferred shortening for Frederick Winslow Taylor. Think of it as an homage—and in no way do I mean to insult the intelligence of Fredo Corleone from *The Godfather*.)

Fredo's principles for managers quickly gained popularity. The foundation of the model was his four principles of scientific management:[7]

1. Develop a science for each element of a man's work.
2. Scientifically select and then train, teach, and develop the workman.
3. Collaborate with the workmen to ensure all the work being done is in accordance with the principles of the science which has been developed.
4. The management will take over all work for which they are better fitted than the workmen.

Taylorism, as it became known, was soon picked up by another notable entrepreneur you might recognize—Henry Ford. In the early days of his entrepreneurial journey, Henry Ford recognized that this new concept of management meant he didn't have to hire workers with skills; he just had to hire people who would follow orders.[8]

That brings me to my favorite Henry Ford quote, one that truly encompasses the beliefs behind an entrepreneur who is heralded as an American hero: "Why do I always get the whole person when all I want is a pair of hands?"

Good guy.

Wall Street investor Steven Berkenfield expanded on this quote in an attempt to modernize it to the logic of the Henry Ford wannabes of today. While being interviewed for *Raising the Floor* by Andy Stern, the former head of the SEIU (Service Employees International Union), he said:

> Why do I always get the whole person when all I want is a pair of hands? If I could just hire someone and put them in a box for 30 years that would be great. But it doesn't work that way. If I hire someone I've gotta train them, manage them and fire them. I got to worry about them getting sick, their parents getting sick, their kids and dog getting sick. If a woman gets pregnant and goes on maternity leave for 3 months I have to figure out how to cover for her. She might feel discriminated against, or harassed. People want to know where they stand, to get a performance review at the end of year and eventually a promotion. I have to work out health benefits, severance and vacation schedules. It goes on and on.[9]

EFFICIENCY

Prior to capitalism, labor was specialized but still task-oriented, meaning workers used to do a variety of tasks, completing each one from beginning to end. With capitalism, a profound change happened. On the very first page of Adam Smith's *The Wealth of Nations,* published in 1776, the author described how dividing the process on a pin factory assembly line into eighteen specific steps across ten workers would result in each worker creating

4,800 pins in a day—and that absent this process, a worker would likely fail to produce even one pin. This breaking up of tasks into subtasks that can be performed by "unskilled" labor became a key workforce strategy.

Another popular model that focuses on the division of labor is called the Babbage principle, named for the mathematician Charles Babbage, inventor of the first computer. This approach expanded the number of workers who could perform a job while reducing the overall cost of labor. This opened up the workforce in many ways. Children and women could be employed on simple jobs that had been broken down from more complex tasks. This increased the potential to hire cheap labor and placed downward pressure on wages. It also just made it easier for managers to exert pressure and control the lives of workers.

MAKING DEALS AND FREE TRADE

In the 1930s President Franklin D. Roosevelt helped workers as the country transitioned out of the Great Depression. Seen as an encroachment by conservatives and business owners, the New Deal made it clear that the federal government would play a part in the lives of workers through regulations, public projects, and financial reforms. The New Deal introduced a variety of new federal programs and initiatives, including the creation of Social Security, unemployment insurance, the establishment of the National Labor Relations Board, and the forty-hour work week.

The modern era of free trade—trade policy that doesn't restrict imports and exports—began in the 1950s. Free trade agreements with other nations would be a big opportunity for American companies by providing access to new markets and investment. It also had some downsides for the American worker by putting workers, mostly factory workers at the start, into direct competition with some of the hungriest workers on the globe.

The effects of free trade agreements were seen as a success for the global economy and providing more buying power for the average American, regardless of wage class.

While it may be true that you can now buy cheaper imported goods in more abundance at your local Walmart, it is also true that we haven't done enough on the wage front for workers whose jobs were directly impacted by these agreements. The U.S. spends far less per capita than countries across Europe on compensating and retraining workers who lose their jobs due to the impact of a free trade agreement.[10]

We'll talk more about this later.

PRODUCTIVITY

Then came the 1980s.

Since the 1940s, data shows that as productivity rose, so did wages. This was the way the model was intended to work—those at the bottom would be able to share in the nation's economic growth. That came to an end in the 1970s under the Nixon administration. In the 1980s, the importance of workers in our economy was reduced even more.

As productivity (including output and GDP) continued to soar from 1979 to the present, wages have stagnated for all except the highest paid. Some have called this separation of wages from productivity "The Great Decoupling." According to the Department of Labor, from 1979 to 2019:

- Worker productivity grew 59.7 percent while worker pay grew by only 15.8 percent.
- Productivity has grown 3.5 times as much as the pay for the typical worker.
- U.S. workers gained an 11.7 percent rise in real wages between 1978 and 2016, while CEOs experienced a 937 percent increase (adjusted for inflation).

This is what the Economic Policy Institute has to say about the period: "Intentional policy choices creating rising inequality: both the top 10 percent and especially the top 1 percent and top 0.1 percent gained a much larger share of all compensation and labor's share of income eroded."[11]

They go on to say in 2021 that if the median hourly compensation had grown at the same rate as productivity (over the period of 1979 to 2019), the median worker would be making $27.00 per hour. A far cry from the federal minimum wage of $7.25 per hour as of 2024.

So, why is this happening?

TODAY

Today, workers fall into two buckets:

1. those selling their time, and
2. those buying the time and profiting from it.

All this while every company is trying to do more with less.

New technological advancements have expanded on Fredo Taylor's principles and Chuck Babbage's philosophy. Just pause and look at the impact on the auto industry. In 1950 each General Motors employee made an average of seven cars per year. In 1990 they made thirteen cars per year, and as of 2023 they make thirty-eight cars per year.

Being more efficient has been the pursuit of businesses for the last century and more. It hasn't resulted in better jobs—just different ones. In 1970, 25 percent of all American workers were in manufacturing. Today, less than 10 percent are in it. They have migrated to the service sector, which now employs eight in ten workers. From 2007 to 2009, in the aftermath of the Great Recession, new low-wage service jobs have taken the place of higher-wage manufacturing jobs. Economists believe these types of service sector jobs emerged as a solution to lagging employment growth and created a new class of low-wage workers that includes workers in the gig economy, healthcare, fast food, retail, and delivery drivers. These workers were also the ones most impacted financially and personally by the recessionary effects of the COVID-19 pandemic.[12]

This has resulted in less security for workers. Over the last few decades, the attack on union organizing has directly weakened union membership and resulted in workers being more vulnerable and having less of a voice about what happens at work. Throughout the 1950s and 1960s nearly 33 percent of U.S. workers were members of a union, but as of 2023 only one in ten belong to one. If you don't know much about unions, you may be opposed to them. Union actions always seem to be trying to mess up your morning Starbucks run or slow down your same-day Prime delivery. At the same time, we aren't necessarily against all unions. Some of our bravest and most respected heroes belong to unions—nurses, police, firefighters.[13]

We just don't like them for certain people.

FRONTLINE WORKERS

We call them frontline workers and essential workers, and they've always already been essential.

—Alissa Quart, author of *Bootstrapped: Liberating Ourselves from the American Dream,* professor at Columbia University, and executive director of the Economic Hardships Reporting Project, in our conversation on the *Bring It In* podcast[*]

As of 2024, 3.3 billion global workers are frontline workers—people who work directly with customers, clients, or other recipients of services. In the U.S., 82 percent of workers are in frontline jobs. Half of those are in low-wage service sector jobs. These numbers mirror some other economies. In the United Kingdom, 83 percent of working people now work in the service sector.[14]

They are servers in a restaurant, nurses in a medical office, clerks in a grocery store, and workers at a construction site. These were the workers in the eye of the storm during the pandemic.

A few more stats on today's U.S. workforce:

- One in three work in either government, education, or the health services sectors (civil servants, teachers, nurses).[15]
- One in four work in retail, leisure, and hospitality.[16]
- One in five work in professional services.[17]
- Two in three jobs are in local services, a number that has been rising over the last fifty years.[18]
- Two in three are women.
- Three in four earn wages below the national average.[19]

---

[*] I have included exclusive quotes taken from interviews I have had with guests on the *Bring It In* podcast throughout the book. Links to each of those episodes can be found on page 363.

Wages

Out of the six industries that make up the majority of frontline jobs, five are in the service sector and a significant percentage of workers make less than 200 percent of the poverty line. These jobs include grocery workers, convenience store workers, drugstore workers, building cleaning services workers, healthcare workers, childcare workers, transit workers, social service workers, warehouse workers, and postal service workers.

Since the Great Recession in 2007, our society has relied more and more on this servant economy that is primarily composed of low-wage workers. These workers are disproportionately women. These workers are disproportionately people of color. And these workers are underpaid.

Race

By May 2020, 41.2 percent of frontline workers were people of color. They are overrepresented in low-wage occupations, like those listed above. This is also true for most of the top ten occupations, in trucking, warehousing, childcare, social services, personal care aides, social workers, and building cleaning services. They are also overrepresented in the top ten healthcare occupations, except physicians, nurses, managers, and secretaries.[20]

Our frontline workers are more racially diverse than any other corner of the U.S. workforce. They are less formally educated than the rest, with fewer than 50 percent having a high school diploma.[21] They also have no room for error. These frontline workers show up every day with basically no financial cushion or paid sick leave that would let them to take time off if they got sick (by let's say a virus?).

Flexibility

During the pandemic, work from home was not an opportunity that everyone could participate in. While high-wage workers had the opportunity to work from home and receive paid sick leave, our frontline workers weren't offered the same deal.

Frontline workers don't get to choose.

They are expected to show up.

Vulnerable

Frontline workers care about when they work, how they get work done, training and development opportunities, benefits, and that their voice is heard. But this isn't happening, especially for contingent workers, better known as gig workers.

Gig workers are basically low-wage labor hired temporarily or as needed for a specific task. They perform all types of work today, including acting as your personal chauffeur, bringing you dinner, doing your grocery shopping, and putting together your furniture.

They often get hired to do all this work via a transaction on an app. You use the app to hire them and aren't burdened by normal employer responsibilities. Isn't that convenient? Of course, you still even conduct your own performance review after they complete their work by rating a delivery or giving a thumbs-up or down. Companies have made it too easy for customers to manage their employees so they don't have to.

WORKERS AREN'T ENGAGED

Sitting at a café in Washington, D.C., I overheard a conversation between two people who work together; one had been out on vacation for the last few weeks:

> Coworker #1: Have you been back to the office yet?
> Coworker #2: Not yet.
> Coworker #1: Good. Don't come back.
> Coworker #1 and #2: [insert laughing]

It's the Manager, a 2019 book from Gallup, is centered on thirty years of research that included thousands of studies of sixty million workers across forty-nine industries and seventy-three countries. The authors also talked with CHROs for three hundred of the largest global companies.[22] To summarize the book: Not many people like work today.

Now, it isn't news to most leaders that workers are struggling with engagement. However, the studies in the book showed that only 15 percent of global employees are engaged at work.[23] Gallup has followed up in reports as recent as April 2023 to estimate that poor management and lack of productivity by disengaged employees is costing the global economy $8.8 trillion a year, or 9 percent of global gross domestic product.[24]

In addition to low engagement, Gallup's surveys found workplace stress levels remained at a record high going back to 2021, with 44 percent of respondents saying they'd experienced stress for a "lot of the day" on the previous day at work.[25]

The interesting part about the Gallup data is employee disengagement has always been a problem, regardless of generation. However, we should take notice of how Gen Z (those born between the late 1990s and early 2010s) is thinking about work, given the reality that this demographic, which makes up about 20 percent of the population as of 2023, is going to make up the majority of our workforce in the near future.

But Gen Z isn't happy. I'd be pissed too if I missed the nineties. But let me stay on track here . . .

Among the four generations currently in the workforce, Gen Z is the most vocal in expressing dissatisfaction with work, according to recent surveys. They're the most likely to say they're frustrated or overwhelmed by work and the most likely to quit quietly. A survey in 2023 of 2,417 U.S. adults found that Gen Z was more likely to report quitting a job and getting a new job in the last year than any other generation.[26] This group isn't really feeling work.

There's a silver lining in the work from our friends at Gallup. In their recommendations on how we move forward and reverse the trend of worker disengagement, they suggested the way to increase employee engagement was not just cash, not bonuses, not benefits, and definitely not free snacks in the breakroom. The way to do it was better leaders. The study found that 70 percent of the variance in team engagement was determined solely by the effectiveness of a manager who embodied a very specific type of leadership style.[27]

They were a coach.

#ANTIWORK

Some cause happiness wherever they go, some whenever they go.

—Oscar Wilde

Been on Reddit lately?

Well, after I missed the opportunity of the Robinhood stock craze, I stuck around for a bit, and another thread emerged.

#AntiWork

Wow.

The stuff on this thread is wild. Talk about the most searing indictments of bad leadership, crappy jobs, and failed workplace cultures. They're all on display on this Reddit forum. Now, of course, grain of salt here. Bad actors exist. But at a recent restaurant industry conference, I heard a CEO bring up the #AntiWork thread from the big stage while he blamed workers for not showing grit, while simultaneously introducing Angela Duckworth and her book with the same title. That's when I knew there is some real truth in here.

Many will say workers shouldn't complain about wages; instead, they should just quit. They say that it's unprofessional for workers to post their grievances on social media; instead, they should confide in their leadership in private. They say that it's unprofessional to no-show for work; instead, they should just do the work.

They will rail against the openness with which workers today can communicate and share their point of view. They get even more upset when the latest trend emerges. It's the one where you just come to work, clock in, do the minimum (sometimes less than the minimum), and ride it out.

Quiet quitting.

But my question is, who quit on who first?

MEET TODAY'S WORKING CLASS

Work has changed a lot since Zeus decided to teach us a lesson.

The working class has changed as well. Today, the working class in America is a group that needs to be more clearly defined.

According to the U.S. Census Bureau, this group is made up of:

44 million adults who make less than $35,000 per year and don't have an associate degree.

One in two live in poverty.

Only 1 percent earn a bachelor's degree by age twenty-four.

The working class passes on their challenges to their children. Research shows only two out of every twenty-five children born in low-income households ever reach the top quintile of the economic ladder. These kids cross all races and ethnic groups.

They, like their parents, are being left out of the opportunity to compete in today's workforce. America has failed to properly invest in its children, whose potential often goes unfulfilled. Today 76 percent of adults say they expect their children's lives to be worse than their own.[28]

By now you should be aware we need a new way forward. A new model. A new approach. Because without it, future generations of young people will encounter a worse experience than their parents.

CHAPTER 2

The Meaning of Work

Hamana Kalili of Laie came to work one day around 1917 at the Kahuku Sugar Mill, a sugarcane plantation on Oahu Island in Hawaii.

The days were always long, and the work was grueling. The work to make the sweet crystals started in the fields with chopping, stacking, and carting the sugarcane.

It would then be passed through a machine by hand to grind it down and extract the juice. The cane juice was then sent on to a sugar refinery to be further processed.

On this day, Hamana was feeding the long green sugar-cane stalks into the crushing machine when he accidentally got dangerously close to the rollers. He couldn't move his hands back fast enough, and the rollers took his index, middle, and ring fingers. All gone.

There is no record that he got any time off or compensation, but we can assume he didn't finish his shift that day. And given his new handicap, he was reassigned as the security guard on the train that transported the raw sugar juice to the refiners.

He was responsible for making sure the local kids didn't jump aboard for free rides. He would make sure the train was clear before signaling the "all clear" to the train conductor.

That's the origin of the shaka wave. A worker on the front line doing dangerous work with long hours and low wages lost a few fingers doing his job. Hope I didn't just ruin your favorite emoji.

Hamana wasn't the only one—many more experienced the same fate on a sugar plantation. But from its start with an industrial accident from unsafe working conditions, the shaka wave turned into a positive sign, evoking good vibes that can mean anything from "hang loose" to "right on" to "take it easy."

Hamana's story is a reminder that the meaning of things can sometimes change. And sometimes they can change in a way that hides what's really going on—like what work really takes from you.

CLOCKING IN

Our relationship with work hasn't always revolved around time.

Medieval monks are believed to be the inventors of the first mechanical clocks. They didn't do it to keep their workers on time. They just wanted to make sure nobody missed their morning prayers. Over the centuries clocks spread across the globe and became widely adopted in town squares as a way to call people to mass or prayer. And it didn't take long before working days started to revolve around the winding arms on the clock tower.

Fast forward to the major achievements of the Industrial Revolution and you'll find historians like Lewis Mumford, who claims in his 1934 book *Technics and Civilization* that the success may not have happened without the clock. Workers were filling up factories and the clock became the secret weapon of the owner and manager.

It enabled businesses to become efficient by exerting more control over the behaviors of workers. As workers worked long hours, often six days a week, clocks kept people showing up on time and directed them to complete the right tasks at the right moment.

The clock gave society a new tool. Time was now something that could be allocated, and it began to be viewed as a resource. And as a resource, it began to be managed, especially by owners who now realized that the pay of a factory worker wasn't just the purchase of their work product but the purchase of their time. If owners control your time as the major driving factor of work output, then by extension a company has a vested interest in the workers' time resource.

This wasn't a natural shift. Up to this point in human history, we hadn't felt that a good life required work. Looking back to the Roman Empire, work was viewed as the requirement to ensure that people could enjoy leisure time. *Negotium*, the Latin word for business, literally translates to "not-leisure." In those days, life wasn't about wasting away in work or business. By the sixteenth century, between religious holidays and seasonal labor, the average worker worked only about 150 days a year.[1]

Companies had to find a way to sell all of us on how great work is for us to part with five months of leisure time. Their answer was to make it mean something different.

If the monks gave us clocks to punch in, another bunch of religions worked to give work meaning.

The idea of the dignity of work has roots in early Christian teaching. Some thinkers believe the rise of capitalism was assisted by the religious teachings and values of Puritanism and Protestantism. Specific denominations aside, it's clear that religion placed an emphasis on the values that have become synonymous with the skills employers value most in their workers. Many of these are exactly the "skills" employers are always whining about their workers being deficient in, like discipline, hard work, and loyalty.

Work wasn't always supposed to be about meaning and passion and all that stuff. But companies had to introduce meaning in order to trick workers into giving up more of their time. Religions chipped in. Philosophers chipped in. And then even governments chipped in.

GRAVESTONES

While I can't recall the last time I found myself walking through graveyards checking gravestones, I am sure that you won't find a gravestone with the word "bartender" or "barista" or "boss" engraved on it.

However, somehow the idea that work gives us meaning has been a widely adopted and acknowledged viewpoint for most workers—either taught to us early or sold to us by our bosses later in life.

The philosopher Aristotle said, "Work in no sense makes you a better person. In fact it makes you a worse one, since it takes up so much time, thus making it difficult to fulfill one's social and political obligations."[2]

The connection between employer and employee has been weakening. We have already talked about the high numbers of disengaged workers today—surveys of workers unsurprisingly raise a variety of concerns by workers, including one where 87 percent of the U.S. workforce is believed to be unable to contribute because they're not passionate about the work they perform.[3]

Given the circus of the last few years, where we have cycled through all types of workforce trends, including quiet quitting, the great resignation, and boss loss, it's no wonder the connection between employer and employee is weak. (Quiet quitting refers to employees who fulfill the bare minimum of their job but do nothing more. It's directly influenced by low wages and lack of job satisfaction; for some, it's because they can't quit and find a better job.)

And now we're talking about BMM—bare minimum Mondays. This is a TikTok trend about easing into the work week by doing the least amount of work on Monday.

These trends of coming up with new sticky naming conventions to attach blame to workers are never going to stop.

WALK OF SHAME

I was recently on a flight from Los Angeles, California, back to Newark, New Jersey, and overheard a back and forth between two flight attendants.

"Do you want to do the walk of shame, or should I?"

One flight attendant then grabbed the stack of credit card application forms, held one up, and walked past me down the aisle.

MOST PEOPLE HATE WORK

The paradox of work today is that so many people's sense of pride and belonging is tied to working for a living. Yet most hate their jobs.

Across the globe, humans spend a major percentage of their lives working. The average American now works five more weeks per year than in 1975. During that same period, income and wealth inequality has risen, while wages have stagnated for the majority of workers.

On average, workers in the United Kingdom don't work the most hours each year—that prize goes to Cambodia —but they don't work the fewest hours, either. Germany gets the win on this one. Some experts believe the U.K. is a good place to get a global assessment of workers today. By the time the average person in the U.K. reaches 80, they will have spent:

- 8,800 hours socializing with friends.
- 9,500 hours in activities with an intimate partner.
- 112,000 hours at work.[4]

In the U.S., workers' lives look very similar. Today, nearly 63 percent of all Americans aged 16 and over are employed workers.[5] That doesn't include the hundreds of millions of hours of unpaid work each day performed by those raising children and caring for parents or loved ones.

TAYLORISM, SOVIET STYLE

In 1929 the Soviet Union wanted to change things up.

In pursuit of greater efficiency from their workforce, government officials launched a plan to restructure society by putting work at the center for all citizens. They were inspired by our friend Fredo Taylor. (You remember him—the efficiency expert from chapter 1.)

Fredo's belief in "scientific management" made him a favorite of the Soviets. They, like him, wanted to squeeze the maximum output from a worker.

Yuri Larin, the Soviet chief economist, wanted to keep factories in the Soviet Union running 365 day a year without any breaks. He decided to redefine the work week. Instead of a week being seven days, it would be reduced to five days, and workers would be given one day off per week. The idea was to stagger work schedules so workers were available every day around the clock. The plan divided citizens into five color-coded work groups (yellow, green, orange, purple, and red). Each group would work a different schedule while staying true to the goal of no days where work ceases. Holidays would also be issued for different groups at different times of the year. Soviet officials claimed the plan had many benefits for the workers, including more days off and shorter lines at the grocery store.[6]

This approach, in the name of creating maximum efficiency for industrial output, greatly reduced leisure time and kept families from enjoying their leisure time together. Its main goal was to destroy the possibility of social life.

HENRY FORD TO THE RESCUE

Religion was one way to get people to care about work. Henry Ford had a better idea.

Consumerism.

Henry Ford developed a different way of motivating workers. His idea was less about survival, compulsion, or a place in heaven. He liked shopping instead. He sold the idea that having an affordable home, an affordable car, and affordable consumer goods would result in driving workers to work harder and care more about spending the majority of their lives at work.

Ford tough.

WORK IS HELL

A guest at a Carowinds amusement park in North Carolina approached the guest services counter and notified a worker that he had seen an exposed crack in the structure on a large rollercoaster.

The worker asked the guest to send her a video of the crack and said they would, "send it to somebody."

The guest later said in an interview with CNN's Erica Hill, "I felt there was no urgency in any of the employees."[7]

Imagine being that worker. It is obvious to you that people are in danger, but you do nothing? Most will say shame on the worker. I say, what kind of leadership has cultivated that indifferent environment?

In *Work, Work, Work* author Michael Yates, a labor educator and economist, says, "For nearly everyone in the world, work is hell. The sad truth is that many are demeaned, worn out, injured, mentally and physically deformed, and all too often killed on the job so that a few can be rich."[8] The people who work for others in an environment where they have limited influence over the quality or how the work is performed are affected personally. And profoundly.

Our workers don't sell just their labor. They don't just sell their skill. They don't just sell their credentials. They sell their time. A lot of it. This is the society we have created. Today it's made up of growing income inequality and too many dead-end jobs with no pathway to a brighter future.

We have worked to survive, we have worked because we were forced, we have worked because God told us it's why we exist, we have worked to make money, and we have worked because it is what our parents told us to do. But if you think about it—there was a time before work. There was a time when we didn't put so much worth into work. We should consider this history and how we all spend way too much time glamorizing the future of work. We should take a second. We should pause. We should consider a new way to work. Or, a better way.

THREE THINGS EMPLOYEES SAY ABOUT WORK

All kinds of friction exist at work today.

Many people find themselves with the wrong skills for jobs today. What makes it worse is that due to a change in the skills we demand, this has more to do with being overqualified than underqualified. Those graduating from college are finding themselves in roles that are less cognitively demanding and less skilled than before.[9] This trend is very visible with young people pursuing degrees in STEM, an area that has been marketed heavily over the last decade as a path that will ensure your job is a good one and resilient to the impact of automation. However, data in the 2021 U.S. Census Bureau study finds as many as 72 percent of Americans with a STEM degree are now in roles that don't require those qualifications.[10]

Challenges exist around the type of work people are taking on. Fast food jobs in the 1950s used to be for teenagers. Today, 66 percent of fast food jobs are taken by adults; 33 percent of those have some college education, and 40 percent are older than twenty-five.[11] Women's jobs are also on the rise, but not in any of the categories they may have hoped. Pink collar jobs out of the reach of robots are mostly in teaching, hairdressing, housekeeping, and social work.

Geographic challenges affect where you can find work. In the U.S., one in two college graduates moves out of their home state, but only 17 percent of high school dropouts do.[12]

These challenges are negatively impacting the types of jobs, wages, and quality of jobs. And they are changing how workers view work.

Workers Believe Work Doesn't Make the World Better

In a survey by YouGov, workers were asked: "Does your job make a meaningful contribution to the world?"

Only 37 percent of workers said yes.[13]

When you consider what workers get from work, a wage to pay our bills is an obvious immediate answer. But, if you look deeper and take into account our history of work being sold to us as having the ability to provide us with "meaning" in our lives—then a second benefit of work should be an opportunity to make a positive impact on our communities. These two are unfortunately at odds with each other in the way work has played out.

Today, the more your work benefits your community, the less likely you are to be paid well for it. It's tragic but true. You can say that our society views the social value of work as being in inverse proportion to its economic value. It is a reality of work that we have come to accept.

President Barack Obama said, in a 2016 interview with *WIRED* magazine, "We must begin to reexamine what we value, what we are collectively willing to pay for—whether it's teachers, nurses, caregivers, moms, dads who stay at home, artists—all the things that are incredibly valuable to us right now but don't rank high on the pay totem pole. The looming problems of inequality, power, meaning—are consequences of unprecedented prosperity."[14]

Plato believed meaning could only come through leisure and

the only purpose of work is to pay for leisure time. Looks like that point of view may becoming popular again.

Workers Believe Employers Don't Care

McDonald's is proud that one out of every seven U.S. workers has been employed at the Golden Arches at some point in their working life.[15] This is a corporation that has effectively built processes and procedures out of everything that touches the business. As a franchise business, they emphasize this fact to new franchisees.

This is a brand that popularized the management saying, "If there's time to lean, there's time to clean," and has created a culture where workers are reprimanded for not smiling. They also spend tens of millions of dollars in lobbying to ensure worker wages don't rise and safety doesn't get better.

What about the stories of Amazon warehouses that offer workers medicine vending machines for on-demand access to single-dose painkillers? All while the company does very little to care much about the workers' pain before they clock in or after they clock out.

We must stop and ask ourselves some hard questions. How are workers supposed to find meaning and purpose in jobs where they are basically working like robots?

Workers Believe They Aren't Fairly Paid

American workers are sold a dream. This dream goes something like this: if you work hard, you will get ahead. Unfortunately, in reality, it's more like if you work and work and work, you fall further and further behind.

Unstable schedules, wage theft, not enough hours, and low wages define work today for too many in our workforce. And the ones being taken advantage of most are especially those on the front line.

Some think that these issues will work themselves out. But work under capitalism has been built to perform this way; it's performing according to plan. Workers are not expected to have control over their work. For many, work is simply something that consumes their lives. Giving workers meaning was merely introduced to make up for wages that you struggle to survive on and environments that care more about profits than people.

WORKERS STILL WANT TO BELIEVE

In 1962, Robert F. Kennedy was touring Cape Canaveral on his first trip to the center of American space exploration.

While he was touring the facility he noticed a custodian down the hall sweeping the hallway. He stepped away from the tour, approached the worker, and asked, "What are you doing at NASA?"

The custodian replied, "I'm helping to put a man on the moon."

Frontline workers spend so much of their lives at work. They spend so much of their energy working the line. Many still believe in the possibility of a workplace that can offer them the opportunity to not just be appreciated at work, but to work in service to a greater cause.

What are we saying about the work they do when we pay them poverty wages? What do the workers around us say when they are starved of access to development opportunities and fulfillment at work?

Unfortunately, the reality of work is many are not feeling the love.

PART II

THE REALITY OF WORK

If you change the way you look at things,
the things you look at start to change.

—WAYNE DYER

CHAPTER 3

Fuck the Future of Work

How's that for an opening?

Everyone today seems to want to talk about the future of work, but I want to talk about the reality of work. And the reality of work is work isn't working for most workers.

The story sold about the future of work is a dream that is often just out of reach. And, because of this, frontline workers don't care about the future of work—and neither do I. I'd argue you shouldn't either.

Instead, you should care about what is happening right now—the reality of work.

Want to know what the future of work has gotten us? A world where those who are paid the least pay the most. This can be observed by simply considering how this future of work thing takes from workers.

Work has been taking a lot from workers.

Work takes your time. Workers don't have much control over their time. The Economic Policy Institute says only 15 percent of workers say they are "free to decide" their work schedule.[1] Work demands workers to work when they see fit and to flex to whatever schedule they're given. Now, this might not seem like a big deal to some of us—it makes sense that our employer can decide our schedule. But employers can also send workers home whenever they want—even just minutes after a shift has started for something as simple as the store not being busy enough. They can even demand that you stay later than your shift to help clean or to carry the extra workload of others. This is positioned as acceptable practice because they are, after all, paying you. However, they can also threaten to fire you if you choose not to stay after a shift or refuse a shift that encroaches on something that you already had scheduled. And by the way, all of this happens with the most frequency for workers who are being paid wages that average between $12 to $14 per hour.

According to Jamie McCallum in *Worked Over*: "This instability is a growing problem, associated with mental and physical stress, unstable income, emotional turmoil, family conflicts, gender and equity, ecological instability, and overall personal happiness."[2]

That someone's time could belong to another person is kind of strange. In work today, a worker's time isn't their own. Rather, it belongs to the one that paid for it. We even go so far as to believe if an employee isn't working, they're actually stealing something from the employer.

But it's not stealing if the employer is doing it. It is now legal to steal the time of a worker. A 2014 Supreme Court ruling was unanimous in its finding around an Amazon warehouse that refused to pay workers for the mandatory security check they had to complete upon entering work. This security check would take a worker around 30 minutes to complete—every shift. The worker ends up losing over 150 hours a year in wages.

Work takes away opportunities. Since 2003, the number of workers in the gig economy has grown 27 percent more than the growth of employees on payroll.[3] These are jobs that rob workers of benefits, security, and protections. They also have ripple effects on these workers as they attempt to transition into full-time work. In the future they will find that the market may not value the gig work they added to their résumé.

Between 2013 and 2023, these gig jobs have been a major source of first jobs for workers—and surged again with the effects of the pandemic on work. This movement to low-wage gig work has long-term effects for the worker. A study of résumés by Strada, a nonprofit education foundation that conducts research and policy work focused on the handoff between education and work, found 43 percent of low-wage workers were underemployed in their first job. They were five times more likely to remain underpaid after five years versus workers who were not underemployed in their first job.[4]

Work takes away family time. In 2022, research by Pew Research Center found that only 48 percent of Americans planned on using their allotted vacation time that year. I would be interested in what that data would look like for our frontline workers. Unfortunately, this would be tough to capture, since only one in three low-wage workers receive any paid holiday or vacation time.[5] The ability to even choose to take a vacation is something that our social and working class greatly determines. Data also shows we are working later and later past retirement age. In 1991, 16 percent of Americans were still working past age sixty-five; as of 2018, that number was 48 percent.[6]

This means workers are having to make work choices that affect them at the stage of their life where they would probably prefer to be experiencing more time with family.

The only way work today is creating more connection at home

has to do with the reality that so many workers are choosing to stay home to take care of loved ones. An increasing percentage of our workforce is performing unpaid work caring for children, disabled and sick family members, and elders.

This was all made worse by the COVID-19 pandemic. While the pandemic impacted every corner of our global economy, from small businesses to large corporations, it made a direct hit on frontline industries by closing restaurants, casinos, hotels, malls, conference centers, theme parks, and strip clubs. In the spring of 2020, nearly 26 million Americans filed for unemployment. The pandemic resulted in a surge of unemployed workers and increased the risk associated with coming to work every day. Look closer and you will see who paid the biggest price. At a time when nearly one in two workers were working in a low-wage job, many of these workers saw their jobs eliminated by the pandemic.

The pandemic further exposed inequities. Schools closed and parents were forced to make sacrifices to care for children, undocumented workers were unable to access government relief and were forced to work in unsafe conditions to survive, workers without a college degree were more likely to be laid off, minority workers in essential jobs couldn't access healthcare and died in disproportionate numbers to workers that could work from home. And with the pandemic now behind us, it still rings true that the concept of working from home is something only a few can access. Our frontline workers can't do it. I guess it kind of makes sense, given their title. Our frontline workers—barbers, janitors, servers, bartenders, housekeepers—didn't have the luxury to work from home during the pandemic and they still don't today.

Too Many Bullshit Jobs

In David Graeber's book *Bullshit Jobs,* he claims that if the majority of jobs were to disappear, we wouldn't be all that bad off. It's a compelling read.

David's formal definition of a bullshit job is "a form of paid employment that is so completely pointless, unnecessary, or pernicious that even the employee cannot justify its existence, even though, as part of the conditions of employment, the employee feels obliged to pretend that this is not the case."[7]

Damn.

He went on to identify the five types of bullshit jobs:

1. Flunkies: Flunky positions are created because those in powerful positions in an organization see underlings as badges of prestige.
2. Goons: Goons are hired due to a dynamic of one-upmanship (if our rivals employ a top law firm, then so must we).
3. Duct tapers: Duct taper positions are created because sometimes organizations find it more difficult to fix a problem than to deal with its consequences.
4. Box tickers: Box-ticker positions exist because, within large organizations, paperwork attesting to the fact that certain actions have been taken often comes to be seen as more important than the actions themselves.
5. Taskmasters: Taskmasters exist largely as side effects of various forms of impersonal authority.

Work has been built this way.

I can't help but nod in agreement that humanity wouldn't suffer all that much were all lobbyists, PR researchers, actuaries, telemarketers, bailiffs, or legal consultants to just up and disappear. Graeber goes on to claim that 37 percent to 40 percent of jobs are completely pointless, and at least 50 percent of the work done in non-pointless office jobs is equally pointless.[8]

This would mean that at least half of all work being done today could be eliminated with presumably little to no negative impact on society. Let's put aside whether you agree or disagree with the math and if you may take offense because your friend is in private equity. It is our moral responsibility to consider the impact of the work we strain to perform.

I agree that we have too many bullshit jobs. I'm not sure how we will ever completely rid the earth of jobs that fail to add value to the worker or society. There are in fact stupid entrepreneurs out there and business owners who will go on treating workers as their cattle, controlling their time and output.

We can do something, however. We should consider the high percentage of jobs that fall into this category of meaningless, empty, or adding little economic value to a society. And then we should ask ourselves why we allow it to happen.

Why are we OK with allowing our markets to reward those in useless roles so much more than those we consider essential?

POINTING FINGERS

In 2015, I wrote a book titled *Not Our Job: How College Destroyed a Generation of Workers and How to Fix It*. It was more of a rant. But I wanted to say it.

I opened by sharing a story about two conversations I had within a week of one another. The first was with a dean of a college who told me he didn't believe it was a college's job to prepare students for work—that was the job of an employer. A few days later, I met with a CEO for a major retail brand who said he didn't believe it was the job of a company to upskill a worker for a job—that was the job of college.

In the book I raised the question: So whose job is it?

It's a question I've come back to often over the years. And I believe we are still waiting for someone to make it their job.

While employers and colleges are pointing fingers at each other, we also have a lot of finger pointing at the worker. But not just any specific worker. We have fallen in love with grouping workers by generation, giving them some futuristic label and then continuing on with our finger-pointing.

Millennials are lazy. Gen Z is stuck on their phone. Boomers let it all happen. Gen X tried and failed.

A quick guide for reference so you can see where you fall based on your birth year:

- Gen Z: 1995 to 2012
- Millennials: 1980 to 1994
- Gen X: 1965 to 1979
- Boomers: 1946 to 1964

Finger-pointing can be fun. It can make a good meme or a good punch line by some old CEO on stage at a conference when he says, "These millennials. . . ."

We must move past finger-pointing, but it's important that we understand the realities of our situation with different generations in the workplace. It's easy to complain. It's hard to correct.

Now speaking for myself, as a millennial, it's nice to have a new group to share some blame with. And Gen Z has been getting hit hard. When you look closer at the generation that is quickly growing into the majority of our workforce, especially for entry-level work, you see it's a generation that's a byproduct of a management style, by which I mean parenting style, that has embraced screen time. Even though data shows a lot of screen time is more likely to result in a more unhappy child and that social media can have a negative impact on a child's mental health, Gen Z grew up on screens.

In Jean Twenge's book, *iGen: Why Today's Super-Connected Kids Are Growing Up Less Rebellious, More Tolerant, Less Happy—and Completely Unprepared for Adulthood—and What That Means for the Rest of Us,* she said this about Gen Z:

> iGen'ers are the safest generation in U.S. history—partially due to their choice to drink less, fight less, wear their seat belt, and drive more safely. More careful and therefore less likely to be killed by crash or homicide. Yet, they are more likely to die through suicide. iGen'ers seem terrified—not just of physical dangers that are made real through everything from Amber alerts going off on phones to school shooter drills—but of the emotional dangers of adult social interaction.[9]

This generation at the center of the future of work has been brought up by parents who wouldn't let them play in the park alone, wouldn't let them apply for a job without talking to the employer themselves, wouldn't let them fail. Instead, their cocoon mentality was embraced by their children and resulted in a generation growing up without the opportunities to converse at dinner, replacing it with screen time.

Now this is obviously not all Gen Z's fault. They didn't get here all on their own. We may have some other generations to thank for that. In Bruce Gibney's *A Generation of Sociopaths,* he said this about our Boomers: "A cranky observation by the old about the young is they just don't make them like they used to. Boomers were more promiscuous, divorced more frequently, had more abortions, saved less, ate more, had more problems with authority, and so on."[10]

We should really stop all the finger pointing. This is a reality of work today. We must approach these new realities as opportunities to strengthen and better prepare our people for work. We must also consider the other lies that are proclaimed by corporations and media when talking about the state of our workforce.

These really piss me off.

LIE #1: WORKERS ARE UNSKILLED

We hear it often: workers don't have the skills.

If you trusted what most employers say, you would believe we have a large majority of workers who aren't able to achieve their full potential just because they lack skills.

Economists call our current situation a skills mismatch. But before we decide if this is actually true, let's define skills mismatch. A skills mismatch can be caused by either a shortage of supply or an excess of demand. It's what happens when a restaurant needs to hire a bartender who knows what they're doing but then claims that after posting the job and interviewing multiple candidates, they still can't find the right new hire.

But what skills are we talking about? A 2016 survey of employers found the skills cited most in demand for recent college graduates were (in order) leadership (80 percent), ability to work in a team (79 percent), and written communication and problem-solving. Note that any technical skill was absent from the top of the list; they were all ranked in the middle or bottom.[11] And a study by DeVry University found the same trend. The study asked managers what attributes they found most important to success in their company. Out of fifteen attributes, only one—communication skills—was related to an academic subject that could be taught in a classroom training.[12] If workers were truly unskilled in the sense of skills that can be taught, wouldn't these skills rank higher by employers in survey after survey? But they never show up.

So, if there is a skills gap, really, then I bet companies are doing everything they can to close the gap. Right?

Nope. The data is clear. Investment in training in the U.S. has gone down over the last twenty-five years and a big part of the believed skills gap has to do more with poor efforts by employers to invest in internal training for either current employees or future hires. In 1979, young workers got 2.5 weeks of training per year, but by 1991 only 17 percent of employees reported receiving any formal training over the past year. And it keeps getting worse. Accenture, a global consulting firm, conducted a recent study that found only 21 percent of employees received any employer-provided formal training in the past five years. If this is true, it would mean that nearly 80 percent of today's workers are doing jobs with no recent training or coaching.[13] On a global level, the U.S. isn't leading here, either. The U.S. is currently ranked second to last in investment in workforce training and education programs. When training does take place, it usually isn't even job-specific or skill-building. Instead, it covers compliance or workplace safety related topics.[14] I call this the "cover your ass" category.

Companies aren't taking the development of the skills workers already have seriously enough. You would think they would be given their point of view around a skills gap. The data makes you think workers aren't the ones that are unskilled. It actually looks more like their employers lack the skills when it comes to people development—or worse, they lack the willingness.

Today, the majority of our workers show up to work every day and don't receive the training necessary to stay up to speed with the changing nature of their jobs. This looks more like an opportunity gap, where our most vulnerable workers are simply not getting the same opportunities as others. In Peter Cappelli's book *Why Good People Can't Get Jobs*, he asks, "Do studies show the United States is among leaders in skill gaps or simply in employer whining?"[15]

Hidden Credentials

Workers are absolutely skilled. The problem isn't the lack of skill but the ability of organizations and human resources teams to properly see and evaluate skills. This means evaluating a candidate and connecting them with opportunities and development pathways to fully unlock their existing knowledge, skills, and abilities.

Unfortunately, the ability to signal their skills is a problem for every worker, but it most harms workers with "uncredentialed knowledge." Knowledge that is uncredentialed is essentially hidden, something that the worker has proficiency in but lacks the paper certificate to prove. These hidden credentials make up all the learning you have done throughout your life, both inside and outside of college, and are of critical importance for an employer to identify in the interview and onboarding process in order to tap into the skills of their worker and activate their abilities within their organization. Low-wage or frontline workers have accumulated the majority of their skills in informal learning that is uncredentialed because their employers don't invest in issuing certificates for this kind of work. Those formal credentials are reserved for college degrees and technical school programs—basically things the employee has to buy as a consumer.

Our workforce doesn't have a skills gap. It has a willingness gap. A willingness to look closer at our people and a willingness to invest so that we can truly unlock the skills and abilities of our workforce.

What does it say about our society that we can so easily throw around the word "unskilled" when talking about people? Economists, politicians, media, educators—they all debate the difference between skilled work and unskilled work and argue about what an unskilled worker need to become more skilled. These labels have even worked their way into how the Department of Labor looks at training programs.

Can you imagine being a worker who is informed that their work is unskilled? How did this become so acceptable? The label has perpetuated a movement of blaming the worker for the shortcomings of society. It's not just employers doing the name calling. Even those that claim to protect workers have gotten in on the action. The Essential Worker Immigration Coalition (EWIC) defines essential workers as the mass of "lesser skilled and unskilled" labor.[16] This from a group that has the aim of fighting and advocating for workers!

Is the UPS driver who delivers your package on time unskilled? Is the dishwasher who washes dishes without breaking any unskilled? Is the maintenance worker who hangs the hurricane shutters to protect your school unskilled? It is not acceptable or just for a society to use such terminology. To pay a worker poverty wages, offer no training assistance, expect them to perform hard work and then label their work and their function as "unskilled" is just wrong.

We do not have unskilled workers. We do have many unwilling leaders. We need to move past this archaic terminology. Words matter.

LIE #2: WORKERS ARE LAZY

Workers are lazy.

This lie has been used repeatedly as a way to put more blame on workers. Anybody remember Linda Taylor? In 1976, President Ronald Reagan delivered a stump speech about the lavish lifestyle of "welfare queen" Linda Taylor. He was attempting to make her the face of welfare, mostly because she happened to be both Black and a woman. During the New Hampshire Republican primary, Reagan said, "There's a woman in Chicago. She has eighty names, thirty addresses, twelve Social Security cards, and is collecting veterans' benefits on four nonexistent deceased husbands. She's got Medicaid, she's getting food stamps, and she is collecting welfare under each of her names. Her tax-free cash income alone is over $150,000."

Taylor was eventually charged with using four aliases, not eighty, and collecting $8,000, not $150,000, but Reagan's ridiculous claims connected with his audience, and the image of the welfare queen was born. False as it is, it remains central to our country's point of view of workers who don't pull their weight and our understanding of public assistance.[17]

Stereotyping a worker as lazy and poor has long been

connected to discrimination and racism. We can go back to slavery to see how white Americans looked down on enslaved people and the work that was associated with their place in society. This trend didn't end with slavery. It has continued throughout the history of the American workforce. It has become an ingrained belief that lets us belittle others to make ourselves feel bigger.

LIE #3: CAN'T FIND WORKERS

I can't find workers.

Have you heard that one before? I have—way too often. What about the talent crunch? The supposed crisis a bunch of MBAs from Accenture say will cost us $8.5 trillion in lost revenues by 2030?

I have to hand it to most employers. They milk this complaint pretty well. The "Now Hiring" signs in storefront windows and the comments made by restaurant managers about being under-staffed are a great excuse for slow service. They've even figured out how to get other employers in on the plot by having them share their complaints and aggravations with customers in an attempt to earn some sympathy.

Think about it for a second! Under capitalism, we're supposed to reward businesses that succeed. But now businesses that are failing by not being able to maintain staffing levels are then turning around and asking for forgiveness and handouts from guests. How the hell did we get turned around like that?

Anyway, no sympathy coming from me. Let me explain.

What is a labor shortage? By definition, a labor shortage occurs when employers can't find enough workers willing to work at the wage they're offering. What usually happens next is when the number of job applicants is low and it costs more money for their labor, the job requirements fall to prevent wages from going up, resulting in employers hiring applicants with less experience. And when the number of applicants is high and it costs less money for their labor, the job requirements rise as employers expect more from an applicant before they will hire them.

I have trouble with this whole labor shortage thing. See, when a company can't find customers, they don't run around saying there's a customer shortage. They don't then go on TV and podcasts and complain about how their customers are lazy and won't come into their stores. Instead, they find solutions. They adjust pricing. They create more value. They change marketing tactics.

Companies could do much better in their hiring process. Companies really struggle here. Poorly developed recruiting and selection processes have only been made worse by accelerated investment in technologies that are offboarding critical decision-making in the interview process. These technologies range from job posting on platforms like ZipRecruiter and Indeed to applicant tracking. They all claim to better organize and assess candidates. These technologies often result in worse outcomes. The hiring process, even without technology, already has all types of problems, ranging from unrealistic employer expectations, poorly trained or absent interview techniques, outdated job descriptions, low-wage jobs, and automation to screen candidates.

The new technologies that use automation are really damaging. By claiming they're "helping" hiring managers at large corporations to make better decisions faster, they're really just sorting tens of thousands of applications per second without understanding them—using who knows what type of algorithm or decision-making properties.[18] Since frontline workers are traditionally short on the formal credentials these platforms value and rich in informal credentials that they struggle to signal, the result is organizations miss out on qualified candidates and still claim they can't find workers.

It also doesn't help that pay for frontline workers isn't showing workers a lot of love.

Employers' failure to offer the wages necessary to attract the skill set they seek can't be talked up as a worker shortage. Look closer at these hard-to-fill jobs and you'll find the ones requiring the least formal credentials are the ones with the "labor shortage"—and are also the jobs paying the least. The labor shortage is more likely just an abundance of bad jobs paying workers poverty wages—and then complaining when nobody takes the deal.

Bottom line: Pay levels are a problem, and not being able to or willing to pay the market price for talent doesn't make it a shortage.

THE NINE REALITIES OF WORK

Build or buy.

This is what companies are thinking every day when they choose between investing in growing their people or paying to acquire a new worker.

Unfortunately, the reality of work today is that employers aren't great builders and they're often on the hunt for discounts. Today, millions of workers in the U.S. alone have potential that goes unrecognized and untapped. It is a reality of unequal access, unequal support, unequal wages, unequal respect. We can't begin to tackle how to fix work if we don't first consider the realities our workforce faces every day. Some will surprise you. Some may not. But all of them should be considered as we decide how we will arrange work for the future.

Now, let's dive into the nine realities of working today.

CHAPTER 4

Misaligned on Work

L'homme est né libre, et par-tout il est dans les fers.
(Man is born free, and everywhere he is in chains.)

—JEAN-JACQUES ROUSSEAU, *DU CONTRAT SOCIAL*, 1762

It was 7 a.m. in Braselton, Georgia. I was preparing for a keynote session at a conference. I came in to the conference center a few hours early to do a run-through of my presentation to ensure everything was in order. I was getting a cup of coffee in the common area when a door opened a bit just a few feet from me and caught me off guard. I could see a young kid through the small crack in the door. She peeked out at me and then quickly closed the door. It looked as if she was peeking out from an office. I didn't think much of it and went back to my coffee.

This went on a few more times over the next few hours. I finished my late afternoon session on stage and was hanging out talking with folks after the session. After my final discussion wrapped up, I began to pack up my stuff. I planned to head to my room to get ready for the evening.

I looked up and noticed that the door was fully open to the office. I was shocked at what I saw. Sitting in a small conference chair was a young girl, maybe six or seven years old. She had on headphones and was watching something on a small tablet. I stood there frozen. She wasn't in an office—she was in a small storage closet surrounded by cleaning supplies. As I watched, a woman in a housekeeping uniform approached her. The girl grabbed a small backpack, slipped her arms through, and then took her mother's hand as they walked to a service exit.

This young girl had just spent her whole day in a broom closet while her mom spent the whole day working.

WE VALUE WORK, NOT WORKERS

Question: How many people work in your organization?
Answer: About half.

—My conversation with a CEO

Work today isn't working for everyone.

A lot of things we've been doing don't work anymore, and they haven't for a long time. The changing nature of work has resulted in one in two workers being an hourly worker in America. Hourly workers deal with unpredictable job schedules that force them to work late into the evening and sometimes come back in the early morning. This may not even be at the same job—reports suggest as many as 8.7 million American workers are working multiple jobs.[1]

The effects of unscheduled work and long hours is harmful to workers beyond just the chaos of not knowing when you will work your next shift. Hourly workers pay for their jobs with lost family time, lost sleep, and lost health. Unpredictable hours makes being an organized adult nearly impossible. You can't plan child care, can't make it to the doctor (and don't have health insurance anyway), can't make parent-teacher conferences. The toll goes further by negatively impacting psychological and mental health. A 2019 study found this kind of scheduling caused workers even more unhappiness than low wages.[2]

Beyond unpredictable scheduling and low wages, work has been built to consolidate control in the hands of the owner. The employer literally owns the labor of the worker. This ownership results in a loss of control over your work. This loss of control extends beyond the specific work activity of the worker and means that the worker, in lacking control, can't defend themselves appropriately against bad bosses, dangerous work conditions, unpaid wages, sexual harassment, discrimination, and racism.

The owner protects their customers. They protect their assets. They protect their work. Not their workers.

It just wasn't built that way.

INVERSE PROPORTIONS

Let's define some stuff.

A job is a political construct. We use job statistics to determine the health of our labor force and economy. A job is different from work, which is considered an activity we use to earn a wage and contribute to our community.

We live in a society that has decided the value of work is in inverse proportion to its economic value to society. Basically, the more your work benefits others, the less you're likely to be paid for it. This is something we have accepted. Some even consider it morally correct and believe you shouldn't be rewarded for doing work that helps or supports the community. Teachers, nonprofit workers, patient aides, and the rest should be paid less than people who create jobs and wealth. Somehow we accept rewarding the destructive behavior of highly paid bankers and Wall Street executives, while reserving low wages for those working every day in a preschool.

How misaligned.

RAISING THE FLOOR

Andy Stern is the former head of the Service Employees Industry Union, better known as SEIU. It is considered one of the most powerful labor unions in the world. In his book *Raising the Floor* he says about work today, "Some companies aren't lowering the ceiling, they are raising the floor."[3]

WAR FOR TALENT

I am what time, circumstance, history have made of me, certainly, but I am also much more than that. So are we all.

—James Baldwin, *Notes of a Native Son*

When did workers become talent?

You could probably assume that some Ivy Leaguehack came up with the term while working for a consulting firm while writing a white paper for publication in a magazine read only by Jack Welch wannabes.

Your guess would be correct.

McKinsey & Company, supposedly the best management consulting firm in the world, popularized the concept of talent in a 1998 *McKinsey Quarterly* article titled "The War for Talent."[4] Kind of an aggressive title, if you ask me. The article said that companies should do four things to help them win the war for top talent:

1. Human resources' primary job is to manage talent (or the vital few).
2. Companies should focus just on the top 20 percent of employees in the organization.
3. Organizations must identify, reward, and develop their talent—but just the 20 percent.
4. The other 80 percent should be seen as just "personnel" who are choosing to just "meet expectations."

The word "talent" has an interesting history. Even from the beginning, it never meant all employees. It was always just a select few.

The word talent was specifically chosen for its historical context and the way we view a worker's abilities as currency. In ancient times, a talent was a unit of weight, and over time the meaning changed to refer to monetary value. The parable of the talents in the Gospel of Luke teaches that individuals should invest the talents they are given, not stash them. Along the way, talent grew to represent a natural skill—i.e., a God-given talent.

Holding a worldview that talent is something you are born with and not developed limits an individual's ability to access opportunities to develop. It ultimately negatively impacts an organization's ability to develop the labor within its workforce due to such a shortsighted, fixed view of worker skills.

The war for talent is really a war on workers. According to Joe Baker in *The Tyranny of Talent*, the rise of the concept of talent means it has become "the 'thing selected for' in programs for talent development, gifted education and employee recruitment."[5]

Work has become obsessed with the concept of talent. It was not done by accident and traditionally favors specific segments of workers who are lucky enough to purchase—I mean access—skills from specific Ivy League institutions, not the workers with the best skill mix. It just hits certain workers harder.

The next time you see the title Director of Talent Development, know this role isn't about the 100 percent. It was built for a select pool of workers. It is a term that is ripe for a redefinition and a new chapter.

HUMAN CAPITAL

Traditionally, economies maintained their strength by focusing on accumulating physical capital. That has changed today. Now, human capital is all the craze. Broadly speaking, human capital is the sum total of the knowledge and skills that make people be productive workers.

Human capital makes up the outputs of the workforce. A strong human capital economy has workers with the right education, connected to the right jobs, producing the right work product. This is a good thing.

A human capital model should be good for all parties. Workers get to access education that lifts their income by making them more productive. A worker would then decide to get more education, resulting in their productivity going up. Ultimately, the nation would get more education, resulting in increased productivity and income. This works if human capital was the reality. The problem today is this isn't the reality.

At odds with a human capital model is a concept called signaling. This occurs when the market rewards workers for education they don't use. In other words, their education is mostly signaling what the worker potentially knows. In the corporate world, signaling means a company would hire a worker who graduated from Harvard over a worker with the same degree who graduated from Rutgers, simply because of the cachet a Harvard degree signals.

Education today has become mostly signaling—and students know it. It means students don't pursue human capital building opportunities. Instead, they favor credentials that are the best market signalers. And since companies mainly pay for credentials acquired, not skills learned, it has been a good strategy for those that can afford to pay for the credentials with the best signals.

A market built on signaling results in education raising income not because you happen to be more skilled and productive, but rather because you *look* more productive. It means that a worker can get more education and have their productivity stay the same, yet their income goes up. It creates opportunities for those who can pay to unlock the right credentials, but skills aren't part of the equation. The current model of work doesn't reward the hardest working. It rewards the privileged—those who can afford to pay for the most valuable credentials. The result is some having human capital that is considered less valuable than others.

This is fertile ground for inequality.

CEO CAPITAL

In early 2024, a Delaware judge voided a compensation plan proposed by the board of directors of Tesla for Elon Musk. It was for $56 billion and would have been the largest compensation plan in public corporate history.[6] The judge called the plan "excessive."

Right after, Musk called for moving Tesla's corporate office to Texas.

Just a few months later, in April 2024, the board of Tesla again asked shareholders to approve his compensation plan—this time for $47 billion. What a deal.

By the way, just two days prior to the board's request for Musk's new compensation plan, Tesla announced to employees that due to declining sales they will be laying off 14,000 workers, or 10 percent of their workforce.[7]

BLAME CAPITALISM?

You have to have a wide [*economic*] *distribution, and we don't have that today.*

—Senator Bob Kerrey, former U.S. senator, governor, and U.S. Navy SEAL in our conversation on the *Bring It In* podcast

The promise sold as the American dream is built on the idea that a job will present itself to anyone willing to work hard.

To keep the promise, America must be a leader on global talent by creating a business environment that attracts the best workers from across the globe. This means infrastructure must be strong, companies must be healthy, tax policy must be just, and education must be accessible. It also means that our society must deliver for its citizens beyond the workplace.

We aren't doing so well here. Out of 146 countries worldwide, America is currently ranked

- #41 in child mortality
- #46 in internet access
- #44 in access to clean drinking water
- #57 in personal safety
- #30 in high school enrollment

This data comes from the Social Progress Index (SPI), a measure of how well countries provide for the social and environmental needs of their citizens. It's an annual ranking put out by the Social Progress Imperative, a nonprofit research organization founded by three Nobel Prize-winning economists.

This is what capitalism has given us. We have to address the upsides and downsides of this system.

The current model of capitalism has resulted in some very wealthy individuals acquiring a greater share of total income than they did at any point in the last hundred years. In 1965, the average CEO earned about twenty times as much as the average worker; today the average CEO earns more than 300 times as much. A retail worker at Walmart earning the median salary at the company, $19,177, would have to work 1,188 years to earn as much as the CEO did in 2018 alone.[8]

A lot of wealth has been created, but not for everyone. The Wall Street bonus pool at the end of each year historically exceeds the combined annual earnings of all Americans working full-time at the federal minimum wage.

In William Kerr's book, *The Gift of Global Talent,* the author says:

> Capitalism will always yield inequality. Some people have greater skills and are more productive, be it for sports, sales, academic research, or computer programming. The promise of higher income also motivates people to invest many years in education or take entrepreneurial risks. Some will work all weekend, whereas others value their time differently. That said, inequality has become obscene, with 25 hedge fund managers taking home the equivalent pay of all

America's kindergarten teachers, and those born to poorer families face significant challenges. Beyond skewing today's consumption, rising inequality makes it harder to spot future talent.[9]

Capitalism has given us a political landscape that is open to donation and influence by lobbyists and the rich. Let's be real. Never before in American history has so few spent so much to influence the votes of so many.[10] The rules let them, so it makes sense that they take advantage. The math is simple. Corporate profits rise when labor costs fall. It's for this reason that organizations funnel cash into PACs and associations like the National Restaurant Association and the U.S. Chamber of Commerce, who spend millions on lobbying efforts to block increases in minimum wage yet support the earned income tax credit and other federal benefits for workers.

All the while, they know that more money in the pockets of their workers is a good thing—as long as it isn't hitting their balance sheet.

We Have an Hourglass-Shaped Economy

Over the last few decades the part of the pie that goes to workers has been shrinking and the part that goes to owners has been growing.

- In 2014, the top 10 percent of income earners made up 46 percent of America's income.
- In 2015, the top 10 percent of income earners took home more than 50 percent of all income and the top 1 percent (those earning $1.4 million or more in income) took home 22 percent.[11]

- The richest 10 percent of people on earth now own an estimated 85 percent of all global assets; the richest 1 percent own 45 percent of all global assets.[12]
- The richest 1 percent in America own more wealth than the bottom 90 percent.[13]
- The wealthiest 160,000 families in the U.S. have as much wealth as the poorest 145 million.[14]
- The richest eighty-five people in the world own as much wealth as the bottom half of humanity.[15]
- The average income of the top 1 percent of income earners has gone up by more than 250 percent to $1.2 million a year. For the top one-hundredth of 1 percent, the average income is now $27 million per year.
- A typical CEO who used to earn about thirty times more than workers now earns 110 times more, while over the last decade the incomes of most Americans have fallen by 6 percent.[16]

This is capitalism.

Working Under Capitalism Takes a Heavy Toll

You and I right this minute are living in what is almost certainly the loneliest era of American history.

—Charles Vogl, author of the international bestseller
The Art of Community: Seven Principles for Belonging

In Michael Yates's book *Work Work Work,* the author says, "Capitalists want our bodies, every part of them. They seek to use us until we wear out. Then we are tossed aside."[17]

It's true that work is demanding for frontline workers. Those hurt the most by the way work has been built aren't the CEOs or the managers. They're not the ones losing sleep, suffering from depression, or dying on the job. These benefits are reserved for the worker on the front line. Manning the machine. Clocking in and clocking out, with no control over their work.

Isn't the goal of capitalism ultimately to allow us to live a life that affords us opportunities and choices? Freedoms? It looks more like its motive is to make us work. And work. And work.

JOBS OF THE FUTURE

They pretend to pay us and we pretend to work.

—Old joke in Soviet Union factories

Jobs are changing.

Today, only 25 percent of global workers have permanent jobs. That means three in four workers are doing work that is either temporary or on some type of short-term contract. Many different types of work are performed this way, from the 3.5 million truck drivers in America to the 700,000 restaurant workers. However, in the years to come work is going to look less like "productive" labor and will be more about "caring" labor. These are the jobs that we humans still prefer to be performed by another human.

Economists believe that by 2030, of the top fifteen occupations adding the most jobs, six will be in healthcare, ranging from home care aides to medical assistants to nurses.[18] Healthcare is becoming the largest job sector in America.[19] The Bureau of Labor Statistics predicts healthcare jobs will grow twice as fast as any other category over the next decade. That doesn't include the 40 million caregivers who provide over $500 billion of unpaid care to adults (usually family members) every year in America;

two-thirds of this work is done by older women.

So, when you picture the future of work, you shouldn't picture a young person working alongside a robot. Instead, you should picture a middle-aged woman, most likely of color, in scrubs caring for a patient in a hospital bed.

BUSINESS CREATION IS SLOWING

We aren't creating enough new businesses.

America's rate of new business creation has been declining for decades. In the 1980s, the rate of new business creation was 12 percent annually. Today, it's 8 percent.[20]

And the types of companies being created today often employ fewer workers.

TIRED

I glance up and see her eyes are closed.

I can hear the other one talking, but the one I can see is leaning against the metal cart, arms crossed and head down.

"I'm just so tired," she says to the other flight attendant. "When do we land? They always give you a trip right when your rest is over."

Workers are tired.

EIGHTY HOURS A WEEK

A worker I met works eighty hours a week in two different jobs. One job pays $7 per hour; the other pays $7.25 per hour.

Bad jobs with bad pay. It is bad for all of us.

CAREERS, JOBS, TASKS

Isn't school supposed to prepare you to function in the society in which you live in?

—Esther Wojcicki, godmother of Silicon Valley,
teacher, and author of *How to Raise Successful People,*
in our conversation on the *Bring It In* podcast

According to the World Economic Forum, 65 percent of children entering primary school today will eventually work in jobs that don't exist yet.[21]

The young people who will soon enter the workforce are going to need to be quick learners. They will have to be agile, nimble, and come to work with a wide foundation, knowing that they will need to find a track that they can fit into. Even then, the job they trained for and are good at may change before they have been able to fully monetize their skills in the marketplace.

That is, if they can even get the job.

The amount of education needed to win a job has risen more than the amount of education you need to do the job. Since 1980, the number of U.S. jobs requiring more than a high school education has grown by 68 percent. Of the 50 million new jobs that will be added in America by 2028, only 37 percent will require an advanced education.[22] This has resulted in a different kind of work with different demands.

While prior generations may have enjoyed a career or a job, more and more it looks as if our work is just a random assortment of tasks.

MEET THE SERVANT ECONOMY

Today, 83 percent of all jobs in America are considered service jobs. These jobs continue to dominate new job creation, where nine in ten jobs are in the service sector.[23]

These jobs will be less routine and will change rapidly as technology and automation continue their steady march forward.

But look closer, and you will notice we don't actually have a service economy. We have a servant economy.

See, in America it's believed we value equality, freedom, and opportunity for everyone. However, when you lack choice in the job (or jobs) you do, you feel vulnerable. When you lack economic security, you're more likely to feel you have no choice but to take a bad job or stay in a job you don't like. Lack of choice makes workers feel scared. It makes workers feel anxious. It makes workers feel powerless.

Like servants.

Many workers have no control. Their employers pull all the strings in deciding when, where, and how work is performed. Just look at the restaurant industry, where workers are overworked, underpaid, and often disrespected while performing dangerous work and experiencing huge amounts of physical wear and tear. In 2022, the average hourly wage for cooks and food prep workers and fast food workers was $13.02 and $11.47, respectively.

WAITING

In Edward Chisholm's *A Waiter in Paris,* the author explores his personal experience working in restaurants in Paris. It's kind of a more recent version of Anthony Bourdain's book *Kitchen Confidential*.

The author shares a conversation between waiters: "All of us have something else. We wouldn't be waiters if we didn't think we were waiting to be somewhere else. . . it's funny, in English you call our job waiting—it's accurate. We're all waiting for something."[24]

GREEN BADGES

Everybody wants to work in tech. It's cool.

Many of Silicon Valley's biggest tech companies have headquarters or even campuses for their workers to come to with all types of cool. From Meta to Google to X, tech giants employ thousands who work in frontline jobs like cafeteria staff, cooks, security, baristas, parking valets, and personal trainers. These workers often have a very different experience from the tech employees—if they even are actual employees.

Many companies employ contractors and contingent workers to perform the jobs that are viewed as nowhere near as mission critical to the companies' success, because these workers don't touch "the product."

When your workplace is broken up into different groups, what do you do? You give them a way to be identified as separate and different. Some tech companies give a "green badge" to workers who work at the company but not on the product. The badge signifies that they aren't really employees and aren't entitled to the same benefits that come with a staff software engineer's badge.

Despite all the hard work a tech company puts in to make working there seem like not just any ordinary job but instead a fun place on a mission to disrupt the world,the fun is only for some workers. It's just another example of how misaligned work is today.

Split up into groups. Identified by a badge. Different colors.

NO MEMBERSHIP

I walked into a building on Broad Street in Newark, New Jersey, for a meeting with a tech company. Big lobby. Fancy security desk.

I greeted the two security guards. One was standing. One was sitting at the desk. I handed one my driver's license, checked in on the tablet, and sat down to wait.

While I sat there, a company executive entered through the revolving doors and approached the security desk. She looked important. She acted important.

She swiped in and then pointed to a video monitor that featured company news and announcements. She pointed to the announcement about a new educational program the company had released and went on to tell both security guards about how great it was.

"Have either of you downloaded and listened to it?"

Both shake their head no. The seated security guard went back to his phone.

"You really have to check it out. It's a must listen."

The executive continued to the elevator, pressed the button, and disappeared.

The two security guards looked at each other. The one sitting shook his head and said, "If only they gave us some access. Then we'd check it out."

Green badges.

Work Was Built This Way

To appraise a society, examine its ability to be self-correcting.

—David Shipler, *The Working Poor*

We can rebuild work.

Looking through old pictures, I come across one from my

birthday in May 2020. I was sitting in the back patio at Apulia, an Italian restaurant in Hoboken, New Jersey.

Frankie, the owner, and Red, his second in command, had become my friends. I had a front-row seat for how these guys fought through the pandemic on a daily basis. They and their team were working on the front lines and carrying, at the very least, the same heavy schedule as before the pandemic, but now definitely with more stress.

They set up a table in the front of the restaurant as a barrier, a signal to everyone from Uber Eats pickup drivers to guests that this is the line. Can't come in any further. But because it's my birthday, they let us past the line and I'm sitting in their back patio. Actually, not so much because of me—I think my three-year-old daughter Nico had a lot to do with it. She would hang in the back and jump off their stairs, eat pizza, run around, and know if she wasn't too much of a pain in the ass then she may get a gelato scoop or three before we leave. The team would hang with us in the gaps between orders. We just wanted to get out of the dungeon that had become our home.

We sat. We ate. We drank. We watched as their team made it all work. And how they made the conscious choice to take care of their customers and their workers—not take care of their customers in lieu of their workers.

We have to build work to look like this for everyone. And here's the deal. We can.

A war on talent, human capital, CEOs making exorbitantly more than their workers, workers as servants. It all shows how misaligned work is today. We now are giving new names to the trends that are a byproduct of this misalignment in order to compartmentalize and explain them away. We have had a great resignation, a great rethink, quiet quitting, and boss loss. These labels don't solve anything other than helping to headline a corporate webinar or the next industry conference program.

Problems are solved by people taking action.

Action to rebuild work will be hard. It will require courage. It will require sacrifice. It will require decency. It's not a question of whether we have the ability to fix the misalignment problem. We do. Instead, it's whether our current approach to work can continue favoring a lucky few while everybody else get screwed regardless of how hard they work.

We understand the problems but have proven unwilling.

It's time to act.

CHAPTER 5

Failing at Education

*Our people compete in a world where what you
can earn depends largely on what you can learn.*

—PRESIDENT BILL CLINTON

After twenty years of teaching at an elementary school in a suburb
of Miami, Florida, Natalie had to make a choice.

She was having a hard time making ends meet; her school
district hadn't raised pay in a decade. Natalie was single and had
two kids, aged 6 and 9. Given her situation, she decided to take
a part-time job to supplement her income. It would mean she
couldn't spend time after school with her kids and would even
have to miss dinner a few nights a week. It would mean she would
have to find childcare, more costs to cut into her extra pay.

She was looking for an extra eighteen to twenty hours a week.
She found it at a Chick-fil-A located conveniently between her
home and her school. She took it.

So, after a full day at school, she would head over to her
second job at Chick-fil-A. Sometimes she'd be there until mid-
night and then get home around 12:30 a.m.

She said: "Most days, I'm exhausted. I work hard at school
and then have times when I see my students come through the

drive-thru after school. What kind of message does that send? I feel disrespected."

I asked why.

"They pay us teachers so little."

WHAT MAKES A GOOD EDUCATION?

A good education requires a few things:

1. Worthy content
2. Skill-based pedagogy
3. Engaged students
4. It also requires teachers. Capable teachers.

17 YEARS

When countries get richer they tend to consume more education.

This is where we are in the United States. The strategy has been to pile up as much formal education as you can as early as you can. The market will then reward you with the best jobs and security.

We get to work on education right away. Starting at age 5 or 6, the educational journey for our luckiest will result in at least seventeen years in a classroom. It's how we're doing in those classrooms that's the problem.

We are failing.

We are failing to teach the right stuff. The educational journey has a responsibility to prepare a student to navigate the world. But most of what schools teach, especially across the over 40,000 public and private secondary schools, is considered to have little to no value in the labor market by employers. Over 40 percent of high school coursework and 40 percent of college majors have received a score of "low" in usefulness.[1]

We are failing to improve. Literacy, numeracy, and problem-solving in U.S. teens trails many other developed nations. In a recent study, almost one-third of American fifteen-year-olds performed below the baseline necessary to thrive in the modern world. The only area where American students really excelled was in overconfidence. They were found to be more likely than kids in other countries to believe they had mastered a topic even when they did worse.[2]

We are failing to properly assess. Today, our goals have shifted to assessments and standardized tests that decide educational funding, all while the tests do more harm than provide valuable insights. Measuring the effectiveness of actual learning continues to be the most outdated feature of our current education system.[3] Research over the past nine decades has shown that schools have failed to transfer learning on any significant level.[4]

With two-thirds of all skills required to win at work believed to be changing in the next decade, what will we do? How will we keep up?

HIGHER EDUCATION: DYSFUNCTIONAL, COSTLY, AND UNACCOUNTABLE

Higher education is the only product where the consumer tries to get as little out of it as possible.

—Arnold Kling, economist at the Cato Institute

Today in the U.S., over 20 million students are enrolled in higher education, including about 40 percent of all eighteen to twenty-four year olds.[5] The total number of colleges and universities has more than doubled between 1950 and today and the combined revenues for postsecondary education (based on the most recent data available for 2015 to 2016) totaled $584 billion.[6]

Check out these numbers:

- We have 4,294 four-year colleges and 517 two-year colleges.
- The average metro area has five colleges and two universities.[7]
- The total number of college students have grown almost nine times since 1950, from 2.28 million in 1950 to 20.2 million in 2014.[8]

Higher education is dysfunctional, costly, and unaccountable for its actual performance of preparing all Americans for lives and careers. It is in dire need of transformation. Data continues to show that we are failing to produce not just the overall number of college graduates our workplace needs, but we aren't producing the right type of college graduate.

Too many students continue to buy degrees in majors for career pathways that aren't pursued. In 2008–09, over 94,000 students earned a bachelor's degree in psychology, but there are only 174,000 psychologists in practice. In the same year, 83,000 earned a bachelor's degree in communications, but only 54,000 work as a reporter or news correspondent.[9] Additionally, according to the Department of Education, the recognized overall number of occupations is up, growing from 269 categories in 1950 to 830 today. Academic degrees haven't kept pace.

We could follow other models of how to respond to the shifting nature of work and the demands of our communities. We could look to European countries with positive outcomes. In Switzerland, for example, over 70 percent of students learn a marketable skill through a vocational track that includes apprenticeships.[10] Their goal is different: to create the right workers for the economy. It may be coders. It may be electricians. It may be drivers.

To make it worse, we make it difficult to fund programs and use standardized test scores to decide where funding goes. In recent years, forty-three U.S. states have cut funding for public colleges and universities, all while increasing tuition and fees.[11] We live in a society where you start out unequal. Inequality is made worse when your ability to achieve is measured by a single standardized test score. These become a way of justifying which groups get more entitlements because of the community the stork dropped them in.

Why is our education system ineffective? Why aren't we getting better? Why aren't we spending more?

WHO'S DOING THE TEACHING?

Too many students are arriving at college unprepared for more challenging coursework. This means the job of topping off their high school education shortfall goes to the college. However, you might be surprised to learn that most of the professors on campus aren't even full-time staff members. Too often, they're underpaid adjunct and part-time faculty. The practice of shifting from full-time faculty to adjuncts has been decades in the making. Today three in four professors at the university level are off the tenure track; 50 percent of these 1.3 million professors are part-time adjuncts.[12]

I can speak from experience here. As an adjunct professor in the Rutgers Global Sports Business program, I teach the Revenue Generation in Sports class every spring semester. It's an experience I value. I feel it's important for me to have a well-rounded understanding of the next generation entering our workforce.

Our universities need to have some adjuncts. I have nothing against the model. Anything that can ensure that the education being delivered is properly up to speed with the state of work just creates better value for students as the consumer of the education. However, adjuncts often are underpaid and not afforded the same opportunities, wages, and protections that tenure-track and tenured professors receive. While we can support the movement by universities to get more instructors in the classroom with relevant work experience, it should also be understood that there is a strong financial incentive for this hiring practice.

More workers with fewer benefits, lower pay, and less security.

NO PLAY ZONE

Let them mess up and screw up.

—Dr. Jeff Brown, professor, psychologist, author of
The Winner's Brain: 8 Strategies Great Minds Use to Achieve Success,
in our conversation on the *Bring It In* podcast

I know we're talking about higher education, but many problems exist long before a student reaches college.

First, let's talk about parents. Snowplow parents. I wish I had come up with that title. They're the type of parent who tries to clear the way for their kids, making their path through life smooth and risk-free. These behaviors are believed to be negatively affecting young people by making them more risk-averse and psychologically fragile.[13]

Parents are definitely taking a more hands-on role. Child development researchers Foster Cline and Jim Fay coined the term "helicopter parenting" to describe the way these parents overmanage their kids, even preventing children from informal play. They claim that the more parents are hyper-engaged with their children, the less their children are likely to participate in physical activities.[14]

Now, let's talk about play and how it ties to avoiding failure. Over 40,000 U.S. schools no longer have recess. Why? Fear of failure is a leading reason—school administrators want students to spend that time preparing for standardized tests instead. A lack of funding for staff to supervise is also a factor, showing pretty clearly where our priorities lie. As of 2023, over 40 percent of schools provided less than thirty minutes of recess per day, and only nine states require schools to offer daily recess.[15]

As Brian Sutton-Smith, author of *The Ambiguity of Play*, writes, "Play is vastly underrated. It gives the brain a workout. It is cognitively challenging. It requires attention. It sharpens senses. It both demands and inspires mental dexterity and flexibility. It thrives on complexity, uncertainty, and possibility. That makes play just about the perfect preparation for life in the 21st century."[16]

The benefits of play are huge. It makes us more flexible mentally and behaviorally. It is proven to help us to adapt, especially to failure and challenge. And given our evolutionary history, you can go so far as to say that we're the most human when we're playing.

Unfortunately, most play today has moved away from just hitting the park with your friends and moved to some travel sports team tournament run by parents as if it were their own real-life career mode sports game. It's not about learning sportsmanship and having a good time. It's all about winning and losing in some sick and twisted parental ego-rich competition.

IMMIGRANTS

Over 5 percent of all U.S. college students—which makes up more than a million students—are international students. In 1980, immigrants were just 7 percent of the college-educated workforce. Today, they make up 17 percent of America's college-educated workforce.[17]

Companies are normally the primary gatekeeper for immigrant workers, but colleges and universities have a major say in what the future of our workforce looks like. They get to decide what the candidate pool looks like for companies when they come to campus to recruit.

AN INEQUALITY MACHINE

The American education system perpetuates inequality.

As you grow up in America you're told to work hard and study hard. If you do, you'll be rewarded with a nice job and be on the path to a good life. We are sold this dream.

But sometimes hard work isn't enough. The disparity in the American education system is evident in economic outcomes. On average, a white household led by a high school graduate earns more than a Black household led by a college graduate. This inequality extends to wealth. The median net worth of white households in 2019 was significantly higher, at $188,200, compared to just $24,100 for Black households.[18]

The higher education system now functions as a mechanism that sorts individuals onto unequal paths. It sorts not only based on the perceived effort and merits of an individual but also by the circumstances of their birth.

A growing trend is the concentration of Black, Latino, and

working-class white students into underfunded two-year and open-admission four-year colleges. Unfortunately, only around 49 percent of those students who enroll manage to graduate. The primary reason for the poor completion rates is not just a decline in college readiness from high schools. It's also because of a lack of resources within the schools themselves.

And, contrary to what you may think, the difficulty of obtaining a bachelor's degree is often lower at highly selective colleges versus less rigorous ones. This is because highly selective colleges offer more resources to help students.

A top-performing high school student has an SAT score above 1000. Graduation rates from the most selective schools for top-performing high school students are 87 percent. The story is very different for top-performing students from open-access colleges—public institutions that admit at least 80 percent of applicants. Here graduation rates for top-performing students are only 58 percent.[19]

Selective colleges are mostly closed off for those without the right family credentials. At these schools, students and faculty primarily engage with those who share similar economic and social backgrounds. Many determined students from working-class and disadvantaged backgrounds, irrespective of race, often find themselves excluded from attending these institutions.

Even when they are accepted, they're never really accepted. It's not surprising that people from underrepresented groups view colleges and universities as country clubs whose primary focus is to help the elite kids get a fast start.

CHECKING BOXES

It's easy to avoid poverty, they say. You just have to check the boxes:

- ☐ Step 1: Graduate from high school.
- ☐ Step 2: Get a good full-time job.
- ☐ Step 3: Get married before you have kids.

That formula doesn't work. I'm not sure it ever did.

If we want to talk about work and how to build high-performance organizations, we have to talk frankly about this stuff. Today, a child's trajectory is largely predetermined by the social class into which they are born. In America today, the likelihood of attending an Ivy League college for children from the top 1 percent of wealthy households is 77 times higher compared to children from the bottom 20 percent of households.[20] Only 5 percent of students in the top 500 colleges nationwide come from the lowest 25 percent of society in terms of family income.[21]

The data shows that "talent" doesn't matter anywhere near as much as where you come from. The most talented disadvantaged young person doesn't achieve outcomes as favorable as those of their least talented but advantaged peers. For instance, a child from the top 25 percent of family income and parental education, despite having low test scores, has a 71 percent likelihood of graduating from college and securing a good job by their mid-20s. However, a high-scoring student from a low-income background faces just a 31 percent chance of achieving the same outcome.[22]

The numbers are worse if you are a minority.

We are leaving real skills on the table.

STUDENTS FOR FAIR ADMISSIONS V. HARVARD

What are the courts doing to tackle our challenges in the classroom?

In June 2023, the Supreme Court issued a split verdict regarding two challenges to affirmative action policies at Harvard and the University of North Carolina. The court ruled against their current programs.

Chief Justice John Roberts, writing for the majority, stated that the existing admission systems lack clear and measurable objectives justifying the use of race, inadvertently employ race negatively, involve racial stereotypes, and lack definitive endpoints. As a result, these admissions programs were deemed inconsistent with the principles of the Equal Protection Clause of the Fourteenth Amendment.

In her dissent, Justice Sonia Sotomayor voiced that the outcome of this decision implies that an individual's skin color might influence the assessment of their potential but is deemed irrelevant in evaluating that person's unique contributions to fostering a diverse learning environment.

THE CHILD AND THE ROAD

At some point, parents will be dead and gone, and God help the child who has led a life so involved with parental involvement that they will not know how to do things for themselves, solve problems, and cope with inevitable setbacks.

—Julie Lythcott-Haims, former dean at
Stanford University, award-winning author, TED speaker,
and activist in our conversation on the *Bring It In* podcast

A common concern is whether we are preparing the child for the road or the road for the child. Parents have a critical role to play in the education process. Not just at home, but by the work they do outside of school that affects the policies and operations of our education system. We are failing on all fronts.

Rich kids often get access to the paved highway that helps them get to their destination quickly.

Poor kids get the dirt road full of roadblocks and checkpoints along the way.

How fast you go is influenced by how we have designed a system that creates too many disparities in learning opportunities. Your success or failure is too predetermined. Where you start on your journey is determined at birth and further influenced by race, gender, and wealth.

We know the helicopter parent manipulates laws and social norms to make things like unsupervised play or walking in the park alone almost a crime. We know limiting these things negatively affects the resilience or mental health of young people. But the helicopter parent has nothing on how slowly our education system is moving to solve the problem of the child and the road.

Paving it for some, not for all. Clearing the road for some, not for all.

WORKING THROUGH SCHOOL

In backward nations young people work. In advanced nations young people study.

I worked through college.

It wasn't easy. It wasn't because of the difficulty of the material. It wasn't because of the grading or the teachers. It was because college didn't care that I was also working a job to support myself.

Higher education hasn't been responsive to the realities of today's working student. Instead, it has created barriers that too often keep adult workers out.

Just because they make it hard doesn't mean they don't have a lot of experience. Higher education works with many older, nontraditional learners. (Apologies for the term "nontraditional learner." It's awkward and ranks right up there for me with "unskilled worker." It's their term, not mine.) Back to my point. In 2016, 8.2 million of the 20.5 million students enrolled in U.S. colleges and universities were twenty-five years of age or older. So, 40 percent of students aren't what most traditionally envision when they think about a college student. By 2025, the forecast is that older students in college will rise to over 9.7 million.[23]

A working student is a different kind of consumer of education. Beyond value, they're looking for an experience that's more flexible and adaptive to their current flow of work. The current way we do education wasn't designed to serve students who work. Support and flexibility are lacking around attendance, technology to support learning, and even compassion in understanding that most workers who are now also students often aren't ready on Day 1. Distance learning initiatives need to be more robust. A working student's biggest challenge is not that they are dollar poor, but that they are time poor. We must adjust our college experience from a model built around the frat kid whose biggest worry is if mommy put their beer money allowance in their account on time to one centered on the reality that too many have responsibilities that are being ignored and thus shut out.

LATE REGISTRATION

I came home and found my mom on the couch.

This was her normal happy hour spot. And while I wasn't surprised by the martini glass, I was surprised to see what she was reading.

Application forms to the University of Miami.

I raised my voice, "I already picked my college. I'm not switching. Don't even try it. If I have to fill out one more fucking application I am going to . . . "

"No, this isn't for you. It's for me."

My eyebrows raised. "OK. What for?"

She didn't look up. She kind of shrugged. Took a sip. And said, "Always wanted to."

I nodded with support. She kept glancing through the papers. My heart sunk. I knew how capable she was. I knew how she would have soared. I also knew how impossible it would be.

A few days later I came home from work. And there it was. I pulled out the drawer that held our trash can and saw the application papers sitting on top.

The papers made it look so easy. But it was just out of reach.

$1 MILLION MORE

Today, we have another problem with messaging. Workers aren't as interested in going back to college, not just because of concerns regarding the cost and the time, but because they also question the value. Only one in five adults thinks college is adequately preparing people for the workforce and over 40 percent of workers believe colleges aren't keeping up with the marketplace for workers.[24]

We need to educate people better on the value that does exist.

Education does pay off.

A college education is expensive. Economists consider college a "positional good," which means its value is more akin to a luxury watch than groceries. Its value comes from its price—and the price is artificially inflated because most can't afford it.

But the data is clear. In the U.S., a year of higher education raises earnings by 5 to 10 percent. Here's a rundown of some other benefits for college graduates:

- They outearn high school graduates in over 90 percent of occupations.[25]
- Their median earnings, if between ages twenty-five to thirty-four, are 70 percent more than a high school graduate.[26]
- They are six times more likely to be able to work from home versus those without a high school degree.[27]
- The more education you have, the more mobile you are. Almost 50 percent of college graduates will move out of their birth state by age thirty, while only 27 percent of high school graduates and 17 percent of high school dropouts will do so.
- The wage advantage of a person with a bachelor's degree over someone with just a high school diploma has risen from 36 percent to 66 percent (since 1970), or to about $1 million in earnings over a working lifetime.[28]
- An investment of $102,000 to get a four-year degree will help you earn over $1 million more in your lifetime. That's more than twice what you would earn if you just held a high school diploma.[29]

It's not just that the value of a college education pays a premium. It's that the value of only having a high school degree is declining. In 2017, high school graduates earned 2.7 percent less than they would have in 1979, adjusted for inflation. Workers without a high school diploma did even worse, earning about 10 percent less. High school graduates out-earn dropouts in 93 percent of occupations.[30]

There are no expiration dates on a college diploma. It has a value that continues to pay off. A college education may be only a signal, but it's a strong one in today's marketplace—regardless of any learning that actually occurs.

While many try, too many run out of time as they pursue a degree.

GRADE: INCOMPLETE

Most people don't have a formal degree or credential today.

It's easy to think an advanced degree is normal when everyone around you has one, but in fact, 65.1 percent of people in the U.S. labor force and 87 percent of all Americans don't have a college degree.[31] It's not for lack of trying. Nearly 14 percent of Americans start but don't complete high school, and a third of the U.S. population spends twelve years in school, gets a high school diploma, and then stops.[32]

Most of those who attend a community college don't complete a degree. Only 27 percent of students who are first-timers at a community college will earn an associate degree in three years and only 25 percent will go on to earn a bachelor's degree in six years.[33]

This is not good news for a popular strategy that has been used to attempt to persuade students to study at a community college for even one year. The supporting data is strong. The median earnings of an associate degree holder are 20 percent higher than those of a high school graduate.[34] Another year of school leads to a 10 percent raise for the rest of your life, along with higher noncash benefits, better quality of life, and lower unemployment.[35] In a 2019 speech, President Barack Obama urged Americans to not necessarily complete college but to just try to do one more year. It's one thing to say it—and another for society to support it.

While employers value the achievements of college graduates, they don't value the skills of those who have failed to finish college. Starting from 1980, earnings have declined for those lacking a college degree, which includes those who have completed some college education.

We should also ask if one more year will even be enough in the years ahead. Will one more year result in the necessary signals to benefit completely, or will it just result in a scenario where a student is left without a degree and with something that may burden them for years to come?

STUDENT LOANS

A millionaire starts a company. Raises capital. Employs workers. Spends exorbitantly. Runs out of money. Can't pay back investors. Files for bankruptcy. Two years later, the former millionaire starts a new company, and their phone rings, asking, "Where can we wire your new funds?"

Across town a student gets accepted into college. Raises money for college by applying for college loans. Does their best to graduate with honors. Works themselves down trying to survive and pay back loans. Runs out of money. Can't pay back the loans. Files for bankruptcy. Two years later, the student's phone rings, saying, "We are checking on the status of your past due loan amount."

BIDEN V. NEBRASKA AND DEPARTMENT OF EDUCATION

In 2020, Joe Biden ran for president on a platform that included a promise to forgive student debt. His executive orders were challenged.

In 2023, the Supreme Court was ready to rule on two cases challenging whether the Biden administration had the authority to eliminate over $400 billion in student loan debt. It would be a major win for President Biden and the over 45 million loan recipients across the nation who are collectively burdened with $1.6 trillion in federal college loans.

The intended action could have constituted one of the most financially significant executive measures in the history of the United States.

The court struck down the Biden administration's student loan forgiveness program.

A TEACHER WILL APPEAR

Parents and teachers are natural enemies because educators look out for all children while parents are concerned only with their own.

—Willard Waller, author of *The Sociology of Teaching*, 1932

Teachers are quitting.

Educational institutions from kindergarten to 12th grade in the U.S. are grappling with a growing challenge in retaining teachers, which holds the potential for significant consequences for society at large. A 2023 research study by McKinsey found nearly a third of U.S. K through 12 teachers are thinking of quitting. This is a big increase over the previous annual turnover rate for teachers of 8 percent. The annual rate is double that for schools designated for Title 1 funding, which is offered to schools that have a high percentage of poor students and need additional assistance. By comparison, the average teacher turnover rate in higher performing academic nations, such as Finland and Singapore, is closer to 3 to 4 percent.[36]

Teacher turnover affects everyone, but some more than others. Teacher turnover continues to disproportionately impact low-wage communities and students of color. The McKinsey study went on to find that:

- 40 percent of teachers in districts where most students received free and reduced-price lunches said they planned to leave.
- 38 percent of teachers are considering leaving in schools where students of color make up more than 75 percent of the student body.

This is not the right direction.

In the popular saying, when the student is ready, the teacher will appear. This may not be true anymore.

DROPPING OUT

In 2022, four million fewer teenagers enrolled in college than in 2012.[37]

Something is happening.

WE MUST EXPECT MORE FROM EDUCATION

Colleges and universities don't think workforce education is their problem.

—William B. Bonvillian, author of *Workforce Education: A New Roadmap*, lecturer at MIT, innovation and technology policy specialist in our conversation on the *Bring It In* podcast

If work expects more of workers, then we must expect more from education.

Perhaps no establishment has resisted change over the last three centuries more than higher education. The U.S. is failing to make sufficient investments in traditional nonprofit institutions like community colleges, while for-profit colleges are now taking in the majority of college-bound students. Research indicates for-profit educational institutions cost more compared to public schools, spend more on activities unrelated to teaching, and experience higher dropout rates.[38] All of this is done while selling the hopes that a college education is effectively preparing them for a career path and a job. Instead, too often the student is just being burdened with loan debt and a degree that more than likely fails to prepare them with the appropriate skills for today's jobs. I recently had a conversation with a business professor who admitted he had yet to even try out any AI application. What future is he preparing his students for?

We can do better.

We should start by better investing in our teachers. Not just in pay, but preparation. It is now that we need our best teachers. Just as I've pointed out the challenges that face working students today, we have to focus on not just retaining but developing our teachers to be prepared to educate students for where work is going. This will require new skills and continued development for not just students but also their instructors.

We need our teachers to feel ready to be teachers of the future. When it comes to teacher preparation, every current and future teacher must have a deep understanding of the science of learning and the workforce demands of the modern worker.[39] They must be able to create an environment that is not just lecture heavy but engagement rich. We're not doing well here. In a McGraw-Hill survey of 600 teachers in 2017, 70 percent said students are less likely to ask questions in class than just five years earlier.[40]

We need to support teachers. Today, over 94 percent of teachers spend between $500 and $750 of their own money every year for classroom supplies, including basic supplies like markers, paper, and pens. This totals nearly $3 billion a year that frontline teachers are out of pocket for, of which only up to $300 is tax-deductible.[41]

We need better technology to offer workers access to learning wherever they go. Schools understand that they can make more money by offering digital learning solutions, but they need to ensure the solution is not just hawking the same goods at a lower price. We have a moral responsibility to offer a quality education, given all the risks of failure that could come with not completing a degree.

A thriving and equitable education system that yields the best outcomes should be one that offers:

- Transparency to understand outcomes and the value of the degree.
- Access to quality instruction.
- Guidance, coaching, and mentorship.
- Opportunities to continue to access education while in the flow of work.
- Affordability.
- Credentials that are relevant for the workforce of today and tomorrow.

To help us get there, we need to make entrance to college more equitable and accessible. Some good places to start are:

- Eliminate legacy admissions.
- Appropriate financial aid better.
- Provide better support for young people when deciding on a major.
- Require admission of a minimum percentage of low-income students.

The worldwide number of people aged 25 to 34 with a college education is going to double by 2030. Even though these degrees are mostly signals, it's still concerning that the U.S. will be home to fewer than one in ten of them.[42]

We know all education often doesn't teach useful job skills. Employers continue to essentially reward workers with college degrees for coursework they used to know. We can't just point fingers at schools—employers have a role to play, too.

A more talented nation won't just happen. We can do better.

CHAPTER 6

Training Is Deficient

We can make those jobs better or worse. We can give
people more dignity or less. Those are the choices we make.

—PRESIDENT BARACK OBAMA

Max came into work at his auto factory job on Friday. It always
happens on Fridays.

This Friday was his last day. Kind of. He was given notice of
termination just after he clocked in. Then, along with dozens
of others, he was quickly given a rundown of corporate BS that
demanded they train their own replacements in order to get
their severance.

The union delegate in the room refused. Over the next few
days it became a major sticking point in the negotiations. The
company then offered an additional $3.50 an hour for any worker
who chose to cross the line and train workers in South Carolina,
and $8 an hour if they were willing to train workers in Mexico.

They eventually found common ground. The company
wouldn't make the severance contingent on training and would
instead seek out volunteers to deliver the training. But if they
didn't get enough volunteers, they would have to fire workers
without severance.

Max said, "At least they got trained. That must be nice. I had to figure all this stuff out on my own."

NOT A SKILL-BUILDING NATION

Many leaders told us they don't have the time in this high-pressure economy for the slow and tedious work of teaching people and helping them grow.

—Daniel Goleman, *Emotional Intelligence*

How are employers doing at investment in workforce training?

A 2016 White House report on AI, automation, and the economy points out that the U.S. spends only 0.1 percent of GDP on programs that help people adjust to workplace changes. The number has fallen every year since 1986.[1]

The U.S. is ranked second to last among industrial nations by the Organisation for Economic Co-Operation and Development (OECD) for investment in workforce training. The OECD tracks historical workforce investment trends and in this study was looking at the behavior of the top 31 industrial nations. When the U.S. does invest in workforce-related programs, the money often goes to those that already have a bunch of education—66 percent of workforce investment goes to workers who already have a college degree.

Here's a breakdown of current workforce investment in the U.S.:

- $177 billion in formal employer-provided training.
  - 58 percent goes to workers with college degrees.
  - 17 percent goes to workers with a high school education or less.

- $1.1 trillion spent on postsecondary education.
  - $655 billion on industry training and certification.
    - $177 billion on employer-provided formal training.
    - $413 billion on employer-provided informal training.

- $47 billion on apprenticeships and other workforce training.
- $18 billion on public job training.[2]

Employers do provide the majority of training for workers, but many report the amount of employer-provided training has declined, from 20 percent of employers offering training to just 11 percent between 1996 and 2008. Note that this reduction was even before the impact of the Great Recession. This reduction affected workers across industries, occupations, ages, education levels, and demographic groups.[3] But it's clear that the workers most affected were the ones in low-wage and mid-wage jobs.

See, employers prefer to hire new workers by using speculative assessments of their future performance, based primarily on where the worker went to school and their highest level of education. If you're lucky enough to have the right mix of credentials, then you'll have the best pick of where to work. The best jobs also offer the most opportunities for learning and development.[4] In the end, those most in need of development get less and less of a percentage of the training and development budgets and resources.

By the way, while the United States has significantly cut spending on these programs, in recent decades, it has significantly increased spending on prisons.

Deficient.

IT COSTS TOO MUCH

What employers really want are workers they don't have to train. Companies simply haven't invested much in training their workers.

—Peter Cappelli, director of the Wharton Center for Human Resources at the University of Pennsylvania

So, we get that our government underinvests in workforce education and development. How are companies doing?

A recent study by Accenture found only one in five employees has received any job training from their employers in the last five years and that 44 percent of companies offer zero upskilling or reskilling opportunities. And even when they do, 82 percent of the training is compliance or regulatory in nature. That we underinvest in training actually related to skills-building is a major problem.[5]

When the Business Roundtable, the most elite cohort of CEOs in America, asked employers, "Why do you not train?" 76 percent said cost.[6]

When we look at where the spending, although small, does go, it tells us not just what but who is valued. Data show that the majority of investment doesn't go to those most in need or the majority of workers on the front line. Instead, $0.83 of every dollar spent on training goes to develop senior managers, not to level up those on the front lines. This affects everybody—I'll talk about it more later in this book.

TRICKLE-DOWN TRAINING

I'm calling it trickle-down training.

It is the belief that if you invest in training and development for one elite group of employees, it will somehow magically trickle down from those sitting in the C suite to the those walking in through the service entrance. It makes no sense that we invest so much to develop senior managers and not to level up those on the front lines who want and need it most.

These investments support those who already have the most access to education, pay, and benefits. They often look more like sending executives to conferences in Vegas, where they can geek out on a Gary Vee rant instead of doing any actual skill development. These events don't get cut as much as they need to, but then again, they aren't about training anyway. They're about access, networking, and happy hours. I love hearing the HR person tell me, "I have no training budget," while they're standing at the lobby bar at the fancy resort hotel, sipping on a mocktail with their team and putting the tab on their corporate credit card.

When companies choose to limit training investment to only their senior leadership, managers, and highest-paid workers, they are sending a message of who they think is most important. It means our frontline workers are the group most impacted when companies are too cheap to invest in their people.

But they can afford those mocktails.

RETURN ON TRAINING

Why do we underinvest in training?

Because too many owners are scared. Companies typically underinvest in skills training out of fear that they won't retain the worker. The way many look at it, after the company provides training to a worker, they will most likely leave and take the investment with them to their next employer—or worse, to a potential competitor. Businesses look at this inability to recoup their training investment as a reason to be more intentional (discriminatory) about who gets access and who doesn't.

The result is that any training companies do tends to be very specific to the company, with little focus on building personal or professional development skills that may be transferable to the next job. According to 1Huddle gameplay data across seventeen million training events for 204 brands, it was found that only 11 percent of game topics created were on non-company, position-specific training. This is a true failure and has greatly contributed to a reskilling crisis in America. In 1979, young workers got 2.5 weeks of training a year. By 1995, young workers got only eleven hours of training a year.[7]

And what's the most common training topic? Workplace safety. Training deficient.

HIGH ROAD VS. LOW ROAD

Give people the opportunity to be able to go into a workplace and have you not just look at them because of the color of their skin or their religion, their background, their disability. Give them the opportunities to educate you.

—Eric LeGrand, renowned motivational speaker, entrepreneur, philanthropist, and former Rutgers football player in our conversation on the *Bring It In* podcast

Companies can take different approaches to developing their workers. Two strategies are most common today.

A High Road policy:

- Prioritizes investments in human capital, skills, and employee well-being.

- Emphasizes quality training, education, and skill development opportunities for workers, enabling them to access higher paying, more skilled jobs.
- Promotes fair wages, good working conditions, and opportunities for career advancement.
- Focuses on creating a skilled and adaptable workforce that can drive innovation and competitiveness.

A Low Road policy:

- Prioritizes short-term cost-cutting, minimal investments in training, and often results in lower wages and fewer benefits for workers.
- Creates flexibility for employers but can lead to poor working conditions, low job security, and limited opportunities for skill development.
- Is a race to the bottom approach where businesses compete based on low wages and minimal benefits rather than on innovation and quality.
- Undermines worker morale, leads to higher turnover rates, and hinders economic growth in the long run.

Imagine the journey to becoming a better worker via workforce development as a race. The difference between the high road and low road policies is like choosing between a well-planned adventure with skill-building pit stops or taking a risky shortcut that leaves you stuck in traffic. When it comes to workforce development, taking the high road might not be the quickest, but it leads to a smoother and more rewarding journey for the organization.

High road policies focus on long-term economic growth through investments in human capital and quality work environments. They aim to create a skilled workforce capable of adapting to changing job requirements.

On the other hand, low road policies prioritize short-term cost savings for employers at the potential expense of workers' well-being and long-term economic stability.

UNSKILLED VS. SKILLED

It's not a good time to be a worker with "basic skills."

Since the 1980s the federal government has defined a worker as skilled or unskilled based on whether they have a college degree.

This misclassification of workers and their abilities isn't just wrong—it results in companies and individuals missing out on opportunities.

We rob workers of dignity when we label their work unskilled.

THE MATTHEW EFFECT

The Matthew Effect is a concept derived from verse 25:29 in the Gospel of Matthew in the New Testament: "For unto every one that hath shall be given, and he shall have abundance: but from him that hath not shall be taken away even that which he hath." This has application today as we think about work, including education and workforce learning. The Matthew Effect suggests that those who already possess a certain level of knowledge, skills, or advantages tend to accumulate more of those advantages over time, while those who start with fewer advantages face increasing challenges in catching up.

In terms of workforce learning, the Matthew Effect can play out in several ways:

1. **Skill accumulation**. Individuals who already have a strong foundation of skills and knowledge are better equipped to acquire new skills and learning. They are more likely to succeed in learning opportunities and gain new qualifications, making them even more competitive in the job market.
2. **Learning opportunities**. Those who have access to quality education and training tend to gain more opportunities for continuous learning and professional development. This further enhances their skill set and employability.
3. **Job placement and career advancement**. People with strong initial qualifications might secure better job placements and advancement opportunities. This could include access to positions with more training, learning, and growth potential.
4. **Learning curve**. Individuals with prior knowledge find it easier to learn and adapt to new information and technologies. They can pick up new skills more quickly, which can be an advantage in rapidly changing industries.
5. **Networking.** People who already have some advantages are more likely to connect with mentors, influencers, and industry professionals, which can lead to more learning opportunities and career growth.

The Matthew Effect is at play at work today. It explains how initial advantages for some can lead to a cycle of accumulating more skills, opportunities, and success, while those with fewer advantages face challenges in accessing the same level of opportunities and growth. It's why providing equitable access to education, training, and career development is critical to ensure a more inclusive, skilled, and high-performing workforce.

CREDENTIAL INFLATION

There is nothing worse than sitting through professional development that's meaningless. It's really demoralizing.

—Patrice Bain, author of *Powerful Teaching*

Today, six million jobs that formerly didn't require a college credential now demand one. At the same time, a college degree won't be required for two-thirds of jobs by 2028.

You do the math.

Today, over 738,000 unique credentials flood our workforce.[8]

SOME GET TRAINED, SOME DON'T

In the fall of 2022 I had a conversation with leadership at RWJ Barnabas Health, a large network of healthcare providers in New Jersey. They told me that their chief human resources officer had retired and an interim role was being determined. While this was happening, they would pause all investment in training and development.

In July 2023, RWJ Barnabas Health was preparing to avert a strike by nurses.

In an interview, COO John Doll said, "I'm really disappointed we are at this point. We really have tried everything to avoid the workers going out. And we're continuing to do so."

The hospital was preparing for the potential that 700 full-time nurses would strike. They responded to this by investing in nurses from other areas of the country, flying them in and putting them through intensive training in preparation for a strike. It is believed that the hospital has spent over $17 million on strike preparation.

It would be interesting to see how that investment could have been put to better work, say by caring for their existing nurses.

RESISTANT TO CHANGE

Sitting at a conference and listening to a panel of directors of training talk about how they approach training their workers:

- "Nothing is better than shoulder to shoulder."
- "I'm old school."
- "Like the 95 percent of brands that cut training in the last three years, we had to just get people to work."
- "One of the best things about us is we don't change much."

My interpretation below:

- "We have no money for a digital learning solution."
- "I'm cheap."
- "We don't care about training."
- "We don't like to learn new things."

Failing to invest in workforce training and development infra-structure has resulted in a workforce that is fragile. Workers aren't able to quickly adjust to new jobs as automation and its impact comes to fruition.

Deficient.

ROI

When somebody says somebody's unskilled, they're not. They've got a lot of skills. You just haven't recognized which ones.

—Dr. Fergus Connolly, performance coach for Liverpool FC, Boston Bruins, San Francisco 49ers, and Carolina Panthers; speaker; author of *Game Changer: The Art of Sports Science* in our conversation on the *Bring It In* podcast

What is the difference between a $100 customer and a $10,000 customer? One comes a hundred times and the other comes just one time.

Failing to invest in training is a stupid business decision.

Frontline workers are closer to the customer experience than any other individual within an organization. Companies spend significant resources on the creation of campaigns that they hope trickle all the way down to the interaction between a customer and a frontline worker. The perspective to be a cheap ass when it comes to worker investment isn't just shortsighted— it's a weak business decision.

The front line affects the bottom line. And, since customers don't talk about averages, it only makes sense that companies should be pouring more time, energy, and resources into the worker experience and development. Not less.

BILL GATES AND CONGRESS

In 2007, Bill Gates spoke in front of Congress and shared three ways we can improve U.S. competitiveness:

1. Better education and training for students and workers.
2. Encouragement of more research and development.
3. Greater immigration for high-skilled workers.

How about we just start with #1.

Who is responsible?

Talk to workers today, and they'll tell you they believe it is the responsibility of their employer to provide them with the learning and training opportunities necessary to perform the job. They also believe it is the company that is responsible for actively participating in their reskilling as work and their job changes.

Gallup found the same thing in a survey of employees. Sixty-one percent say companies should be responsible for retraining workers, yet only three in ten U.S. workers strongly agree that there is someone at their workplace who encourages their development.[9] Given the speed at which tasks at work will be affected by change, we should invest in technology that allows us to build skills on multiple fronts, whether for leveling up a worker for the current job, reskilling them for a new job, or upskilling them for whatever the next job may be.

We also must ensure the technology we use enables us to train the worker while they are already working—in the flow of work. This is a major pain point today. Companies are stuck with outdated desktop-based technology that can't reach the majority of workers, who are mostly hourly, deskless, or frontline. These systems have been created more out of administrative convenience rather than being grounded in any learning science. Too many organizations still invest in learning management systems and bulky e-learning platforms that require you to click and watch videos without any real data showing this mode has any lasting impact on learning.

We can look for these misses in action in a large sector of our workforce, such as retail. Back in the day, retail training was pretty bare bones. Stores and chains that were comfortable with old-school retail setups and staff that barely got any training are now in for a big wake-up call. They've got an uphill battle to keep their workforce up to speed, given their lack of technology adoption. They likely will need to supplement any in-person training experiences with an online platform that can meet workers where they are—especially if they want to get workers up to speed quickly. Additionally, they will need to invest in additional training for frontline managers to ensure they are prepared to respond to the changing nature of their front line.

These are big investments. At a time when automation and technology are knocking loudly and publicly on the door, it will be easier than ever to tell which side companies are taking.

I find it unjust that we live in a time of an abundance of technology but only 1 percent of workforce training, education, and development today is mobile-first. We need to use all the tools at our disposal to help our workers succeed.

Isn't that leadership? Don't we owe it to them?

People who have repeatedly failed can't succeed until they learn they are capable of success.

We need to change how we develop our people. And fast.

We need to consider that the way organizations approach people development are going to change in three major ways:

1. What we teach.
2. How we teach it.
3. When we teach it.

Before we approach these three questions, we must start by seeing work through the eyes of our workers. When new hires come on board, they already carry ingrained notions about learning and stepping out of their comfort zones. These notions have been molded by their past experiences, the good and the bad.

They have a direct impact on the confidence of the worker. High-performing organizations must be great at not just hiring workers with confidence but also at developing confidence in their workers, who may enter their organization with experiences that have weakened their belief in themselves and their abilities.

Workers need a strong sense of self-confidence in order to set goals, execute difficult tasks, reframe failure as learning opportunities, and work through difficult situations.

We need to do the right thing by the people that trust us with their labor. The effectiveness of any training and development program is greatly impacted by the knowledge, attitudes, and behaviors of the ones doing the teaching. Our leaders must consider that workers who have repeatedly failed—in school, sports, work, life—can't succeed until they learn they are capable of success.

INVEST

Pray for the dead. And fight like hell for the living.

—*Mother Jones*

Many say the best job training is a job. In reality, the best job training is a job that trains you.

Workers want to grow.

Time and time again, in every survey of workers, we're surprised to learn how interested workers are in their own career development. According to a survey in 2022, retail employees on the front line said they were quitting because they didn't have enough flexibility on the job and lacked career growth opportunities.[10] It's time for companies to approach training and development as more than just a safety seminar or a harassment and discrimination module. We should take risks on our people, not just check boxes by deploying useless training that is solely focused on mitigating it.

This is also true in our choice of the technology we invest in. Many workers today are long on time and short on experience; others are short on time but long on experience. This means companies need to create an environment where workers at all corners of the workplace can access learning and development opportunities within their existing flow of work.

While mobile solutions for workforce education makes sense, many companies underinvest out of fear of litigation for a worker doing what might look like work off the clock. Many of my favorite conversations are with HR "leaders," who spend more time being concerned about a worker accessing learning and education on their mobile phones outside of work than if their strategy is actually helping their people. There are ways to reduce risk while still giving your worker the development opportunities they deserve. But they require a caring employer.

Companies must also stop thinking about training and development programs as a sunk cost. In fact, it's more likely that costs go up when you fail to replenish skills. They need to keep in mind that when workers are prepared, they feel confident, and when they are confident, they smile at work. Their smile brings a smile to the customers' faces. They go together.

Better and happier employees don't just result in happier customers. They result in higher sales.

But the people responsible for employee growth are not always positioned or prepared to offer it.

CHAPTER 7

Human Resources Is Under-Resourced

The forest was shrinking, but the trees kept voting for the ax.
Because its handle was made of wood, they thought that it was one of them.

—TURKISH PROVERB

Alyssa was the head of human resources.

I was on a call with her, talking about her frontline workers. As the person responsible for human resources at a major sports hospitality company whose name must not be spoken, Alyssa was logged on to the call from her desk. In other words, from the kitchen counter in her Upper East Side home.

We were set to talk about how global workers across their properties were utilizing the 1Huddle mobile game platform for training. They had some amazing results—near perfect gameplay. But this was a cancellation call. She told me they were canceling our mobile training solution in favor of a desktop-only platform that would be used for onboarding and safety training only.

I shared with Alyssa that a few players on their platform were playing games outside of working hours. Alyssa stopped me as I was showing her a young woman from Cleveland who had played nearly 70 percent of all her games before or after work, presumably as a way to learn more and prepare for work.

Alyssa rolled her eyes. Then she leaned back and said, laughingly, "Why would she even do that?"

This was the person responsible for training and development, someone who was privileged enough to WFK (work from kitchen). I found it sad that she would look down upon a worker for trying to improve and get better.

I GOT A PROBLEM WITH HR

Ready to talk HR?

Former SEIU leader Andy Stern tells a story in his book, *Raising the Floor,* about a group of HR managers who were tasked with deconstructing the job of a human resources specialist. They were asked to break the job down into its component tasks. The group determined that 65 percent of tasks performed by this role could be immediately automated.

The group went on to say, "If we had 1,000 employees in HR, 300 were great, 400 were okay and the rest didn't have a clue in terms of getting people in the company the information they needed."[1]

This ain't baseball. Batting .300 isn't going to work here.

It is my belief that the United States has the weakest human resources departments in the industrialized world. They have only been made worse by the deterioration of unions and the slimming down of the functions of human resources to caring more about reducing corporate risk and legal exposure than improving the performance of the people they supposedly fight for.

There are a few reasons I have a problem with HR as a way to develop workers.

They lack the skills. Check the résumé for most people in human resources roles, and you'll rarely find formal education in the science of learning or skill development. Lack of formal education in these areas of human development is a major problem for the human resources function today. I believe that if companies were taking these roles seriously, they would require professionals with advanced training or certification in these areas. Most don't.

They have a conflict of interest. The role of human resources is to find, hire, onboard, certify, warn, and terminate. Not develop. Some even admit that the human resources job function was designed to keep workers in order. Their ultimate responsibility is a fiduciary responsibility to the shareholders. Not to the workers.

They have a bad title. Any job that calls humans "resources" is fundamentally fucked. People aren't human resources. People are people. At work they are all unique in their needs, aspirations, and life stages. Start with people, not resources.

This is the way human resources was built. Remember our old friend Fredo? His original view was that the conflict between workers and managers could be overcome to a company's benefit if the right structure and techniques were present. This belief formed the foundations for the creation of the human resources job function.[2] If you look up the definition for "human resource management," you'll find something like this:

> Human resource management is the hiring, management and firing of employees with the aim to motivate them and maximize performance in service of an organization's strategy.

Nothing in the definition above says that any of their work is about training and development, or in service to the human becoming a better human. It's in service to the organization. Nothing more.

HR SKILL GAP

We need to fix the system in companies, instead of trying to fix the people.

—Zeynep Ton, author of T*he Case for Good Jobs: How Great Companies Bring Dignity, Pay, and Meaning to Everyone's Work*, professor of practice at the MIT Sloan School of Management in our conversation on the *Bring It In* podcast

In a *Harvard Business Review* article titled "Where Companies Go Wrong with Learning and Development," the author argued "Not only is the majority of training in today's companies ineffective, but the purpose, timing, and content of training is flawed." The article goes on to highlight several challenges:

- A majority of managers aren't happy with their company's approach to learning and development (75 percent of 1,500 managers surveyed are dissatisfied).
- Most employees say they aren't prepared (70 percent of employees said they don't have the skills needed to do their jobs).
- Most of the skills learned aren't even utilized. Only 12 percent of employees say they apply new skills from their learning and development program to their existing work.[3]

Human Resources has a skills gap.

HR professionals might not always focus heavily on learning and development for a lot of reasons:

1. **Different focus.** HR managers often juggle many responsibilities, including recruitment, employee relations, benefits administration, compliance, and more. This broad range of tasks leaves less time to specialize in learning and development.

2. **Lack of specialization.** Learning and development can be a specialized field within HR, and most HR managers admit to having limited expertise or training in this particular area.

3. **Resource constraints.** Depending on the size and structure of the organization, HR managers might not have access to the resources or tools needed to become experts in learning. There may be budget limitations, time constraints, or other obstacles that prevent a deep focus on learning and development.

4. **Lack of training or interest.** Some HR managers might not have the interest or haven't received the training to become experts in learning. If learning and development aren't a priority for the organization, they may not be emphasized in the HR manager's role.

5. **Changing nature of learning.** The field of learning and development is rapidly evolving with new technology, methodologies, and tools. Keeping up with these changes requires continuous learning and adaptation, which might not be feasible for HR managers focusing on other core areas.

The alignment of HR with learning and development varies widely depending on the organization. Some companies have HR managers get deeply involved in employee training and learning, while in others, the functions might be handled by separate teams or individuals. This lack of consistency points to a problem: most organizations don't know how to best use their HR professionals.

WHY I WON'T ATTEND SHRM

Several times a month, I get an email inviting me to attend, sponsor, or speak at an HR conference. While I get bombarded with emails from SHRM, my favorites often come from some HR related magazine or publication.

A recent invite I received is below:

Subject: Top 10 Global Human Resources Solution

Hello Sam,

This opportunity might appear like just another expense for your marketing, but what clearly didn't resonate in my earlier email is the amount of positive benefits that this recognition will bring at a nominal cost.

A clear cut way to stand out from the rest of the competition when you're selling solutions/services to your prospects is by letting them know that you are one among the selected few chosen to be on this list and whose offerings are aligned with the goals of their business.

There's no better time than the present to let the community know that 1Huddle is one among the "Top 10 Global Human Resources Solution Providers 2022."

If you have a few minutes, I would like to hop on a brief call to share with you how our previously featured companies have leveraged this recognition to drive sales and marketing.

I will look forward to speaking with you.

Warm regards,
Richard

Pay to play. My favorite.

It's why these so-called educational conferences don't educate at all but rather are filled with the same people, same vendors, and same ideas—unless you pay to speak, that is.

This is why nothing changes.

THE WORKFORCE'S SOCCER MOM

People who are bred, selected, and compensated to find complicated solutions do not have an incentive to implement simplified ones.

—Nassim Taleb, author of *Skin in the Game: Hidden Asymmetries in Daily Life*[4]

During an open dialogue at the Aspen Environment Forum back in 2012, the biologist E. O. Wilson expressed his concerns about what he termed the "soccer mom syndrome." He explained that this trend toward being overprotective, commonly seen among white suburban soccer moms, is harming bio-education by shielding children from direct interaction with nature. Wilson argued that taking a child to a botanical garden, where every tree is labeled and identified, is detrimental. Rather, he suggested, parents should allow their kids to explore nature by visiting the seashore with a pail and shovel, letting them experience nature firsthand.

Soccer moms are known to protect their children by eliminating trial and error or any type of threat from their child's environment. The environment they create lacks rigor, randomness, self-discovery, and challenge. That sounds a lot like what happens with HR teams today when it comes to employee development.

The level of control that HR exhibits over the employee's access to learning and development opportunities makes our workforce weaker and more fragile. It is common today for training and development to be limited to a manual, a PowerPoint presentation, or live classroom experience. In too many situations, HR approaches development with the view that only they are the single source of knowledge, thereby limiting or in some cases completely restricting a worker's ability to discover new learning by exploration or their own search. Emotional discomfort is avoided and even seen as traumatic. This overprotective HR style has had a direct role in the creation of workers that they sometimes label "generation snowflake." They complain about the lack of toughness and grit in their workers, all while failing to challenge workers in the learning process.

Many people in organizations stick to what they know and resist learning new things. They prefer to continue their usual practices rather than embrace new ideas and delve into more complex methods to achieve different outcomes. Leaders at all levels must reflect on whether they are hindering or helping growth. Building a successful team focused on high growth is challenging. Effective leaders don't shy away from the difficulties complexity brings.

Back to Wilson and the Aspen Forum. A woman from the audience said she would "forgive him" for his comments against soccer moms.

He responded, "Don't. Think on it."

THE PANDEMIC'S IMPACT ON HR

Every company is trying to do more with less.

The effect of the pandemic made life much harder for HR departments and, by extension, their workers. Companies that began laying off workers and reducing costs often started in the human resources department. They quickly terminated and downsized the people responsible for worker recruiting, selection, onboarding, and development. This had an obvious impact on organizations' ability to return to normal worker levels. Instead of taking ownership of the true source of their operational challenge, however, they instead decided to blame workers. The news that you couldn't get away from in the aftermath of the pandemic included phrases like "labor shortage" and included pointing fingers at workers as those to blame for simply not being willing to return to a prior place of employment.

These challenges also extended to training, where the time and effort related to getting a new hire up to speed was not something companies had the infrastructure to manage—especially given their recent downsizing. While I don't believe the human resources role was ever really built to optimally train and develop workers, it was the only one that had some semblance of a playbook on hand. When this group was gutted, it had a long-term impact on organizations when they wanted to bring workers back. They had to start by bringing back their human resources leadership first.

So, I find the complaints by companies that said they couldn't find workers laughable. They laid off the human resources workers, who are the primary points of contact for managing applicant tracking systems, job postings, hiring processes, offers, and onboarding, and then had to simultaneously re-onboard them while also bringing back workers or hiring new ones. Of course they were having trouble. They brought it on themselves, but it's much easier to blame the workers for being lazy.

Another negative effect of these cutbacks to HR was that no longer was anyone left to push back on biased, unclear, or unreasonable job descriptions. This left the HR role disincentivized to speak up out of fear of new hire failing.

DON'T RATE YOURSELF

I hate self-evaluations.

They are a weapon of weak human resources departments. They're another control mechanism used to try to get an employee to report something that can then be used against them in the future.

Never complete one.

CLOSED HIRING

Human resources have been at the forefront of adopting technologies and resources directly aimed at reducing friction in finding new job candidates. Applicant tracking technology and outsourcing recruiting to external recruiters have become major trends and the source of new activity for HR. They have also had an overall negative impact on the workforce.

A wide range of automated tools has emerged to help HR teams find new candidates, track communications, and select applicants. We have to consider the effects of automated technology on the hiring process when we already know that it is affected by built-in racism, discrimination, and bias. The automated tools have the same baked-in flaws. In a famous 2003 research study, fake résumés that featured very white-sounding and very Black-sounding first names—but were otherwise identical—were sent in response to help-wanted ads. The white résumés received 50 percent more callbacks than the Black résumés. This is the equivalent to eight years of work experience, which white applicants didn't actually have.[5]

A similar study in 2024, nearly twenty years later, found identical results. White-sounding names received 50 percent more callbacks for interviews.[6]

Imagine a world where every employer uses automated résumé screening algorithms that all use the same biased heuristics. Job seekers who don't pass those checks will get rejected everywhere.

My own experience hiring external recruiting firms and their technology platforms bears this out. In 2022, I interviewed multiple recruiting firms with the intention of hiring several workers for roles in our Newark-based office. Among other requirements, I wanted candidates from the Newark area. But the motivation to fill jobs with a specific model of candidate resulted in weeks of frustration as three separate firms continued to match me with candidates who all largely looked the same, with the same experience—and none from Newark. I was surprised. Newark is a big, diverse city. Something was at play that I couldn't see.

Oh, and I ended up firing all three recruiting firms. Our company did our own direct community outreach. We filled the open roles in three weeks.

OVERHEARD

I was standing by guest services at a Philadelphia 76ers game. I overheard a human resources manager talking to a colleague.

She said, "They don't want to complete the required training and feel that it's not relevant. Honestly, I just don't want to deal with this."

She then opens her phone and leans against the counter.

FLUSHING THE TOILET

If the professor is not capable of giving a class without preparation, don't attend.

—Nassim Taleb, author of *Antifragile*

You'd think that energy would be focused on how to make the workplace better for workers. Instead, we have grown obsessed with the concept of productivity.

At a recent Society for Human Resources (SHRM) conference I enjoyed watching an HR "leader" talk about recent initiatives to increase productivity and engagement. While I was dozing off mid PowerPoint, something caught my attention. A toilet.

This speaker was sharing a recent purchase aimed at reducing wasted time on bathroom breaks. They purchased the Slanty Toilet, an angled toilet that becomes uncomfortable to the user after just a few minutes. According to the manufacturer, it will "increase productivity by 25 percent."[7]

We have really run out of ideas.

You know how you increase the productivity of your people? You invest in development. Great development.

Companies make a ton of mistakes here.

They put people with no experience in charge of training and development. The experience trap is on full display here. Companies typically value experience in hiring their next manager without taking into account the functional differences between being a frontline manager and a leader of training and development. We really shouldn't be leaving employee education up to novices.

They adopt outdated, time-intensive models of training to protect their jobs. Most HR training is an instruction style called "drill and skill," but many see it as "drill and kill." Learning myths permeate organizations today. Too many still believe that seat time, PowerPoints, and video-based learning on a learning management system is the right approach to disseminating new learning to workers. LMS, the weapon of choice of HR managers, was built by academia because they ran out of colleges to sell to. Now it's being used to make workers feel like they're back in school.

They have no skin in the game. Human resources don't get bonuses or incentives for the things they're responsible for. If we really want to drive the right behaviors of our HR teams, we should treat them like sales managers. Tie a percentage (25-50 percent) of their compensation to key success metrics like:

- Success rates of new hires
- Customer service scores
- Sales performance
- Knowledge retention
- Speed of onboarding

They forget about the front line. Josh Fuller from Harvard

Business School said, "Companies don't yet perceive middle skill workers as strategic assets." Well, by looking at the behaviors and the investment, that sounds about right. Forty-four percent of employers offer zero upskilling or reskilling opportunities. According to a report by the Association for Talent Development (ATD) in 2020, U.S. companies allocated an average of 2.5 percent of their total payroll for employee training and development. Employers often overlook the potential talent within their existing workforce, failing to recognize it as a vital resource that could be essential for future success.[8]

In 2019, a survey conducted by SHRM found that approximately 33 percent of organizations in the United States offered no formal training or development programs to their employees.[9] This indicates that a significant portion of companies in the country still do not prioritize workforce training as part of their organizational strategy.

It's time to flush down the drain this outdated approach to developing our workers. We need better strategies, better systems, and better support. We need leaders who teach from a position of experience and have skin in the game with the success of their workers.

SEEING AND BELIEVING

My wife has plants all over the house. Tons of them.

Over time I've observed how she cares for them all. Some get water daily, some don't. Some get a lot of light, some get none. Some do better upstairs, some downstairs. She recognizes what works for each plant. And then she behaves in a way to help each plant grow and be healthy.

A company that doesn't see the skills of its individual workers is like a gardener who has a variety of unique and valuable plants but treats them all the same. Some plants need more sun, others more shade; some require more water, others less. By failing to recognize and cater to these individual needs and qualities, the gardener may never see the full bloom of their garden. Similarly, a company that fails to recognize and utilize the individual skills and talents of its employees may never realize its full potential.

HR's one-size-fits-all approach and failure to provide the adequate resources to help their people grow result in workers who are disconnected, disoriented, and disengaged.

UNION BUSTING

What goes through the mind of HR when a company spends millions of dollars and resources to bust the efforts of its workers to unionize?

The dinner-theater chain Medieval Times in New Jersey broke the law by getting a union's TikTok account banned. Labor board prosecutors say the company illegally fired a union supporter and withheld raises from workers who organized.[10]

When a company works to bust unionization efforts by its workforce, it's similar to one parent sitting on the sidelines, afraid to speak up.

WORST OUTCOMES

If your goal were to create a system that yielded the worst possible outcomes, how would you build it?

- Allow only certain workers to access the system.
- Offer no learning opportunities outside of the worker's current role on the system.
- Only let workers access the system on the clock.
- Don't pay workers to use the system.
- Make using the system a requirement, but make sure it has little value to the worker.
- Put people in charge who aren't incentivized by the outcomes of the system.

MAKE PEOPLE THE POINT

It ain't so much the things we don't know that get us into trouble. It's the things we know that just ain't so.

—Josh Billings, nineteenth-century humorist

There's a big difference between making a worker feel important and making them important. Great leaders know their people are the point.

And while I know my fair share of HR people who are well-intentioned and do come to work every day focused on elevating their people, the fact is we have too many HR operations that are worried more about compliance than performance.

Organizations are never going to perform at the level they're capable of until they turn the human resources function into a human development function. Organizations must become enablers that create the right environment for employees to learn, grow, and thrive. These environments must produce leaders as enablers by transforming managers into coaches deliberately focused on people development and removing institutional obstacles to growth.

Again, this requires the human resource function to be transformed into a human development function. Leaders need to come to work every day thinking about not only how we level up workers but fire up workers. Knowing that knowledge is never static or complete and that a leader who is through learning is through. Until we do that, they're always going to be behind.

It's time for leaders to stop and ask themselves: Are you the obstacle blocking your people's growth, or are you supporting it?

Companies need to see their workers. I believe that if they did, then they might acknowledge them. And if they acknowledge them, they might talk to them. And if they talk to them, then they might understand them. And if they understand them, then they might care about them. And if they care about them, then they might invest in them. And if they invest in them, then they might unlock them.

It starts with seeing them.

CHAPTER 8

Vulnerable on Wages

An imbalance between rich and poor is the
oldest and most fatal ailment of all republics.

—PLUTARCH

Over six years as a cook at a Pizza Hut in Alabama, Juan remained stuck at the federal minimum wage of $7.25 an hour.

He woke up one day and walked to the bus stop, where he took a seventy-five-minute ride to get to work. He arrived for an afternoon shift. As he went to clock in, his manager stopped him and told him to go home—don't even clock in.

"Why?" asked Juan. The manager replied, "Business is slow, and you aren't going to be paid for the day."

Juan left and went back to the bus stop.

WE HAVE BECOME A LOW-WAGE NATION

The nature of low-wage work is going to change because workers during the pandemic reached their limit and realized that we actually can and should be demanding a lot more.

—Saru Jayaraman, author of *One Fair Wage: Ending Subminimum Pay in America*, attorney, activist, president of One Fair Wage, director of the Food Labor Research Center at UC Berkeley in our conversation on the *Bring It In* podcast

A recent report from the Brookings Institute found one in two jobs today are bad jobs.[1] They aren't talking about a job that has to deal with angry Karens complaining about their avocado toast at their 11 a.m. Tuesday brunch after yoga class. Nothing against yoga.

They're talking about jobs where an unexpected $400 expense could put a worker into poverty.[2] That means an unexpected water leak, car accident, or parking ticket. (I live in New Jersey, so believe me that a $400 parking ticket is possible.) Any of these could put you into a desperate cash position.

When workers live on the edge, day in and day out, it's impossible to bring your best self to work. The effects ripple through communities, where now 76 percent of adults expect the lives of their children to be worse than their own.[3]

America is a nation of working poor, with some of the lowest wages on the planet. Many Americans now work close to forty-seven hours per week, yet earn far less than decades ago. In a survey of full-time workers, 40 percent reported working over fifty hours per week and 18 percent said they work over sixty hours per week. Most of this work is also being done on the edges of what most people consider a workday. For workers on the front line, nearly 50 percent of hourly workers who make less than $22,500 a year work a night shift. The demands of this type of shift take in so many ways from a worker. It takes from the time they can spend with family, it takes from their ability to live a balanced life, and it takes from their health. It's much different for those workers earning $60,000 or more, where only 25 percent report working a night shift.[4]

Here are some more startling realities about how vulnerable workers have become at work today:

In 2008, 60 percent of the job losses during the Great Recession were mid-wage jobs, but only 22 percent of the job growth during the recovery was in this range. While low-wage jobs made up only 21 percent of Great Recession job losses, they were 58 percent of all recovery job growth. By 2014, there were almost two million fewer jobs in mid- and high-wage industries and almost two million more low-wage workers than before the Great Recession.[5]

The job losses were so heavily skewed toward low-wage earners that the median wage actually rose by 7 percent from 2019. This gave the economic downturn a misleadingly positive appearance.[6]

Today 85 percent of lower-paid workers fear they won't even meet expenses, up from 60 percent in 1971.[7]

In 2017, the average income of the top 20 percent of Americans was sixteen times the average income of the bottom 20 percent.[8]

The top three employers in the U.S. are Walmart, McDonald's, and Home Depot. The median pay for 21 million retail workers is $15 per hour. For the 5.1 million fast food workers, it's only $12 per hour.[9]

Since 2010, wages for new college graduates have been declining. Up to 50 percent of new graduates are now forced to take jobs that don't even require a college degree.[10]

The Bureau of Labor Statistics says two out of three of new jobs created by 2020 were low-wage and only required a high school degree or less. These bad jobs are blue-collar jobs with low wages; they lack benefits, and they pay by the hour, compared to the white-collar jobs that are salaried with a fair wage, benefits, and more security.[11]

We're now seeing the largest employment shift in recent history, where low-wage workers are working 24 percent more hours than they did in 1979.[12] And where does that lead them? Sadly, many are stuck. Only 13 percent of workers without college degrees find themselves in better-paying jobs after ten years.[13] This isn't the promise America has made to workers.

Employers have transformed time into a tool to demand more from their workers, insisting on extended hours, mandating overtime, and providing inadequate shifts, even encroaching upon the sacred space of weekends. Believe it or not, something as common as daylight savings time has been manipulated to extract more labor from the American people.

We find ourselves at a crossroads. For too long, the choices we've made favor capital over the workers doing the work. They've weakened unions and kept wages stagnant. If we had only allowed the federal minimum wage of 1968 to keep up with inflation and productivity, hard-working Americans would be earning $27 an hour today, not $7.25.[14]

We should be better. We must do better. We should create a community where every worker has a fair shot at success and where time is a tool for progress, not a weapon against those striving to make a living.

PRODUCTIVITY: HOW WORK WAS BUILT (AND MEASURED)

The media has overwhelmed us with messaging around the future of work. But it rarely tells the whole story. The future of work story paints a picture of workers being forced against their will to come into work one to two days a week. Or on how AI is making work easier and robots are coming to create cooler and better jobs.

Wake up. This future of work dream is more like a nightmare for most workers. Today, we have become a nation with an unreasonably high number of vulnerable low-wage workers. These workers are more productive than ever but aren't getting the same respect as workers in similar roles in other nations.

It is more common to find a worker in a rich country being more productive while working fewer hours. However, this is not the case for U.S. workers, who average 289 more working hours per year just to maintain current productivity levels. Data shows that in 2018 U.S. workers were only slightly more productive than workers in Germany, despite working 31 percent more hours. By the way, that's the equivalent of an additional two plus months of work.[15] So much for your holiday on the Amalfi coast.

We used to tie wages to productivity growth. Increases in labor productivity are the main way society has become more prosperous—they're the lever to elevate the standard of living. Increases in GDP per person stem from increases in productivity. Productivity, from an economics perspective, is our ability to get more output from the current level of inputs, and starting in 1938, this is the way the system worked. The idea was that those at the bottom would share in the economic growth that their labor created.

From 1995 to 2015, across twenty-four countries, productivity has continued to go up, rising an average of 30 percent. During this period, global pay has increased by only 16 percent.[16] In the U.S., wages haven't been growing proportionately. As of the late 1970s, the trend of wages growing with productivity started to separate.

Productivity has tripled since 1968. If wages had kept pace

with the growth in worker productivity since then, adjusting for inflation, today's worker should receive a minimum wage of $27 per hour. Instead, the minimum wage sits stuck at $7.25 per hour, basically a quarter of what it should be. The federal minimum wage has been $7.25 an hour since 2009.[17] While Democratic lawmaker's[18] have tried unsuccessfully[19] to increase it to $15 an hour several times, as of 2023, 21 states still use the federal minimum wage as their wage floor. We've been told that if we raised productivity, wages would go up as well. This is no longer the case. The result is more workers than ever being more vulnerable than ever.

This isn't an accident. It's the way work was built.

A $20 SALAD

I walked into Tropical Smoothie Café for lunch.

The store was empty. After getting my salad I started a conversation with the worker behind the counter. Small talk. I asked what her favorite salad was. She said she didn't eat there—it was too expensive.

She looked like she wanted to say more. I nodded encouragingly.

She continued, "And, you know it really bothers me. I sell $20 salads. It's like double my hourly wage. It pisses me off."

WHAT IS A QUALITY JOB?

Today, many workers face a job quality problem. They're stuck in lower-end service jobs that lack fair pay, predictable schedules, and benefits. What should a quality job do for workers?

- A quality job should treat you right regardless of how you look. But this isn't true. Too many jobs treat people of color worse. Black workers earn less. White workers earn more. Black men earn less than three-quarters of the wages of white men, and this gap is present regardless of their level of education.[20]
- A quality job should consider your mental health. But this isn't true. Too many jobs stress you out. A brain on excessive stress is a brain in crisis mode—that's not good for mental performance. Think of a frontline worker who comes to work and is worrying about how they can't make rent.
- A quality job should treat you as part of a team. But this isn't true. Many workplaces in today's economy expect teamwork, yet too many jobs treat you as if you're on your own.

Multiple studies over the years have pointed to the relationship between the quality of a product and the wage of those doing the producing. It has been found that the greater the disparity in pay between leadership and hourly workers, the lower the quality of the products that were being produced. These findings point to not just an economic issue but to a moral one as well. It calls on us to consider what kind of values we want to prioritize in our businesses and our society.

Quality work goes up when quality jobs go up.

HERE'S A TIP

After the Civil War and the abolition of slavery, newly freed Black

Americans sought opportunities to work. Many found work in service industries, such as restaurants and railroads.

However, it was in this time of newfound freedom where a new practice emerged and has been around to this day. Employers, unwilling to pay former slaves the wages they deserved, instead employed a practice known as tipping, allowing them the ability to pay certain workers less— sometimes even nothing—expecting that their income would be made up in gratuities from patrons.

This practice didn't remain isolated. Instead, it became more entrenched, spreading across various service sectors, and soon tipping became a customary practice in the United States, one that we still see today.

The federal tipped minimum wage is a reality for workers in the hospitality and service industries. As of 2024, sixteen states use the federal tipped minimum wage of $2.13 an hour. The level is below $5 an hour in another thirteen states. It's all over the place from there. Only four states have eliminated it: Nevada, Oregon, California, and Minnesota. This is a reality of work for some workers today. They're vulnerable not just to a minimum wage, but to a tipped minimum wage.

I guess the word minimum has multiple meanings. Policy advisors at the Economic Policy Institute say, "Research indicates that having a separate, lower minimum wage for tipped workers perpetuates racial and gender inequities, and results in worse economic outcomes for tipped workers. Forcing service workers to rely on tips for their wages creates tremendous instability in income flows, making it more difficult to budget or absorb financial shocks."

They go on to say workers in tipped minimum wage positions are the victims of greater discrimination, especially since the data showed white servers earn better tips than Black servers.

Tipped workers are also victims of wage theft at higher rates than other workers.[21]

But we must not overlook the underlying issues that this practice has brought with it. It has perpetuated wage disparities and injustices that continue to affect those who labor in our service industries. It's a reminder that some are valued differently in our economy and that the work of making work a place where every person can earn a fair wage for a hard day's work is not done.

FREE MEMBERSHIPS

While traveling to Charlotte, North Carolina, for meetings, I stopped into a Life Time Fitness club with my colleague Roger to get a quick workout in before the day.

On the way out I asked the front desk person, "What's the best part of working at Life Time?"

She said. "The free membership."

AND NOW YOU CAN'T TIP . . .

We know tipped minimum wage environments make workers more vulnerable.

We now have brands removing tipping. A DCist/WAMU article in 2021 talked about changes happening at Washington, D.C.-based Compass Coffee. The coffee brand made the decision to change their tipping policy at all fourteen stores, removing tipping as an option and instead raising the hourly pay of their workers. The owners reasoned that 42 percent of customers didn't tip, and the other customers said they tipped out of a feeling of "obligation." Thirty percent chose to tip the lowest amount of 10 percent.

Messaging to the stores was disjointed. Many Compass employees felt they were misleading customers when they explained that tips had been eliminated and prices raised in order to pay them higher wages.

A barista in the store said, "When the tipping was taken away, it was explained that the raise— our wage increase—made up for that. It might have been true for maybe two cafés, but for the vast majority of us, we were losing significant amounts of money." They went on to explain why coworkers aren't speaking out against the change. People "want to try to move up as fast as you can so you're making more money [because] clearly, you're not getting it in tips."[22]

No more tips. But still vulnerable and forcing certain workers to take sides. This is what it's like on the front line.

WAGE THEFT

If I'm running a business and I can't afford to pay my electricity, I can't say, "The electric company is lazy." The pressure comes on workers, which is a human being, and job creators say, "Oh, you should work for less.

—Gordon Lafer, author of *Job Training Charade*, former senior labor representative for U.S. House of Representatives, economist in our conversation on the *Bring It In* podcast

Tipping aside, sometimes workers don't get paid even when they do the work.

In June 2023, three supermarkets in northern New Jersey had to fork over more than $1.8 million. Why? Because they were caught by the Department of Labor not paying 226 of their employees the overtime rates they deserved. Federal investigators found stores in Hackensack, Oakland, and Waldwick were deliberately cutting corners on pay. The investigation led to the recovery of $917,455 in back wages and an equal amount in liquidated damages. The DOL also assessed $80,428 in civil money penalties for the willful nature of the violations. And the violations were all over the place. The employers were caught paying employees a flat day rate and conveniently "forgetting" the overtime pay. Some got checks and cash at regular rates, even if they worked overtime hours. Short breaks? They were actually deducting those from hours worked. And bonuses? They didn't even include those in the regular pay rate.[23]

In the same month, a few states away, another Department of Labor investigation resulted in the recovery of $505,000 in back wages for Mississippi Delta farmworkers after 161 workers were found to have been cheated of wages. The Department of Labor found that forty-four employers were in violation. Wage and Hour Division Director Audrey Hall said this about the report:

> "The outcome of these investigations confirms that employers in the Mississippi Delta denied a large number of marginalized farmworkers their lawful wages, and in some cases, violated the rights of U.S. workers by giving temporary guest workers preferential treatment. Though we were alarmed by the allegations from Black farmworkers in the Mississippi Delta, we applaud them for their willingness to come forward and shed light on these widespread violations. The courage they showed has helped workers across the Delta finally receive their long overdue wages."[24]

Wage theft has always been a problem. It impacts our low-wage workers the most. A 2018 Politico report found employers ripped off $15 billion in wages that should have gone into workers' paychecks because of poor enforcement of minimum wage laws.[25] A research team from Rutgers University analyzed federal data and minimum wage violations during the Great Recession. They found for each percentage point increase in a state's unemployment rate, there was almost a full percentage point increase in the likelihood that a worker would experience a minimum wage violation.

Janice Fine, a professor in the Rutgers School of Management and Labor Relations and director of research and strategy for Rutgers Center for Innovation in Worker Organization, said, "We know that low-wage workers who care for our elders and our children, harvest our crops, and process our meat, cook our to-go orders, staff our factories and warehouses, stock our shelves, and clean our homes and hospitals are literally risking their lives for us during this pandemic. What this study of the Great Recession tells us is that there is a strong likelihood that many—particularly women, immigrants, Latinx and Black workers—won't even be paid the paltry wages they are owed."[26]

The economics of wage theft can mean big margins for businesses, especially at scale. For example, if each of the 150 hourly workers in a Home Depot store worked just one hour of unpaid overtime per week, it would result in 600 hours per month. Multiplied by the federal minimum wage of $7.25 an hour, which would result in an annual savings (or wage theft) of $104 million across 1,997 stores.[27]

Employers pushing their higher costs onto low-wage workers who can barely make ends meet isn't right. These folks can't afford to be underpaid or miss a paycheck. That's exactly why we need government to step up, especially if business owners won't.

When things get rough, that's when those working the hardest need protection the most.

A CONVERSATION

In 2023 I was hosting a webinar called *Workforce Trends for Hospitality in 2023*.

In the middle of the webinar, I began a conversation on wage theft and how bad it is for workers—especially those surviving on subminimum wages and tips. I was talking about this in the context of training time, saying it's something that should be compensated under certain conditions. A CHRO from a major restaurant brand dropped this message into the chat:

CHRO: What is wage theft?!?

I addressed it quickly by providing the explanation that wage theft occurs when a business expects a worker to do work prior to clocking in or after clocking out and doesn't compensate them for that time. I went on to say it is basically stealing from your workers.

She left the webinar.

I continued.

TRUE CRIME

The Strand Book Store in New York is massive, touting that they have eighteen miles of books across multiple floors. On this day I find myself in the basement seeking out the section marked "Labor."

I find it. And as I begin to browse, I can't help but notice out of the corner of my eye the section immediately next to the five shelves of labor books.

It was True Crime.

Pretty soon they may want to combine both of these sections into one.

PAY WORKERS MORE

Today's global corporations have no permanent home, recognize no national borders, salute no flag but their own corporate logo, and take their money to anywhere where they can make the most and pay the least.

—Andy Stern, former president of the
Service Employees International Union (SEIU)

You can tell a lot about a system and a society based on how it takes care of its workers. Ours steals their money. In 2021, U.S. CEOs made 399 times what their average worker made.[28]

We should pay workers more. It's good for business. Economic data supports the concept of the multiplier effect, where every extra dollar in the pockets of low-wage workers adds $1.21 to the economy. The same extra dollar in the pocket of a high-income worker adds only $0.39.[29]

In 1964, President Lyndon Johnson declared a war on poverty. In the process, the government realized it didn't have a metric to define who is and isn't poor. They adopted one used by Mollie Orshansky, a social research analyst for the Social Security Administration. The thresholds she developed became the federal government's official statistical measure of poverty. The Orshansky Index was used to help researchers measure poverty and was never intended to be used to select who would receive government benefits, but that's what it has been used for.

Her model used the cost of a nutritionally adequate diet to

calculate cost of living. The U.S. government used her model for the least expensive meal plan to officially set the poverty line at three times the food expenses of the cheapest possible way to feed a family. The same formula is still in use today as the way we officially define poverty. The model has been adjusted for inflation, but it doesn't take into consideration the changes in the other kinds of expenses families have. For example, an average family in the 1960s spent one-third of their income on food. Today, however, Americans spend only about 11.3 percent of income on food while other costs have risen, including housing, healthcare, childcare, and transportation.

This model leaves low-wage workers more vulnerable. Imagine how it feels to be so vulnerable and look around and see so much wealth.

- Today, the richest eighty-five people in the world have more wealth than the poorest 3.5 billion on the planet combined.[30]
- In the U.S., the richest 1 percent earn more than 20 percent of all income.[31]
- Prior to the pandemic, only one American was worth $100 billion. By 2021 there were nine with wealth topping a cumulative $1.4 trillion.[32]

And one more thing. All these multibillionaires pay a lower income tax rate than the frontline workers who risked their lives coming to work for them during the pandemic.[33] Never have people who take so much given back so little.

WELCOME TO MY OFFICE

I was sitting at the bar in Negril. I'd been here many times before. And especially at this exact time—happy hour.

Behind the bar was my good friend Delroy. Over the years we have had many conversations at this same spot as I would hide from the sun that blazed down on the Seven Mile Beach in Jamaica.

On this day he was making it all happen, a packed bar with rum and Red Stripes all around. A woman walked up with a menu in her hand and her brow furrowed in a way that I recognized. She was about to start trouble.

"Excuse me. But, we got charged for four Red Stripes and this menu here says a Red Stripe is $2.25. Why did you charge me $10?"

Delroy picked up the menu and read it. Shook his head and walked over to a stack of menus behind the bar. His eyes glanced back and forth comparing both menus and then he came back and apologized, "It was supposed to say $2.50 like this one but looks like that menu didn't get changed." He pointed to another menu that clearly had the new pricing.

She stared and shook her head. Demanding her $1 back.

Delroy told her not to worry about it and she stormed off. I then watched as Delroy pulled the $1 from his pocket.

A few minutes later he came over with two shots of Appleton Special for us and said, "Welcome to my office."

We toasted to "respect" and Delroy got back to work.

SEVEN LIFETIMES

You'd have to work seven lifetimes to make what your CEO makes in one year.

Here's the math:

- Average American annual pay: $54,132
- Average length of work: 45 years

According to the AFL-CIO's Executive Paywatch, the average pay of the CEO of an S&P 500 company was $16.7 million in 2022.[34]

A low-wage worker earning $24,000 a year would have to work fifteen lifetimes to make that much.

The CEO of American Express "earns" $48 million per year. That means he earns $23,076 per hour. Not a bad hourly wage. He makes more in one hour of work than an average restaurant server earns in a year.

What's in your wallet?

THE HUNDRED-HOUR WORK WEEK

A 2022 survey by the United Way of the National Capital Area found in many major U.S. cities, minimum wage workers must work over fifty hours per week to afford rent on a one-bedroom home.[35] It also found that minimum wage workers in New York City needed to clock over a hundred hours a week to afford their rent.

OECD data has found as much as sixty-one hours per week of work is necessary to break the poverty line.[36]

What happened to the forty-hour work week?

I'm not saying pay more, but . . .

A 2015 study by researchers at Cornell University found raising the minimum wage did not force restaurants to cut staff, increase prices, and reduce revenue.[37]

On the other hand, it did find that it resulted in happier, more productive workers and happier customers.

FOUNDATIONS

Many companies have nonprofit foundations that donate to community programs, yet most of their workers receive federal assistance, such as Medicaid and SNAP benefits.

Makes sense.

It's misleading for major corporations to advocate publicly against increasing taxes, yet privately advocate for social support programs for workers to reduce their reliance on increasing wages.

Major corporations do this. YUM! Brands, Walmart, McDonalds, Amazon . . .

EARNED INCOME TAX CREDIT

It's why major corporations have supported the earned income tax credit (EITC), an anti-poverty program that helps low- to moderate-income workers and families making below $46,600 to $63,400 (depending on marital status and children) per year.

In 2020, the average EITC was $3,099. Some 25 million working families and individuals received it.[38]

That is a big number. The U.S. had 83 million working families in 2020 and 25 million of them needed extra help to get by.

LET'S PLAY A GAME OF WHO WOULD YOU HIRE?

Bam. I just made you the manager of Sam's Spaghetti Spot in Hoboken, New Jersey. It's a cool spot. Since you have no HR team, and you must have read my earlier chapters, it's up to you to make a hiring decision.

Candidate #1 walks in and applies to be a dishwasher. He says he has no experience but will only cost you $15 per hour.

Candidate #2 walks in and applies to be a dishwasher. He says he has three years of experience as a dishwasher and will cost you $18 per hour.

Who do you hire?

Most owners will say they want to pay less. Which means they would pick Candidate #1.

However, let's look at this a different way. If you hire Candidate #2, will it really cost you more? Someone with experience will run a cleaner, safer, and more efficient station. Because they know the demands of the job, they will be less likely to miss a shift and less likely to break glasses and dishes as they navigate the chaos of the kitchen.

Owners should think long when it comes to labor. But too many think short.

UNEMPLOYMENT IS DEBILITATING

You live fighting or die working.

—Jamie McCallum, author of *Essential: How the Pandemic Transformed the Long Fight for Worker Justice*

Ultimately, our lowest-paid workers can be vulnerable to more than just being paid poverty wages or experiencing wage theft. They could experience the complete loss of work.

Unemployment is a debilitating problem. Today, out of every 100 working-class adults, fifteen work part-time, thirty-eight work full-time, and forty-seven are jobless. Unemployment has a major impact on workers over the long haul. Workers who are out of work have a very hard time returning. Companies look elsewhere for younger workers who may seem more dynamic; job skills decay with time and become outdated; and they lose motivation. Their ability to find the next job diminishes because employers seem to actively discriminate against workers who have been unemployed for a prolonged period.

Unemployment is also a major policy issue for American cities. A worker's salary and job prospects depend more on where they may live than on the experience on their résumé. If a local economy has a high percentage of college-educated residents, that has a direct impact on the kinds of jobs available and the productivity of all workers. The result is a rise in wages and a reduction in unemployment for all categories of workers. Earnings of a worker with a high school education rise by 7 percent as the share of college graduates in their city increases by 10 percent.[39]

Look, when jobs disappear, it's not just about the money. We're talking about real, human consequences. People's self-esteem takes a hit, families struggle to hold together, and problems like substance abuse, homelessness, and even child abuse can spike. One study found that for every 1 percent increase in unemployment, child neglect went up by a staggering 20 percent.[40]

When you lose your job, you lose so much more along with it.

THE WILL TO GET IT DONE

As an economist I am always asked: Can we afford to provide the middle-class life for most, let alone all, Americans? Somehow, we did when we were a much poorer country in the years after World War II.

—Joseph Stiglitz, American economist

What is the purpose of working if you can't even live?

It's true that economic security leads to better choices for workers. You can even say that a higher wage reduces depression, aids in sleep, and relieves stress. The stress that affects workers in poverty has been shown to affect those workers at even a cellular level. A study of 5,500 premature deaths in New York City from 2008 to 2012 claimed the deaths likely would have been prevented if the minimum wage in the city for those workers was $15 per hour.[41]

We also need better wages to allow workers to continue to learn and grow. A longer work life, along with the speed of change in technology, is going to require organizations to build robust learning environments so workers can continuously learn. In the future, more adults will face multiple career transitions that will challenge them to acquire new skills. We have to make this easier for workers if we truly want to prepare them to contribute to our organizations. If we paid more for workers, I believe it would incentivize us to invest more in training instead of just letting workers leave and starting over again with new people.

We must stop complaining about raising the minimum wage. Why is a worker wanting to make more money a bad thing but a company wanting to profit more good business? While I believe raising wages is necessary, some businesses have built business models that are too fragile to handle this change. Data continues to suggest that increasing the minimum wage has negligible effects on employment. Time and time again, research shows raising the minimum wage results in happier and more productive workers—and even happier customers.[42]

The solutions to bad jobs are straightforward: higher wages, better predictability in work schedules, paid leave, help with childcare, unions, health benefits, worker ownership, labor-friendly schedules, and great work. We don't struggle with the solutions. We struggle with the will to get them done.

It's time for business leaders to step up. Invest more in people and create an environment where they can bring their best selves to work. Instead of lobbying against workers, focus energy on building better products, systems, and cultures to offset whatever negative impact you believe raising the minimum wage would have on your business. Go sell something! Drive revenue. Stop cost-cutting your way to success.

We must act now. Especially because another reality workers are starting to face is technology, which looks like a storm heading right at our front lines.

CHAPTER 9

Retreating on AI, Automation, and Technology

I would bring a hammer.

**–JAN HEIN DONNER, DUTCH CHESS GRANDMASTER,
WHEN ASKED HOW HE WOULD PREPARE FOR
A MATCH AGAINST A COMPUTER**

Melissa drives for Uber. She used to go to a community college but dropped out because she could never make the class schedule work. When I stepped into her car in Newark, she was on a call. I didn't mind.

"I want my bonus. This is the second time you all did this to me. I am not hanging up till I talk to somebody."

She gets put on hold, looks back at me, and shakes her head. She tells me how this is the second time this month that she was up for a quest bonus and the app crashed. A quest bonus is a game you play against yourself where you have to complete a hundred or more rides in three days. If you do, you can unlock cash bonuses, generally around $100.

Melissa was pissed. She says this is the second time where she got to within three rides of the bonus, with just a few hours left on the promotion, when the app crashed and sent her quest number back to zero.

"They do this shit and then I have to call customer support and they are always in some other country. I can't even get a real person—just some robot and so they just play with me. They play with me and hope I am just going to hang up and give up. I ain't doing that shit again. They gonna pay me my money. I am a damn diamond driver!"

Melissa worked twelve hours a day for the last three days in a row. She's gotta fight for her money. The robots will decide when her queue is up.

TOO MANY TWENTIETH-CENTURY SOLUTIONS TO TWENTY-FIRST-CENTURY PROBLEMS

Karl Marx once called humans "appendages to the machine." And today, this has never looked more accurate.

Every kind of work will be affected by technology at a time when we have failed to adopt technology in the right places for our people. Whether you're a restaurant worker on the line in the kitchen or a driver making deliveries to the restaurant—your job is in the eye of the storm.

Technology has always impacted work. It has been changing the nature of work and skills that are valued over the last two centuries. From industrial technology devaluing the skills of artisans who handcrafted products to the early twentieth century, when electricity allowed us to study longer and work

in factories later, to the adoption of managers to control labor and efficiency. It's been a wild ride—and technology has been there at every turn.

Technology is not just reshaping work but deciding the skills that will be required of workers. For every $1 invested in computer hardware, companies are going to need to invest up to $9 in software, training, and business process design to keep up.[1]

And technology isn't just coming for the low-skilled worker. It's coming for all workers, from the street to the C-suite.

WHAT IS AI?

Artificial Intelligence (AI) is a term for computer systems that claim to extend human capability by sensing, comprehending, acting, and learning.[2] In other words, machines that can think like humans. AI systems can process large amounts of information and perform tasks that previously required humans, such as recognizing speech and identifying patterns.

According to my recent convo with ChatGPT, AI is

> The simulation of human intelligence in machines that are programmed to think like humans and mimic their actions. It involves the creation of algorithms that allow computers to perform tasks that typically require human intelligence, such as understanding natural language, recognizing patterns and images, making decisions, and solving problems. AI technology can range from simple rules and automation to complex learning and prediction systems that can adapt and improve over time. It is a broad and rapidly evolving field that intersects with

various disciplines, including computer science, mathematics, neuroscience, and engineering.

You just got it from the source.

Definitions aside, AI is changing the very nature of work. We need to be ready, because machines are going to continue to get better at performing tasks humans used to do. This means education will need to transform into a lifelong journey that enables workers to acquire new skills continuously as they try to keep pace. All workers will need to retool on an ongoing basis as machines acquire new skills.[3] Entire categories of work will be eliminated. No job is truly safe.

In survey after survey, workers share this concern. An Accenture study revealed that less than 50 percent of people have confidence in the safety of AI systems, only 33 percent of people aren't fearful of AI, and 25 percent go so far as to believe that new technology will harm society.[4]

ARTIFICIAL INTELLIGENCE AND JOBS

Based on the current trends in technology advancement and adoption, I predict that within fifteen years, artificial intelligence will technically be able to replace around 40 to 50 percent of jobs in the United States. Actual job losses may end up lagging those technical capabilities by an additional decade, but I forecast that the disruption to job markets will be very real, very large, and coming soon.

—Kai Fu Lee, author of *AI Super-Powers*

Kai Fu Lee was the head of Google China from 2005 to 2009. Today, he speaks often about how in the past new technologies caused big changes in the economy, such as turning farmers into factory workers during the 1800s and 1900s. But the arrival of AI is happening even faster than those changes.

The effects are global and are especially real for frontline low-wage workers. Automation fueled by artificial intelligence can make a direct hit on factory workers by reducing the need for low-wage labor. This has been a key development for certain global economies, such as China and South Korea. Lee believes that this will potentially result in factories moving closer to big markets, taking away the opportunities these countries used to grow into wealthy, tech-driven economies. This means that the wealth gap between rich and poor countries could grow even wider, and the control of AI technology might end up concentrated in the hands of a few big companies in China and the U.S. The result will be more inequality that could create massive unemployment and instability.

This is the real danger posed by artificial intelligence.

Within ten to twenty years, Lee estimates we will be "technically capable" of automating 40 to 50 percent of the jobs in the U.S. He cautions that this will not happen all at once due to regulatory restrictions, inertia, and the creation of new jobs along the way. But it's happening. The ultimate result will be a new normal where intelligent machines could experience full employment and the average worker will be looking for a way forward.

In his book, Lee shares two charts that show which jobs he thinks will be most at risk of replacement by AI.[5] They fall into two categories: cognitive labor and physical labor.

For the cognitive roles, he believes that the jobs requiring social interaction and the use of creativity or strategy will be the jobs least at risk to automation. For the physical roles, he believes that the jobs requiring social interaction and the use of manual dexterity will be the jobs less at risk to automation.

Quadrant 1: Danger Zone

The jobs in the danger zones include tellers, cashiers, translators, customer service reps, and fast food preparers. All of these jobs are in trouble—and are already in many ways under attack. Restaurants are buying robots to flip burgers, companies are automating customer service calls, and the cashier line at Whole Foods is longer for the self checkout than the one open lane with a human. These are on their way—and totally qualify as the danger zone.

Quadrant 2: Slow Creep

The jobs in the slow creep category are supposed to be fine for now but will begin to see disruption. These jobs include graphic designers, columnists, artists, taxi drivers, plumbers, and security. I'm not sure how slow we are talking here, given that columnists and graphic designers are already under attack by ChatGPT. There's really nothing a live security guard can do that digital systems can't completely replace. But damn—we're talking about artists and designers. This is crazy. These are on their way, I think a little faster than Lee may have thought.

Quadrant 3: Human Veneer

The jobs in the human veneer category aren't fully replaceable right now, but the reorganization of tasks could put this list of jobs at risk. These jobs include doctors, tour guides, teachers, wedding planners, bartenders, and hotel receptionists. These jobs have some tasks that already put them at risk of automation. Their underlying social component is their only defense.

For example, the ability of a machine to diagnose like a doctor or provide answers to a hotel guest isn't really the problem—we just prefer to deal with a human in these environments. These jobs will see the need to work closely with AI as it becomes responsible for the behind-the-scenes computations and the human worker acts as the social interface. How quickly these jobs disappear will depend on the speed at which companies work to restructure work. I am not optimistic.

Quadrant 4: Safe Zone

Finally, some good news. A safe zone!

A safe zone category is where jobs are expected to be safe for the foreseeable future. These jobs include nurses, concierges, CEOs, and even dog trainers. The belief is that these jobs require a greater percentage of tasks that are social and require manual work or creativity, putting them off limits for the time being.

WHERE WILL WORKERS GO?

I could fill a book with research by economists on the percentage of jobs that automation will impact. Here are a few recent predictions:

- According to McKinsey, as much as 70 percent of jobs are vulnerable to partial automation over the next fifteen to thirty-five years.[6]
- According to an Oxford University study, 47 percent of Americans work in a job vulnerable to automation in the next two decades.[7]
- According to the Nevada Independent, between 38 percent and 65 percent of hospitality jobs will be auto-

mated by 2030. We are talking 500,000 and 860,000 gigs disappearing by 2035.[8]

According to an IBM report, 40 percent of workers will need new job skills within a few years. To succeed with automation, companies will need to "prioritize with purpose" and "make work more rewarding."[9]

Displaced workers will need to find their next gig. But where? And how will it play out?

Historically, when workers are displaced by new technologies it results in one of three outcomes:

Replacement

In this scenario, machines will have displaced workers from certain jobs due to their impact on the tasks that make up the work. However, in the process the worker has been made more productive for other tasks at the employer.

Transition

In this scenario, machines will have displaced workers from certain jobs. However, workers are able to find work for new goods that are now in demand.

Creation

In this scenario, machines will have displaced workers from certain jobs. However, workers are able to find work in another industry or sector in the workforce.

A worker's ability to be in demand is not guaranteed. It depends on their ability to find tasks that they are best suited to perform and that the economy demands. While many economists are optimistic that humans will always be in demand in some way, nothing is certain.

Especially when employers aren't concerned with every worker having a job but rather with maximizing revenue.

HOLLYWOOD

If big corporations think that they can put human beings out of work and replace them with artificial intelligence, it's dangerous. And it's without thinking or conscience. Or caring.

—Fran Drescher, president of SAG-AFTRA

In July 2023, the Writers Guild of America and the Screen Actors Guild (SAG-AFTRA) went on strike. These unions represent a large percentage of TV and film writers and actors.[10]

What was the reason? Well, pay was a big piece, but so was their future. During negotiations, Hollywood studio executives revealed they were considering replacing background actors (also called extras) with likenesses created by artificial intelligence.

Because studio executives don't want to have to pay for bringing background actors back on set for multiple days during a shoot, they wanted to be able to scan a performer once and pay them for only one day of work. The studio would own the scan and be able to use it for the rest of the project, which would most definitely reduce the earning potential of the actor. This would be a major hit for actors who often find entry-level opportunities as a background actor.

The strike was settled about six months later. The union won important concessions, including on the digital replication and payment of background actors.

Many believe that the power of AI will be a complement to the work of Hollywood writers and producers. It can be used to eliminate swear words in post production, de-age actors, and support the writing process. This all could be true.

HUMAN vs. ROBOT

Soon.

Humans are already competing with robots and technology. In the future a human is either going to be the one telling the robot what to do or the robot is going to be the one telling the human what to do.

Very soon.

Chances are your already being served by robots. Let's meet some.

Autocado

Chipotle has decided to take a different approach to growing their business. The company has cited high job openings in the U.S. restaurant sector as a major challenge. In May 2023, job openings in the restaurant sector hit 1.2 million. To put that in perspective, since 2003 job openings in the industry have surpassed the 1 million mark only once before.

Chipotle decided the solution to worker shortages is to invest in their workers by raising wages, doubling down on workforce development, increasing benefits, and launching an internal labor committee that will give workers a voice at the table on all compensation and workplace changes.

Ha. Got ya. Nope. They ain't doing that.

Chipotle does have a solution, however. Leadership claims

it is less about replacing human workers and more about supporting them. Their new "collaborative robot" is designed to speed up the production process for an item that is its star on the menu: the avocado.

"It's essential for us to maintain the experience of preparing the guacamole to our exact standards," explained Curt Garner, chief customer and technology officer at Chipotle. He emphasized that the robot, specifically designed for Chipotle, will ease some of the identified pain points for restaurant employees.

By the way, by pain points he means the whole end-to-end creation of the guacamole.

Here's how it works: An employee loads up to twenty-five pounds of avocados into a machine called the Autocado. The fruit is then robotically peeled, cored, and sliced; the prepared slices are collected into a bowl. To create this tailored solution, Chipotle partnered with Vebu Labs, a California-based robotics startup. Together, they analyzed the preparation process across various Chipotle restaurants to pinpoint the most time-consuming tasks. In fact, Chipotle has even invested in Vebu Labs as part of their $50 million venture, Cultivate Next.

The innovation doesn't stop at guacamole. Chipotle hints that dishwashing robots could be next on the horizon, and they're already testing "Chippy," a robotic kitchen assistant that utilizes artificial intelligence to make tortilla chips to dip in Autocado's guacamole.

Steve Ells, the founder and former CEO of Chipotle, is reportedly seeking funding for a new tiny restaurant concept that would use robots and only three staff members. (By the way, he stepped down from Chipotle in 2017 after repeated foodborne illness outbreaks at their restaurants.)

I assume he likes the lighter staffing models in the new venture.

Chipotle's move to automation isn't a surprise move by a brand that has flip-flopped over the years in their position around how important labor is. At times, they claimed they can't find workers and need to invest in technology to create "labor efficiencies." At other times, they claimed that full employment and investment in robots would create those same "labor efficiencies."

Speaking of flipping . . .

Flippy

In 2020, the fast-food chain White Castle introduced a new robot called Flippy. Built by Miso Robotics, Flippy was originally launched in a kitchen in the Chicago area. The robot can cook ten different items, including fries, and uses artificial intelligence to identify the ingredients. The robot costs restaurants around $3,000 per month. Executives at White Castle point out that a major benefit is that robots are immune to the stressors and distractions that humans feel, so they don't make mistakes or miss work. The plan is to install Flippy 2, an upgrade that's smaller and can mimic even more human functions, in the majority of the 360 White Castle restaurants.

Jamie Richardson, vice president at White Castle, and Mike Bell, the CEO of Miso Robotics, the company that created Flippy, both say the robot isn't supposed to replace workers. Richardson, in multiple interviews, has pointed out that the robot will free up workers to do other tasks and that Flippy is "like any other investment we make in the kitchen that just makes the work easier, and allows us to hire more people over time to do other things."

Mike Bell says that their robot "can work around the clock. It doesn't require benefits or days off."

The shift toward automation and the increased capability of robots to perform human-like tasks is a concerning sign for those worried about the potential loss of jobs and the dehumanization of the food preparation process.

Presto Voice

Ready for AI drive-thru?

CKE Restaurants (owners of Hardee's and Carl's Jr.), along with several other fast food brands, has begun adopting AI technology to make the drive-thru process more efficient. Companies reason that using AI to converse with customers and take orders will lead to more consistency in upselling, which will result in more revenue.[11]

Another company using AI at the drive-thru lane is Wendy's. Their former CEO, Todd Penegor, has talked about how the slowest point of service in the entire restaurant is the drive-thru lane. When talking about their goals for adoption of AI, what Penegor says is very telling about the way restaurant executives look at the impact of AI and their workforce: Wendy's is "trying to make our lives a little bit better for our employees and a heck of a lot better for our customers."

A "little better" for employees. A "heck of a lot better" for customers.

The current CEO of Presto Automation Inc. is Xavier Casanova. He was appointed to the role on August 1, 2023, succeeding Krishna Gupta, who returned to his position as Chairman of the Board of Directors for Presto, the AI company partnering with CKE and many other restaurants with AI for drive-thru. Gupta says that their AI "upsells in every order" and that the companies "want faster speed of service. They want better customer satisfaction, and they want higher check sizes, and they are getting it all with Presto Voice."

So, I guess we can't increase speed of service and improve customer satisfaction using humans. They probably aren't so good at that. CEOs of automation and AI companies have zero concern for their impact on workers. Their goal is singular: profit. The restaurant executives continue to speak down about their workforce when they make claims that AI and robots make them "more efficient." If they truly wanted more efficient workers, they could get there by investing more in their people. This would mean investing in state-of-the-art training and development programs and supportive employee culture-building initiatives.

The productivity that comes from the adoption of new technology is making it easier for CEOs to get rid of their biggest headache—people.

COMPANIES QUIETLY FAVOR AUTOMATING AWAY WORKERS

A team of two robots from Richtech Robotics fills in for roughly three human workers.

—Shawn, in a testimonial on the Richtech Robotics website

Today, it takes an average U.S. worker 11 hours of work to produce as much as 40 hours did in 1950.[12] Workers are faster than ever. But they're still not fast enough for companies today.

And it isn't just about speed. Many other reasons explain why companies prefer robots over humans. Robots don't get sick, they don't complain, and they don't try to unionize. Conversely, they can increase revenue, upsell, and deliver the same greeting in every customer interaction. A 2020 survey by the nonprofit World Economic Forum found 43 percent of companies plan to reduce their workforce through new technology. Employers want robots. And they are going to get them.[13]

Flippy the kitchen robot is just the tip of the iceberg. Everyone in the food business wants a piece of the robot action these days. Take Inspire Brands, for example. They own Buffalo Wild Wings, and guess what they're doing? Testing out a robot called Flippy Wings. Yep, the same folks who made Flippy are behind this one, too. And startups are raising money left and right to create robotic kitchen helpers, with investors like SoftBank putting $375 million into a robotic company called Zume in 2018.

On the bright side for workers, many of these technologies aren't turning out as expected. After raising close to $500 million, Zume shut down[14] in 2023, and the salad robotic startup Chowbotics also shuttered.[15] While some of the battles are being lost as the technology figures out its footing, we should all be concerned at the amount of funding being directed at startups that only focus on taking and not giving back.

In a recent conversation, I spoke with the CEO of a startup in Newark that built a robot vending machine to make burgers on demand. I asked what brought them to Newark, and the CEO answered, "Free parking." I asked a few more questions to try to understand if maybe there was a driver behind the technology that focused on creating a better community or better working conditions for workers in the restaurant industry. He didn't let me down. His response was simply, "Now we don't need as many workers."

Nice.

TECHNOLOGICAL UNEMPLOYMENT

They call the trend technological unemployment, and it isn't new. Technology has been impacting the nature of work for centuries. In a 1930 essay, economist John Maynard Keynes popularized the term by saying it arises, "due to our discovery of means of economizing the labor outrunning the pace at which we can find new uses of labor." He also went on to call it "a new disease" that is affecting our community.

Between 1910 and 2000, jobs that were in "professional, managerial, clerical, sales, and service" have tripled, growing from 25 percent to over 75 percent of total jobs. The increase in this type of work, which technological unemployment and displacement directly affected, has resulted in the disappearance of jobs that were used to be labeled as productive.

These jobs are different. And the effects are often felt more by folks with less formal education. When workers who have accumulated formal education and credentials push those that don't down the ladder toward jobs that require less and pay less, this is called the "deskilling process."[16] Technology supports, and in many ways leads, this charge of "deskilling" by reducing the effort required to produce high-quality goods that in the past may have required more skilled work to create.

MAKING WORK WORSE

There is a lot of talk on the positive impact of automation on workers and how robots will somehow make the day-to-day for a worker easier. Is this true?

It is true that automation has replaced some of the most dangerous work performed by workers, especially for workers in factories, construction, and physical labor. But it hasn't necessarily made the lives of workers better. Today, humans find themselves working faster, longer, and harder just to keep up with their new coworking robots. Americans work some of the longest hours among major countries. According to the OECD, the U.S. is ranked eleventh-highest among countries with workers working over fifty hours per week.[17] And according to a 2019 Gallup Poll, 39 percent of workers work at least fifty hours a week, and 18 percent work at least sixty. It's incredible.[18] The story that new technology and AI would make our work life easier has simply not been true.

Want another example? No problem. Let's look at Amazon, where warehouse workers are surrounded by all kinds of robotics and automation. They're constantly pressured to work faster and faster. In 2021, workers organizing in Alabama brought up several complaints about their work conditions that are affected by technology. Workers shared that they felt they were under constant pressure to mimic the machines they were working alongside and that they were not even given enough time to go to the bathroom.[19] And these technologies may still have a ways to go when it comes to safety. In 2023, almost two years following Jeff Bezos's announcement that Amazon would dedicate $300 million to enhance workplace safety, a group of labor unions is alleging that the company accounted for a startling 53 percent of all severe warehouse injuries in the U.S. last year.[20]

The adoption of new technology used to make us safer. Now it's actually hurting workers—physically, financially, and emotionally.

OUT OF STOCK

A leaked 2022 internal memo from Amazon has sounded an alarm that the company is facing a shortage of potential employees to hire.[21]

The report states: "If we continue business as usual, Amazon will deplete the available labor supply in the U.S. network by 2024."

It makes sense that Amazon is investing so heavily in automation. They're out of workers.

But I thought this stuff didn't replace people?

Better never means better for everyone.

Innovation brings both promise and peril. Nearly all developing technology aims to enhance productivity and cut labor costs. As tech advances, robots will eliminate jobs, create jobs, and preserve some jobs. It will also create value that will not be shared evenly.

Better never means better for everyone. It always means worse for some.

As technology races forward, it's leaving some behind. This has nothing to do with a worker's willingness to work. Instead, the speed of change will leave many with the wrong mix of skills for the changing nature of the available work.

Low-wage workers are the most vulnerable. Frontline workers in restaurants and hospitality have got to be nervous. I hope they aren't reading their industry trade media, because it's littered with articles about changes that will affect their future work lives:

- McDonald's is replacing cashiers with kiosks.
- Domino's is replacing delivery teams with self-driving robots.
- Home Depot is replacing greeters with robotic greeters.
- Sweetgreen is replacing the process of cooking vegeta-

bles and grains and putting them into bowls using their new robot Spyce.

Creator (formerly Momentum Machines) is another robotics company in the restaurant industry. They have a robot that can make 360 hamburgers per hour from scratch. Alexandros Vardakostas, CEO of Creator, said "Our device isn't meant to make employees more efficient. It's meant to completely obviate them."[22]

We must have a sense of urgency about the challenges and the opportunities we're facing.

In 2018, Yvette Cooper, a British parliamentarian and former Secretary of State for Work and Pensions, said this in an op-ed for *The Guardian*:

> The robots are coming, artificial intelligence is expanding, yet no one is doing enough to make sure workers benefit rather than losing out. According to a new survey, a quarter of the workforce think their job won't be needed in the future. Many of us expect the technological revolution to be as disruptive as the industrial revolution. This could bring amazing opportunities and emancipation, but also new forms of exploitation, deeper inequalities, injustices and anger.[23]

MORE TOWELS PLEASE

While checking in on a recent family trip in the Florida Keys, I was asked if I would prefer the room to be serviced and towels replaced every two days or every three days. I responded by requesting it daily.

Automating away work by trying to make me feel bad about servicing a room so that you can reduce hours and reduce payroll will not fly with me.

Not everybody can proceed like Trader Joe's, who in 2023 publicly stated that it will not add self-checkout lines to its stores.[24]

But you can do the small things:

- Avoid using self-checkout.
- Avoid opting out of servicing your room.
- Avoid checkout on tablets.

I get some of these are harder than others. But this is how you speak up.

RACIST TECHNOLOGY

The digital divide creates unequal access to computers and the internet. The divide falls along predictable racial, class, and gender lines.[25] This has been a reality for decades—and puts many people in minority communities at a double disadvantage, given the adoption of new technologies at work and school. Not only will they have their work affected by new technologies, but their lack of educational opportunities using technology puts them at a disadvantage for their next job.

Since technology is built by humans and since some humans are racist (even if unconsciously), technologies can exhibit racist behavior. In the case of AI's impact, as machines learn to think more like humans, they are likely to become more racist.

In *Race After Technology,* author Ruha Benjamin talks about the "New Jim Code," where new technology reflects and reproduces existing inequities. The technology is promoted and perceived as more objective or progressive than discriminatory systems of previous eras, but actually incorporates the same baked-in racism.[26]

Let's consider some examples. Take using the rating platform Yelp the next time you're looking for a new place for dinner. Reports show that Yelp has engaged in behaviors that have made it harder for Black business owners to have their restaurants found by users. One reason is that the platform penalizes small businesses that don't advertise on it. Another reason is low check-ins because Black individuals are historically less likely to use the check-in feature on apps for personal security reasons. Yelp hard-coded these actions. It was a design choice that discriminated disproportionately against one group. Benjamin considers this to be "a slippery slope between effective marketing and efficient racism. The same algorithmic filtering that ushers more ethnically tailored representations into my feed can also redirect real estate ads away from people 'like me.'"[27]

Another impact of review sites like Google or Yelp is that it encourages consumers to evaluate the competence of workers, including waiters, drivers, retail associates, mechanics, doctors, and more. Employers can then use the ratings and reviews to discipline and control their workers. Political scientist Joshua Sperber refers to the continuous surveillance of workers as a "digital panopticon." Employees are perpetually under observation, and it's unclear what actions might lead to an unfavorable customer review.

Of all the stuff I read and see about technology, my mind always comes back to the infamous memo that was leaked to the media in 2017 after James Damore, a software engineer at Google, uploaded it to an internal Google mailing list. In the memo, Damore took a stance against Google's diversity initiatives, implying that the underrepresentation at the company, particularly of women and people of color, could be attributed to biological differences rather than discrimination or underlying structural inequality.[28]

Inequity can be literally coded into our world. Whether it is by software engineers deciding whose business gets featured or even in hardware like soap dispensers that, because they weren't designed to see a wide range of colors, fail to dispense soap to Black skin.

Technology can be racist.

LOW BATTERY

The Belgian newspaper *Derniere Heure* claims in a 2023 report that Uber is linking charges to phone battery levels.[29]

The reporters did a test with two smartphones: one with an 84 percent battery and another with a 12 percent battery. When they requested the same ride from their office, the results showed a big price difference. The low battery phone was charged €17.56 and the high battery phone was charged €16.60.

THE SILVER LINING: WHAT AI WILL CHALLENGE US TO BECOME

One machine can do the work of fifty ordinary men. No machine can do the work of one extraordinary man.

—Elbert Hubbard, American philosopher and writer

If you're staffing the checkout line at your neighborhood grocery store, brace yourself. That scanner over there might just take over your job. And watch out if you're steering the wheel as a bus driver, taxi driver, Uber operator, or trucker. As we speed into the age of autonomous vehicles, your job might be left in the rearview mirror.

The future's moving fast, and it's not waiting for anyone. AI is going to bring dislocation, disruption, and challenges to many. A McKinsey study claims that 50 percent of today's work activities that represent $15 trillion in global wages can be automated by 2055. As work changes, the skills necessary to perform the tasks will also change. The majority of jobs are likely to have a significant part of their tasks change at faster rates. This trend will continue. Today the half-life of a job skill is only five years. It means the skills you have today could be meaningless for your next job.[30]

Companies have been using technology to move faster. In 2015, Airbnb managed three million listings with 2,500 employees; Marriott managed 1.2 million rooms with 175,000 employees. This trend will continue.

We can't continue retreating. We must move forward meaningfully by considering technology's impact.

We need to consider the impact on our society as a whole. Let's play a game for a second. What if technology actually replaced every single job? If that were true, we would then have to consider our next question. What do we do with people?

When a worker loses a job, it often results in depression, aggravation, sadness, and, of course, lost income. What would happen if an entire society became unemployed?

In the spring of 2020, during the COVID pandemic, the number of individuals reporting anxiety tripled compared to the previous year, and those reporting depression quadrupled, according to the Centers for Disease Control and Prevention. An alarming statistic reveals that over a quarter of young people confessed to having thought about suicide in the past month. Stress levels are notably and disproportionately high among Black, Hispanic, and younger people.[31]

We need to consider the work we do. If your job has elements of repetition or redundancy, your job will carry real risks of being taken over by a robot.

Technology also has an impact on how we classify workers. The sales team at DoorDash is part of the family, but the people delivering the orders are told they aren't. A consumer may see the delivery person as an extension of the brand or an actual employee, yet brands like Amazon, DoorDash, and Uber go to great lengths to make sure drivers know they are their own boss.

Will AI eliminate jobs? Yes. A lot of them. And we can't be certain the new ones that pop up won't be ones that the robots will become better than us at too! For this reason, we must consider the work we do beyond the task. Will it be worth it?

We need to consider the impact on our workers. It is essential that we provide all people with the education, training, and support they need to win at work.

Companies investing in robots and AI systems have a moral obligation to modernize their people development and learning strategies in order to better attract, onboard, and retain their workers, especially since AI is going to demand new capabilities and processes across the entire business.

One area that will need to be looked at closely is the human resources function, which may well become the "machine relations" function. I talk to many HR people who are using AI to auto-create learning content and write courses, without realizing that in the process they may be automating themselves out of a future role. They're failing to see the moment as an opportunity to leverage the new technology to save time, and then reinvest the found time into more employee development activities for their people. And that's something that is greatly needed, given the current underinvestment in workforce training and development time.

The jobs of the future are going to require creativity and the ability to learn quickly. Organizations need to get much better and faster at developing their people.

In 2016, the Obama administration released its final report on automation, saying,

> Accelerating artificial intelligence (AI) capabilities will enable automation of some tasks that have long required human labor. These transformations will open up new opportunities for individuals, the economy, and society, but they have the potential to disrupt the current livelihoods of millions of Americans. Whether AI leads to unemployment and increases in inequality over the long-run *depends not only on the technology itself but also on the institutions and policies that are in place.*[32]

It's our choice. Continue retreating or start rebuilding? We need to make a decision. Hating on AI is one approach—and it may not get you very far. In fact, I think AI is great. I think it's going to force humans to be the best form of the one thing that we can be but that robots never can: human.

We must lean into our humanity. Design technology with human intention. Create a workplace that is human.

We can give robots hands and fingers. We can give them

heads and a face. We can even give them names like Flippy. But they can never be us. They can never be human.

Let's not treat them better than us.

CHAPTER 10

Blinders on Government

Marissa became pregnant while working as a Whole Foods cashier in Texas.

After several weeks, her eight-hour shifts became more and more difficult. She was always tired, and aches and pains were starting to take their toll on her. It didn't make it any easier that as a cashier, she was expected to stand the whole time. Her back hurt, her legs hurt, and her feet were swollen.

Her manager let her use a stool to sit on for a few hours during her shift, but one day a regional manager visited the store and approached Marissa.

"You can't sit on the job. Cashiers aren't allowed to sit, and stools aren't allowed. You shouldn't have been told you could do that."

Cashiers aren't allowed to sit.

HOLDING WORKERS BACK OR MOVING WORKERS FORWARD?

Let's talk government.

It definitely has a role to play at work. Government plays a major role in writing the rules that directly affect the way work happens today. Some say we have too many regulations; some say we don't have enough.

Some countries are aggressive with regulations to create worker opportunity. In Sweden, mandated benefits cover paid sick leave, parental leave, vacation, and healthcare. Some countries are aggressive with regulations to limit opportunities. The World Bank claims 93 percent of countries in the Middle East and North Africa have restrictions on the kinds of jobs women can hold.[1]

If they wanted, governments could transform cities into growth engines—knowledge spillover and multiplier effects have the potential to accelerate the sharing of ideas and the circulation of capital.

One of the big impacts of multiplier and spillover effects is that workers with less education can gain new insights and ideas when interacting in the same community as workers who have a robust formal education. While the average metropolitan area has five colleges and two universities, most workers can't get to them while they're working, especially low-wage frontline workers. Policies that enable this mix can result in rapid skill transference in an informal setting and a more connected community. It would also make a community more resilient to the changing nature of work brought on by technology that can threaten communities by leaving workers with the wrong mix of jobs and skills.

Data even supports the economic impact of such interventions by government. Earnings of a worker with only a high school education rise by 7 percent as the share of college graduates increase in the city by about 10 percent.[2] Sharing knowledge and skills through formal and informal interaction generates significant knowledge spillovers.

The type of jobs we create also matter. According to Enrico Moretti in *The New Geography of Jobs*, "For each high tech job in a city it creates five additional jobs outside of the high tech sector." He goes on to point out, in defense of a multiplier effect, how companies like Microsoft made a big impact on Seattle by creating 120,000 jobs for service workers with limited education (cleaners, taxi drivers, real estate agents, small business owners) and 80,000 jobs for workers with advanced degrees (teachers, doctors, nurses).[3]

Government has a responsibility to every worker. With all of this possibility, a reality of work today is that government isn't doing enough. They operate with blinders on to the challenges faced by the people they represent—or they're just unwilling to work to bring about the change that they promised in their last election cycle.

We live in a society based on work. It is a place where if you are unable to get or keep a job, then you are excluded from being able to fully partake in American life. You are then placed in a vulnerable position where you are more likely to experience homelessness, poverty, and poor health. This is where government has a role to play—to help workers achieve.

Too often the work of government is just holding us back.

MEET YOUR MEMBER OF CONGRESS

The International Franchise Association represents 800,000 franchisees across 300,000 brands that use franchising as a business model. Franchises represent over 3 percent of GDP in the U.S. The leadership at IFA works hard to protect the business model.

In the summer of 2023, the International Franchise

Association held a roundtable with franchisees and elected officials at McDonald's corporate headquarters in Chicago.

This is where I heard Congressman Raja Krishnamoorthi of Illinois tell a story about his first job working in a McDonald's. He described how on his first day he was working the line (I guess they really throw you right into the mix there). He said as he was working the hamburger station he watched as the person next to him was building a burger. Half of the bun fell on the floor. The employee then picked up the bun and placed it on top of the burger and continued working. A voice from the back room yelled, "You're fired!"

Congressman Krishnamoorthi went on to make the point of his story to the audience of lobbyists, franchise owners, politicians, and McDonald's executives, saying, "That was the day I learned about leadership."

Really? The congressman was working his first day with no training. And on a separate note—I guess that required ServSafe food safety training really failed them here. Back to my point—what is so representative of quality leadership when you have a manager screaming through an entire restaurant at a worker?

This is a failure, not a talking point—unless his point is to poke fun at a low-wage worker who wasn't trained properly.

The congressman went on to close his remarks by saying, "There is nothing stopping people from getting the education they need."

Sure.

TRADE ASSOCIATIONS SCREW WORKERS

There are 92,000 trade associations in the U.S. They exist to represent their members and speak on their behalf to policymakers, media, agencies, and more. Basically, they are kind of like their agents.

But who they are specifically representing is something that often gets confused. While all trade associations will say the work they do is for the good of the "industry," they will also claim they work to not just protect the member companies who pay them, but also the employees of the member companies that make up the labor force of the industry.

Trade associations have a very simple business model. Revenues flow into the association from member companies through membership dues, sponsorships of events and conferences, and donations. Expenses flow out of the association for the annual convention and events, staffing, and, most importantly, lobbying.

Associations build financial war chests and aim the dollars primarily to advocate for policies that benefit the member companies. When you look closer at their motivations and behaviors, you'll notice that their lobbying efforts don't always care so much about the employees of the member company as much as they do about the owners.

Several behaviors of trade associations screw workers today.

Suppressing

And one way to keep prices low is to massively suppress the pay of the workers that helped create it.

—Talmon Smith, economics reporter for *The New York Times*, The Institute of Politics at Harvard University national campaign ambassador in our conversation on the *Bring It In* podcast

The National Restaurant Association, sometimes known as the "other NRA," represents the restaurant industry and has long opposed increases in wages, investing tens of millions of dollars to maintain the federal tipped minimum wage at $2.13 per hour.

According to a study by UC Berkeley, this low base pay has led to a situation where half of restaurant workers who were laid off during the pandemic didn't qualify for unemployment insurance. Their earnings were too low to meet the minimum eligibility criteria.[4]

Associations like the NRA too often suppress the voice at trade shows by limiting speaker lineups to sponsors and their most giving brands.

Stealing

If I was a waiter at the same restaurant right now in 2023, I would still get paid $2.13 an hour, the same I was paid in 1996.

—David Fahrenthold, Pulitzer Prize-winning reporter for *The New York Times* on how restaurant workers pay for lobbying to keep their wages low in our conversation on the *Bring It In* podcast

Let's stick with the National Restaurant Association, given the high percentage of low-wage workers on their front line.

ServSafe is a food and beverage safety training and certificate program owned by the National Restaurant Association. The program is designed for food service professionals, such as chefs, servers, and managers, to learn about food safety practices. ServSafe covers basic areas like food handling, food preparation, cooking, sanitation, personal hygiene, and more. The curriculum is designed to comply with the regulatory food codes and to promote safe food handling practices that prevent foodborne illnesses. The training typically involves attending a course taught by a certified ServSafe instructor and then taking an exam. The courses can be taken in a classroom setting or online, and the exams are typically proctored to ensure integrity. This program has varying price points: $15 for a food handler, $152.95 for a manager, $30 for alcohol safety, and $22 for allergens. And, of course, additional fees for retesting.

ServSafe wasn't always owned by the National Restaurant Association. It was bought in 2007 because the association saw a huge revenue opportunity. After all, this program essentially charges low-wage service workers a tax in order to work in their subminimum wage environments. Let's not forget that the subminimum wage of $2.13 an hour, affecting nearly 5 million workers reliant on tips, has its roots in a dark chapter of our history. After emancipation, many restaurant owners employed formerly enslaved individuals without pay, forcing them to work for tips only. This practice, a remnant of the era of slavery, has been carried forward to the present day in the form of a subminimum wage. It's a living testament to an unjust past and a stark reminder of the work still to be done to ensure fair wages and treatment for all.

Now you might be saying you don't see anything wrong with an association investing in a safety program that makes consumers safer. Well, let's break it down. The National Restaurant Association is using the ServSafe program to generate tens of millions of dollars that they can turn and use to fund their lobbying efforts. Cash in, cash out, remember?

Nothing could be eviler than charging a service sector low-wage worker $15 to do a training on stuff they already know. Like don't wipe your ass and then make a hamburger. And on top of it, the restaurants make workers take the training not to upskill them but because they want to protect themselves. What's cute is making a worker pay $15 to protect customers. What's evil is to then take the money and pay K Street lawyers to suppress workers' wages. We have to recognize as a society that we can't do this shit. We can't blame the lawyers. They're like plumbers—they have a skill set and you pay them to use it. Blame the people at the top of a restaurant association who dream up this stuff.

All those dollars will end up in a super PAC somewhere, alongside the promise not to touch any issue that raises the costs to the business by making work safer for the worker.

Attacking

And what about when trade associations directly attack workers?

During the pandemic, several state business trade associations were trying to crack down on workers not showing up to work. It wasn't a problem they thought up. They were responding to concerns being voiced by their paying members.

Of course, they had to act in the best interest of their members. So, they launched special portals on their websites that would allow employers and employees to report workers they believed were voluntarily not coming into work, whether because they wanted to get fired to claim unemployment, or otherwise.

The worst part is they didn't just market it as a tool for employers. They sold it as a tool for employees to report on each other.

Misanthropy

Misanthropy is defined as the general hatred, dislike, distrust, or contempt of humans.

It's what comes to mind when I think about the actions of groups that exploit their workers. Too many of these organizations talk about teamwork, hard work, and the American dream, all with a mission statement and core values on a wall somewhere.

The corporate leadership can't recite them, and they don't just take advantage of workers; they consume them. Along the way, they dehumanize them, rob them of their autonomy and purpose, and charge them $15 to be safety-certified.

And when they're done with their labor, or when they've hired Flippy the robot, they let them go. They let them go with less than when they found them, hire new resources, and get back to work.

TAXES

In a debate between Jon Stewart of *The Daily Show* and Bill O'Reilly of Fox News, Stewart interrupted the Fox News personality by saying, "Why is it that if you take advantage of a tax break and you're a corporation, you're a smart businessman, but if you take advantage of something you need to not be hungry, you're a moocher?"

The U.S. government gives the most help to those who need it the least.

Taxes tell you a lot about values. Some taxes are progressive—the tax burdens grow as incomes increase (income tax). Some are regressive—those with less income have to pay a larger share of their earnings (sales tax). Currently, Americans in the poor and middle-income brackets allocate roughly 25 percent of their income to taxes, whereas wealthier families face an effective tax rate of only 28 percent. Interestingly, the 400 richest individuals in the country are taxed at a lower rate of 23 percent.[5]

In some instances the work of government has resulted in discrimination affecting who we target when collecting taxes. The IRS confirmed a Stanford study on racial bias in audits. In the study, Daniel Ho of Stanford Law School "found that Black taxpayers are 3 to 5 times more likely to be audited than are other taxpayers."[6] The researcher expressed that they didn't believe the IRS was intentionally targeting any particular racial group. Instead, they suggested that the outcome might have resulted from the way the systems and algorithms were constructed. Factors such as the influence of tax credits, including the earned income tax credit, could have contributed to this result.

One way tax policy could be used better would be to make benefits more accessible for companies that invest in their workforce. Improved tax policies could effectively encourage companies to invest more in their people by providing more training opportunities. Since the 1990s, even though jobs have become more technically demanding, businesses have cut back on both the funding for external education and on-the-job training. While this short-sighted, cost-cutting, lazy ass, scared approach may boost short-term profits, it threatens a company's long-term prospects by negatively affecting employee morale and embracing a strategy of cost cutting to profitability instead of investing for growth.

OPPORTUNITY ZONES

Sometimes we put a plan together that we think will knock it out of the park. Opportunity Zones are one of them. An Opportunity Zone is an economically distressed community where new investments may be eligible for preferential tax treatment. The idea is to use the tax advantages to spur private and public investment in underserved communities.

Tax benefits have gotten venture capital and tech investors into the mix with Opportunity Zones. The concept was introduced as part of the Tax Cuts and Jobs Act of 2017. Opportunity

Zones are having an impact in several ways:

1. **Investment**: By providing tax incentives, Opportunity Zones attract venture capital firms and investors to invest in startups located within these areas. This can lead to increased funding for new and emerging businesses.
2. **Underserved areas**: Since Opportunity Zones are often located in economically distressed communities, they encourage venture capitalists to explore investment opportunities that might have otherwise been overlooked.
3. **Gentrification**: While Opportunity Zones strive to promote economic growth in struggling areas, they can displace existing residents without providing new opportunities.

Opportunity Zones have the potential to significantly impact venture capital and startups by directing investment into underserved areas, encouraging long-term commitment, and possibly increasing diversity in entrepreneurship. However, the success of these efforts depends on careful alignment between the goals of Opportunity Zones, the interests of venture capitalists, and the needs of the communities they are meant to serve. A 2021 paper concluded half of Opportunity Zone investments went to only 1 percent of the 8,000-plus zones, including projects like a luxury hotel in Miami Beach.[7]

The Opportunity Zone program evolved into a real estate tax credit, although a few businesses also utilized it. Experienced in leveraging the tax code for access to inexpensive capital, the real estate industry has built an extensive sector around this practice. They rely on an abundance of intermediaries skilled at identifying every loophole in the tax code. All this while the average small business owner lacks the knowledge and connections to find affluent investors or understand how to engage with a program like this.

STOCK BUYBACKS

In 2022 we saw the highest level of share buybacks by S&P 500 companies in any calendar year on record: $922.7 billion. The buybacks resulted in more wealth for executives, not an increase in wages or more jobs for employees.

In 2021, CVS decided to buy back $10 billion in stock.[8] That amount would work out to a $33,333 bonus for each of its 300,000 workers. In the same year, CVS paid $5 billion in a settlement for its negligence and role in the opioid disaster.[9]

CVS's corporate mission statement, according to their website, is to "Help people on their path to better health."

PRIVATE EQUITY'S PROFITABLE PINK-COLLAR JOBS

Recently I found myself in the emergency room. My mom had a fall at home and after breaking a hip needed surgery to fix the fracture.

While in the hospital under a nurse's care she fell again and broke her other hip. It was a rough week.

After a few days she was moved to a rehab center to begin the recovery process. While we were still in the lobby, seconds after arriving, a nurse's assistant stormed past me and yelled back at the nurse she had apparently been working with, something that you don't want to hear in a care facility for a family member: "I don't need this shit. I'm going to go work at Kroger's where it makes sense."

Today, seven out of ten hospice care agencies are now for-profit, putting profit maximization over the well-being and care of patients in the final days of their lives. The investment in pink-collar businesses by private equity is creating a world where our most vulnerable are working in unsafe environments and being forced to care for our most fragile.

Today, over 5,500 hospices provide services for the dying; less than 3 percent are publicly owned.[10] Private equity has taken advantage of both the sector's fragmentation and significant oversight lapses by federal agencies, such as the Centers for Medicare & Medicaid Services (CMS) and the Federal Trade Commission (FTC). Even though in-depth reports from the *Los Angeles Times* and the *New Yorker* have recently highlighted concerns about hospice fraud, there has been insufficient focus on systemic issues, especially how private equity can capitalize on these regulatory gaps. Providers owned by private equity have taken measures to enhance their profit margins, such as reducing the duration or intensity of patient care or employing underpaid and less experienced staff in potentially unsafe situations. Studies indicate Medicare beneficiaries under the care of for-profit hospice agencies often receive a more limited set of services compared to those in nonprofit agencies. Since there are no specific criteria for the essential needs of terminally ill patients—especially in their last days when the demand for pain management and comfort treatments is most critical—patients in for-profit hospices risk facing significant neglect during their final moments.

This is what the future of work looks like. Low-wage workers, mostly female, in scrubs being forced to provide care with limited resources and training in an environment where the goal isn't care but maximizing profit.

CAREGIVERS OR CARETAKERS?

One of the most underpaid jobs in the world is that of a caregiver.

While the business of caregiving is a lucrative one, a high percentage of revenue goes to admin costs and overhead related line items ranging from insurance to rent. This leaves for-profit businesses with the decision to prioritize either profits or patients.

Who do you think they choose?

SCAN TO PAY

Every once in a while some multimillionaire CEO makes a comment about how much tax they pay. They complain bitterly about the taxes they and their corporation get hit with on various fronts.

But then again, every once in a while, billionaire investor Warren Buffet or someone like him says that they're "trying to do the right thing" with their personal income tax. They point out that they pay a lower tax rate than their secretary. Well, guess what! This can be easily fixed!

They should just head on over to pay.gov, where you can chip in and contribute to lowering the national debt. These disgruntled and concerned billionaire patriots can, if they choose, adjust their tax rates to whatever level they like. Problem solved!

A closing stat. In fiscal year 2023, the U.S. Treasury reports that they had only collected a total of $1,044,391.27 via this virtual donation box.[11]

Guess I'm not that surprised.

UNIVERSAL PRE-K: OUR FUTURE WORKERS

Government shouldn't be blind to the fact that what happens outside of work affects a worker at work.

Workers with children have a lot they need to think about and juggle to bring their best selves to work every day. Today, the U.S. is trailing other developed countries, including Norway, Italy, Sweden, France, and Germany, in offering universal prekindergarten for children ages three and four. Versions of universal pre-K exist in only about a dozen states, ranging from Georgia to New York. Boston, the city that established the nation's first public school in 1635 and then, four years later, its first public elementary school, has a long history of commitment to early childhood education. In 2023, two-thirds of the city's four-year-olds attend one of the public or private programs in Boston's pre-K system.[12]

A major part of their effort is outreach to low-income families. A 2021 study found that free pre-K programs significantly increased the labor supply for women with incomes below 200 percent of the poverty line.[13]

In 2022 an investment of $20 million was launched in Boston to create educational opportunities for three-year-old children.

This will allow small, in-home childcare programs to participate if they meet certain standards. The goal is to serve an additional 1,000 children, focusing on neighborhoods that haven't had enough access to such services. Boston is using teaching plans made by some of the best early childhood experts in the country. One key belief is that 4-year-old children can learn complex things. Even at this young age, they can start building thinking skills they'll use later in life. The teaching still uses fun, play-based learning with lots of hands-on activities in bright and colorful spaces that naturally draw the children's interest. But these activities aren't just fun and games. They follow a planned theme throughout the year and include important basics like sounds of letters (phonics), new words (vocabulary), and counting numbers. Teachers introduce these ideas through storytelling and group activities, and then the children practice them through art, music, and games.

TeeAra Dias, one of the top deputies at the early childhood office since 2015, says, "You can have a great system, but if you don't have the right people implementing it, it's not going to be great—it's going to be useless."[14]

Many opponents of universal pre-K argue that the data on its benefits isn't conclusive. This is just another example of a community that doesn't value investment in education. How much science do you really need to conclude that enrolling a person in an educational program at a younger age will yield positive results? Especially when compared to the alternative, which would be a child stuck at home with a parent who can't get to work.

Lack of access to universal pre-K disproportionately impacts our most vulnerable frontline workers, who are often forced to pick between work and caring for their family.

FAIR LABOR AND STANDARDS ACT

Back to that New Deal thing again. Back in 1938, the Wage and Hour Division created the Fair Labor Standards Act of 1938 (FLSA).

It is this move that established the minimum wage, overtime pay, established the forty-hour work week, and set restrictions on child labor. It was a powerful move and important at its time.

The challenge today is that it isn't 1938 anymore. And while several elements have stood the test of time, others need revising. In 1938 folks didn't envision an internet or a world where people were head-down on trains swiping up, down, right, and left on everything from pictures of puppies to their future spouse. It's fair to say that carve-outs for a world of work where workers use personal devices were not part of this plan.

The FLSA was modified under President Nixon when he raised the minimum wage. Nixon supported the Equal Rights Amendment, which would have helped ensure wage parity between men and women. Interesting side note: President Nixon even took a shot at a universal basic income. He had the idea to scrap welfare in favor of a guaranteed minimum income for all Americans, but the move was obviously too radical and wasn't adopted.

Today's challenge with the FLSA exists around how it classifies training time that must be compensated by a company. Under the current FLSA, if a worker is accessing training voluntarily—even if the training is voluntary and not mandated by the company—the company is still liable for compensation to the worker because the training content is considered non-transferable. It is classified as nontransferable because, under the overly academic and outdated labor mindset, when training is company-specific, it has no spillover value to a worker at another company. Obviously, this makes no sense today. If a bartender is doing job training on a mobile application for their current restaurant the training itself is enhancing the knowledge and skill level of the worker and therefore has a transferable value to the worker—even if that specific cocktail menu may not exist down the street at another bar.

Because the FLSA designates this type of training as non-transferable, it has resulted in an environment where companies are overly careful about who they provide training to and in which format. This has an outsized negative effect on our most vulnerable low-wage workers because companies are unsure about investing in training. If they invest in a digital learning technology for their workers, for example, does this increase their legal exposure if the workers were to access the material off-premise and off the clock?

At one time, the FLSA created more opportunity for more workers. It is now doing the opposite when it comes to skill development.

0 FOR 71

In 2021, I began the process of trying to directly lobby for change to the FLSA.

Citing my prior points, I began the process of engaging with members of Congress to initiate a conversation around why now was the time to amend this dated regulation in order to create more opportunities for more workers. I engaged a lobbying firm for support and crafted a bill that would amend the FLSA to allow workers the flexibility to engage in job training, regardless of whether the training is company specific or generic, as long as the training is offered as optional by the employer. Of course, if the training was required, then the organization should be required to compensate the worker for their time.

This bill was rightly named the Flexibility for Worker Education Act.

After just a few months, we had a victory with Congresswoman Ashley Hinson from Iowa coming forward and agreeing to introduce our bill in the U.S. House of Representatives.[15] The bill would be introduced as H.R. 7365.[16] Pretty cool.

While this was a win, it is a long road for a bill to navigate the halls of Congress before it officially becomes law. Our next step was finding a Democrat to co-sponsor the bill so it could be introduced in front of the House Committee on Education and Labor and have a shot of moving on to the U.S. Senate, where it would again need a Republican and a Democrat to come together to co-sponsor the bill.

Over eleven months I had seventy-one calls and meetings with Democratic members of Congress.

And I had seventy-one say they couldn't support the bill.

While the majority voiced surprise the current FLSA was creating a barrier to opportunity for our most vulnerable workers, they all stated a variety of reasons for not being able to support the bill. They largely came down to partisan politics. Not the good of the people.

In 2023, while continuing to advocate for the bill, we won the support of Senator Ted Budd from North Carolina. He introduced the bill in the U.S. Senate. In a press release he said, "At a time when small business owners across our state are struggling to find qualified candidates, now is the time to cut the burdensome red tape that has stifled the upward mobility of thousands of workers. I'm proud to put forward a proposal that supports access to innovative education options, skills development tools, and career growth."[17]

Whether you are a Democrat or a Republican—I really don't care. I do care that elected officials come to work and do their job for the people. All elected officials share collective responsibility for the social and economic impact that their work has on our workforce.

WORKFORCE DEVELOPMENT PROGRAMS

Milton Friedman, a Nobel Prize winner in economics, observed a canal project in Asia and asked why the workers had shovels instead of modern tractors and other machinery. The government official responded, "You don't understand. This is a jobs program." Friedman responded, "Oh, I thought you were trying to build a canal. If it's jobs you want then you should give these workers spoons, not shovels."[18]

On-the-job training in most workplaces can largely be summed up by a single instruction: copy the worker next to you.

In 1999, a new federal program called the Workforce Investment and Opportunity Act (WIOA) was created. It continues to be criticized by lawmakers on both sides of the aisle. Under WIOA the responsibility for training was divided among twenty-two different offices within the Department of Labor, plus fourteen other federal agencies outside the department.[19]

Today, over 2,500 job training centers exist in America. Even with the amount of infrastructure and investment under WIOA, it's still not enough. Job training programs are still too small and serve too small a percentage of the population. According to Gordon

Lafer, author of *The Job Training Charade,* "No more than 5% of the eligible population" gets access to government-funded job training programs.[20] And when they do, there are questions about how effective the programs are. Studies show retraining programs, as currently practiced, tend to show few, if any, benefits. In Michigan's "No Worker Left Behind" program, only one in three workers found any work after participation in the program.[21]

I could easily fill the rest of this book with a critique of WIOA. The most important thing to know is we have invested here; it hasn't been enough, it's a start, and we need to do more.

These programs have several challenges we should be aware of and work to address.

Challenge #1: Failing at Placement

The goal of job programs isn't just training but also connecting workers to jobs. However, the U.S. spends millions on workforce training programs that often don't find people jobs. Since 2018, just 54 percent of people who attended WIOA-approved programs became employed after completing their program.[22]

Challenge #2: Bad Partners

Workforce development programs have limited resources and are often reliant on volunteers and local boards to ensure progress on initiatives and to do the real work. However, many workforce development boards are inundated with local career and technical for-profit schools and vendors that are solely focused on selling certifications. They're not incentivized around placement and performance of their students.

These programs can take three to nine months to complete and cost thousands of dollars, some of which may be covered under local WIOA funding and the rest by the candidate. Reporting requirements by these partners can be hard to track, so workforce development programs lack the ability to gain critical feedback on effectiveness. That leaves under-resourced workforce centers with the difficult task of making recommendations to clients who are not just wage poor but time poor.

Challenge #3: Failing to Finish

Many students receiving federal grants for workforce training fail to finish or don't become employed because of life obstacles. Students who receive federal grants may also struggle with the seemingly simple requirement of getting to the workforce training programs. Federal requirements of "seat time" mean candidates must be able to commute to a physical location to sit in a class and log the necessary hours.

Federally funded workforce programs aren't required to offer students a credential upon completion. Some see this as a gap in the federal workforce training system. A credential is what the market values—remember signaling from back in Chapter 3? The workforce development boards should ensure candidates have a certificate of some sort they can use to signal to the market that they have acquired a valuable skill. In some cases, a formal certificate may be available via a partnership with an academic institution or a technical school.

Challenge #4: Locked Out

"We have to build a system where workers can plug into a relearning, retraining environment.

—Harry Holzer, former chief economist for the U.S. Department of Labor, professor of public policy at Georgetown, senior fellow in economic studies at the Brookings Institution in our conversation on the *Bring It In* podcast

In 2021, workforce programs spent $547 million to upskill more than 220,000 people. That isn't a lot of people in a workforce of over 165 million workers.[23]

Some programs require passing a standardized test to even access job training resources. The CASAS (Comprehensive Adult Student Assessment Systems) or TABE (Test of Adult Basic Education) are assessments that are required for candidates to pass in order to access many local services. These tests are like SATs and test an individual in areas such as reading comprehension and math.

They are discriminatory. These standardized tests do little to predict a worker's ability to succeed in a workplace environment, but they do much to block a worker's access to job skill training and employment services. Failing the test requires the candidate to enroll in a test preparation program—another program that requires seat time and often results in low completion rates. When a candidate doesn't pass their state's required standardized test, the likelihood that they will try again is very low. When I worked in Newark with their One Stop Workforce Center, only 12 percent of participants returned if they failed the TABE test.

Challenge #5: Lack of Staff Resources

"Some workforce boards are persistently under-resourced, and they lack an understanding of how to best use WIOA money," said Justin Birch, program director of workforce development at the Rural Local Initiatives Support Corporation.

Candidates often struggle to navigate workforce development centers that have more of a feeling of a DMV than a welcoming educational and support office. They may even have a metal detector and an armed guard at the door.

Once you make it through the door, it's a constant challenge to connect with a counselor or maintain one. Staff turnover is a challenge in most workforce development centers.

Challenge #6: Lack of Follow-Through

Government should provide retraining programs to help workers transition into new jobs.

Some good policies are being recommended.

Skill accounts aren't a bad place to start. But we need to do more to encourage and incentivize companies to invest directly in credentialing workers while they're on the job, instead of programs that can only be accessed by attendance when you're off the clock. When will workers putting in 60 to 80 hours a week ever get time for that?

The direction is correct, however we need more programs that allow workers the ability to invest in their development. This will require government to do a better job of sharing clear insights and providing coaching to individuals to help them make the right choices about how to invest in their own education. The Department of Labor has seven pages of regulations on how to use a ladder and none on guidance for upskilling workers. While I appreciate their concern for safety, it's time for us to start to lay down some foundations on how to properly deliver a workforce development program that doesn't just connect people to work, but arms them with the skills necessary for a long work life.

PRIORITIES

Our priorities are out of whack.

In June 2023, OceanGate's *Titan* submersible carried four guests and the CEO of the company on a journey to the wreck site of the famous *Titanic*. The ship lost contact and imploded. Over the next week, the world watched as the media reported on a search operation looking for five lost people. It was a massive search that employed global search and military resources.

At the same time, hundreds of miles away off the coast of Greece, another ship ran into trouble. Over 700 people were lost at sea. This time there was no search operation, no immediate resources dispatched by the U.S. Coast Guard. Why? Well, those 700 people had lives that we value differently. They were illegal migrants who died in an attempted smuggling.

This made nowhere near the news of the five lost on the tourist expedition that the passengers paid $250,000 each for. How much did the U.S. government spend searching for five millionaires? They won't tell you.

It's so hard to sustain a democracy and a future of work that helps everyone have a chance when you have such massive concentrations of wealth—and such tiny efforts to care for all.

Unless we make more people feel economically secure. Make them feel like they are taken more seriously. Make them feel like they are heard.

IMMIGRANTS GET THE JOB DONE

Today, 25 percent of the innovation workforce in America are immigrants.[24]

America wouldn't be America if it weren't for immigrants. Government policy has a direct impact on the ability to recruit new workers from other countries into the economy. Failures on this front can be felt across the entire economy.

Look at the number of patents in America held by a Chinese

or Indian inventor in San Francisco. In 1970, one in every 220 patents were from this group versus one in every 11 today.[25]

However, the trend may be shifting from immigrating in to immigrating out. By 2030, nine in ten young college graduates worldwide will live outside the United States. According to the *Journal of Labor Economics,* between 25 and 50 percent of current U.S. jobs could be moved abroad in the years to come.

So, let's get back to building walls.

THE SUPREMES

We can't talk about the government without including the Supreme Court.

These nine judges lead the judicial branch of the U.S. government—and are having a rough patch. In 2023, Justice Samuel Alito and Justice Clarence Thomas were found accepting lavish gifts and vacations from billionaire benefactors. The situation seems to paint the Supreme Court as a body representing the interests of billionaires who financially support them. Does this reflect the true nature of democracy?

In a landmark ruling in 2023, the Supreme Court terminated race-conscious admission policies at educational institutions nationwide. The decision, split along ideological lines, saw the six-justice conservative majority strike down the affirmative admissions programs at both Harvard and the University of North Carolina. We closed the door on the classroom but kept it open for affirmative action to be used for the military. Makes sense.

And, what about another 2023 Supreme Court ruling striking down student loan debt forgiveness?[26]

In the case of *Biden v. Nebraska,* Justice Amy Coney Barrett concurred with the decision that nullified President Joe Biden's student debt forgiveness plan. Within her concurrence, she defended the Supreme Court's conservative majority's application of a disputed legal theory. Utilizing analogies related to babysitters and grocery store owners, she detailed her perspective on how this legal principle should be applied going forward.

Justice Barrett's hypothetical example involved a grocery store owner who normally stocks 200 apples and then tells a clerk to "go to the orchard" to buy more. She wrote, "Though this grant of apple-purchasing authority sounds unqualified, a reasonable clerk would know that there are limits." She explained that if the grocer usually has 200 apples in stock, the clerk doesn't have the actual authority to buy 1,000 apples; if such an extraordinary purchase were intended, the grocer would have provided more specific instructions. Barrett further noted, "A clerk who disregards context and stretches the words to their fullest will not have a job for long."

Something tells me Judge Barrett has never worked in an orchard or a grocery store. Just a hunch.

Just to break it down. The outstanding student loan debt of $400 million would have been erased for 38.6 million Americans. This pales in comparison to the $1.9 trillion total in Trump tax cuts that only benefitted a very small percentage of people—primarily the wealthiest.

A recent survey by *Slate* looked to understand if people would feel a certain way about having an AI judge instead of a human judge. They found that humans scored better—but not by much.[27]

Not sure our supremes are helping the cause.

OPPORTUNITY, BUT NO ACCESS

Many applicants have a criminal record because we've incarcerated more people than anywhere in the entire world, ever, in history.

—Luke Shaefer, author of *$2.00 a Day: Living on Almost Nothing in America*, professor of social work, and public policy expert in our conversation on the *Bring It In* podcast

Today, too many young people in in urban communities are provided opportunities but no access.

We see what happens when there isn't a clear handoff from education to workforce. When you're not able to take the next step in developing your education and skills for work, bad things happen. You don't go to college and you may not immediately get a job. What do you do instead? You stick around. And when you stick around, you may get into trouble.

It may mean getting a ticket you can't pay. It may mean that ticket turns into a suspended license. It may mean that suspended license turns into you not being able to travel to apply for work. It may mean you put yourself in a position where you can't pass a drug test. It may mean a criminal record.

Now you have barriers. These barriers only make it harder to break through a pattern of employer discrimination that exists. Employers that hire based more on what you look like and where you live than on what skills you actually have.

We need to teach young people about opportunities. We don't tell kids that a carpenter gets paid $80 an hour, or a plumber gets paid $80 an hour or that if you attend a CDL program for three months you can be earning $100,000 a year. Young people attend high school and sit in classrooms where teachers have diplomas on the wall so to them success only looks like you go to college or bust.

We need to arm them with marketable skills to better position them to win a job or for them to create their own.

We also can't be naive and think that a workforce program or certificate alone is going to solve this problem. I have seen millions of community dollars invested in workforce training programs to teach people to do jobs they weren't allowed to perform up until the last few decades—and then these individuals acquired the skills and achieved the certificate but still couldn't win a job. Recruiters from local employers would then continue complaining about not being able to find workers.

Opportunity, but no access.

DON'T EXPECT MORE, DEMAND MORE

You're supposed to just do what the people above you have told you to do. My argument is that doesn't work to make good government.

—Jennifer Pahlka, author of *Recoding America: Why Government Is Failing in the Digital Age and How We Can Do Better*, former U.S. deputy chief technology officer, founder of Code for America in our conversation on the *Bring It In* podcast

Government creates the rules of the game.

But the world we're living in has stretched government in directions that the founders didn't expect.

Work was different. And the future of work wasn't something they were thinking about. But we're thinking about it now. And we need our government to think wider, think broader, and take the blinders off.

The first step is to vote out those no longer fit to serve. We need elected officials with skin in the game. We should therefore remove those in office or pursuing office that are running up additional debts or supporting policies that they may not have to experience.

Our democracy will not be healthy with the levels of inequality we've seen generated by the bad policy choices by elected officials. They've led to the decline in unions, automation, globalization, and unacceptable levels of inequality.

I pause and look at the companies that always seem to win, like Uber and Amazon. These are businesses that have spent many millions to change regulations to fit their business models. They have re-written the rules. They didn't do it for the betterment of society or for some bottom-line social impact BS. They did it for profit.

I'm not arguing for imposing heavy labor regulations. Some policy folks who have limited business experience have blind spots on certain policies. I have experienced this first-hand when lobbying members of Congress on a variety of issues. However, we must wake up to the fact that we are living in a world where profits take priority, skills are changing quickly, and people are living longer.

We must demand more from the government. We must be willing to rewrite the rules. We must take our blinders off so that everyone can participate.

CHAPTER 11

Unforgiving on Mass Incarceration

Hector had returned from prison just four months earlier.

On most mornings Hector reported to his car wash job in Miami at 9 a.m., as directed, but his boss usually wouldn't let him clock in until 11, sometimes not until noon. Maybe sooner if customers began lining up. Many days his boss paid him for seven hours of work, even though he worked ten.

One day, a car came out of the wash too fast, surprising Hector. The car hit him, knocked him down, and ran over his foot. He missed two weeks of work and didn't receive any pay or workers' compensation.

Hector complained about the unpaid hours and made safety suggestions to avoid another incident. The car wash owner didn't listen. Instead, he threatened to complain to Hector's parole officer and then fire him.

MASS INCARCERATION IS AS AMERICAN AS APPLE PIE

We're good at incarceration.

That's not a good thing.

In 1970, the U.S. had fewer than 200,000 people in federal or state prison. Then things changed. Incarceration rates soared more than nine times. Today, in the land of the free 1.9 million Americans are incarcerated.[1]

Want some more numbers?

- One out of five prisoners in the world are incarcerated in America.[2]
- Nearly one in every hundred Americans is in prison today.[3]
- One in seven Americans in prison are serving a life sentence and nearly half of them are people of color
- Two million people are in jail daily and 3.7 million are on probation or parole.[4]
- One in three people behind bars are in a jail and 80 percent have yet to be convicted in a court.[5]

The United States has the largest prison population in the world despite being third in population. The U.S. has 331 million citizens compared to China and India, which each have roughly 1.4 billion citizens.

Less than 5 percent of the world's population is in America, yet 20 percent of the people incarcerated on the planet are here. And the U.S. locks up more people per capita than any other nation on the planet.[6]

The impact is felt throughout our communities. And, of course, in our workforce. The percentage of working-age adults that are incarcerated (1.07 percent of the population) is more than the total percentage of adults that are incarcerated (0.88 percent of the population).[7] Families, business, and communities are impacted.

We have a prison system that doesn't forget. Returning from prison doesn't cleanse you of your past deeds. They stick with you. They affect, in many cases, every move you make going forward. In the worst cases, and all too often, they may even result in you returning to prison. Recidivism rates in the U.S. are some of the highest in the world. Almost 44 percent of criminals released from prison will return within their first year out.[8]

Unforgiving.

That is what I think about when I think about mass incarceration in America.

It is a reality for so many workers. Too many workers.

THE 38TH STATE

The corrections system is so big that it has literally become a state within a state.

As of 2022, it would make up a sizable enough population to be America's 38th most populous state. That's larger than Nebraska, West Virginia, or Hawaii.

Want to know what's scarier? Well, if you include the over three million individuals on probation, then the number of individuals incarcerated or on probation, represented as a state, would be the 24th biggest, ahead of Alabama and Louisiana. That would also make it the 125th biggest country—about the same size as Ireland or Norway.

It's interesting to compare the size of the U.S. prison industrial complex to Norway, which couldn't be more different. Norway's criminal justice system emphasizes restorative justice and the rehabilitation of prisoners, aiming to turn them into productive members of society. The country's prisons are known for humane treatment, with strict laws against torture and cruel punishment. Norway has one of the world's lowest overall crime rates and also has one of the world's lowest rates of repeat offenses, with only 20 percent of inmates reoffending within two years. The country's prison system is considered one of the most effective and humane globally. There is no capital punishment or life imprisonment.

PRIORITIES

The nearly two million incarcerated people in America are imprisoned across: 3,116 local jails, 1,566 state prisons, 1,323 juvenile facilities, 820 state psychiatric hospitals, 181 immigration detention facilities, 98 federal prisons, 80 Indian country jails, and 36 military prisons.[9]

That's over 7,000 facilities.

Which, by the way, means we have more jails and prisons than colleges and universities.[10]

Most people in prison are parents.

Half the people in prison are parents to minors.

This leaves 1.25 million kids with a parent behind the wall. At the state prison level, one in five of those children are age 4 or younger.

The number of marriages in the U.S. would increase by as much as 30 percent if we didn't imprison a single person.[11] It begs the question: What is the criminal "justice" system doing to families?

Mass incarceration and the policies that make them happen can be considered the most anti-family social policies that can be written.

"When Will I Get to Know You?"

I still remember where I stood in the hallway.

I was seventeen and had arrived at my dad's new apartment. Only a few hours earlier, he had been released from federal prison. I arrived just before his parole officer did. When you're released early from prison, before you complete your full sentence, you're typically assigned a parole officer whose job description is "to provide supervision and guidance to an assigned caseload of offenders released from state and local correctional facilities to ensure and assist in their compliance with the terms and conditions of release."

I didn't know what to expect.

My dad answered the door, and after a brief hello, a man dressed in khakis, loafers, and a Hawaiian shirt—looking more like he was here in Miami on vacation—pushed in past my dad before he had a chance to invite him in.

I stood in the hallway as he started forward, giving himself his own tour of the place. He stopped in front of me and turned his head but maintained his posture, communicating that he was stopping just to acknowledge me for a moment before getting on with his inspection.

While looking at me, he shouted back toward the door, "This your son?"

My dad responded, "Yep."

Then the man nodded with the kind of smirk you only make when you are accessing the creative part of your brain.

Then he said, "When am I gonna get to know you?"

NOT MUCH IS BEING CORRECTED

The degree of civilization in a society can be judged by entering its prisons.

—Fyodor Dostoyevsky

Many believe that behind the wall is a place where the corrections system lives up to its name. But not much is being corrected today.

A correctional system is a group of organizations that manage prisons and community programs like parole and probation. It's a component of the broader criminal justice system, which also encompasses the police, prosecutors, and courts.

Some call this system of mass incarceration the "prison industrial complex," meaning the many institutions, both public and private, that reinforce a system more focused on imprisonment and control (and profit) than rehabilitation and respect.

Beginning in the late 1970s, coincidentally around the same time we started to see the separation of wages and productivity, the prison population started to skyrocket in America.

Policy changes started a shift that transformed jails from systems designed to improve and correct into tools for mass confinement.[12]

Today, the U.S. spends more on prisons and jails than it does on educating children—and 15 states spend at least $27,000 more per prisoner than they do per student. California taxpayers spend $64,642 per inmate each year versus $11,492 per student. Both numbers are wrong—and both show our priorities today.[13]

By the way, we act the same way at work. Budgets for education and training are sparse and leaders often favor a command-and-control approach over one of education and development. We don't just underinvest in education for individuals early in life; we also fail to offer training and development opportunities while an individual is incarcerated—I mean being "corrected."

Today, three in four of America's inmates receive no job training while incarcerated. When job training is offered, it's often because a private company has found a way to profit from it—not because the prison industrial complex wants to invest more. Today some states are investing in technology, from tablets to computers, to offer more opportunities for individuals. But these technologies are often just more ways for the prison to profit off an inmate. Devices purchased by prisons aren't used just for job training. The majority also offer services, like phone calling and controlled internet use, that the inmate must pay to use.

Many states are talking about investment in platforms like virtual reality. Let's not even talk about the challenges of scaling a system like this inside of a prison—it has to be extremely challenging and prohibitively costly. Even major U.S. corporations that have invested in virtual reality systems have admitted that the system has trouble scaling and it is hard to create consistency so all employees can access the tools. Even so, several states have bought virtual reality platforms through a government vendor that is profiting from the sale of their technology into a prison. Today, virtual reality is being talked about as the new opportunity, yet these prisons have historically underinvested in even live classroom training or computer-based programs. What makes us think they're going to invest broadly in virtual reality programs?

Many others are skeptical. Dr. Cyndi Rickards is an associate teaching professor at Drexel University who leads weekly criminology courses inside Philadelphia prisons. She says people who are incarcerated:

"wear the label of inmate on their back. It's a dehumanizing system, so to suggest that VR is going to reintegrate them into society after being in a punitive system . . . just further objectifies folks, it continues a pattern of dehumanizing folks, and I've not read any compelling evidence that this is the route we should use to integrate people to be members of a healthy and contributing society."[14]

When you speak to for-profit companies that sell technology into prisons, many have a good mission or vision story lined up. They will say things like learning basic skills that an inmate missed before being incarcerated will ensure a reduced chance of recidivism upon release. They will say their technology is safer given the challenge of offering educational opportunities inside a prison environment. They will even reference the truth that many inmates may have never used the internet or a smartphone.

I believe we can be better. Given the over $300 billion spent annually on the criminal justice system, we should be able to find a way to make the environment more conducive to rehabilitation and development.

And while we're talking about training and education, we need to remember that this is just a small piece of the puzzle. Individuals returning from prison need access to a wide array of wrap-around services, to ensure they transition successfully back into the community. Reentry programs, although nowhere near enough and often tough to access, help those returning from prison to cover their bases beyond employment by helping with access to healthcare, medicine, identification, banking, parole, and more.

The whole process takes more than it gives.

Unforgiving.

JOB TRAINING

Education is the oxygen of work.

—Sanjay Sarma, professor at MIT, author of *Grasp: The Science Transforming How We Learn* and *Workforce Education: A New Roadmap* in our conversation on the *Bring It In* podcast

If you're incarcerated, you have something in common with most workers. You don't get access to training.

Job training is crucial for people in prison and those rejoining society, especially since many have less formal education or might have left high school without a diploma. Lack of education is a significant problem in places like Washington, D.C., where three-quarters of available jobs demand a bachelor's degree, but only 4 percent of those returning from jail possess such qualifications.[15]

When it is offered, job training in prisons and jails historically misses the mark. The programs are often outdated and often aren't teaching skills that transfer to the workforce inmates will meet upon release. You may learn kitchen skills, only to find that the techniques you're taught have no application in a modern restaurant.

THE CHAIN GANG

We are treated like inmates! The good pay isn't worth being treated this way! Currently looking for a new job!

—One-star Glassdoor review by a nurse at CoreCivic (formerly the Corrections Corporation of America), one of the nation's largest private prison firms. The company generated $1.9 billion in revenues in 2023.

Not bad.

If you were wondering who benefits from labor inside prisons, it's companies like CoreCivic. A benefit CoreCivic promotes on earnings calls is how they provide inmates with opportunities to work. It's very kind of them.

Prisons depend on the labor of inmates for tasks like food service and laundry, paying them extremely low wages. A study in 2017 showed inmates typically earn between 86 cents and $3.45 per day for common prison jobs, and in at least five states, they aren't paid at all. Additionally, inmates are required to work without much regulation or protection, and they can be punished if they refuse. The small amount of money they do earn often goes right back to the prison, as they are charged for essential things like medical care and hygiene products. This practice of making people work for little or no pay, without benefits, and then charging them for basic needs, helps prisons offset their operating costs onto the inmates themselves, concealing the true expense of running the prisons from the general public.[16]

They also put inmates in harm's way. The state of California has a program to train inmates to be "volunteer" firefighters. A big deal, given the state's challenges with forest fires. Thousands of incarcerated firefighters make up nearly 30 percent of California's wildland firefighters.[17] In 1946, California created a fire camp program that today pays $2 to $5 a day for a firefighter in camp and an additional $1 to $2 per hour if they were on a fire line.[18] The corrections department claims that California taxpayers save $100 million a year by using inmates to fight fires. These incarcerated firefighters put their lives at risk for their community. But when they return from prison, chances are it won't be so easy to fight fires when they are on the other side of the wall. Restrictions against violent offenders or formerly incarcerated individuals can make it difficult to impossible for these individuals to continue working in that capacity.

In 2020, California Governor Gavin Newsom signed into law A.B. 2147 to allow formerly incarcerated fire crew members to expedite expunging their record so they can seek employment in the fire service. This isn't the case in other states.

A REFLECTION ON REENTRY

The only difference between us and them is we didn't get caught.

I've heard this line countless times over the years. Every time it makes me feel lucky, ashamed, and determined. Lucky because I know it's true. Whether it be driving too fast or getting in scuffles nobody saw, it could have gone differently. Ashamed because I know many have been penalized for crimes they didn't commit or penalized unfairly for those they did. And determined because I know my actions can affect change, even if it's just changing another person's point of view.

In April 2023 I had the privilege of speaking at New Jersey Reentry's annual conference on "Training and the Dignity of Work."[19] The event was held at Saint Peter's University in Jersey City. It was a powerful and moving event, with community leaders, government officials, business leaders, and reentry program clients that included chairperson Governor Phil Murphy (NJ), former Governor Jim McGreevey (NJ), Newark Mayor Ras J. Baraka, Congressman Josh Gottheimer (D-NJ), and Don Katz, the founder and executive chairperson at Audible.

The all-day conference covered a wide range of topics around the challenges facing people returning from prison. We explored solutions as we tried to create a world where every person has the opportunity to compete.

Here are a few of my biggest takeaways from the day.

1. A Job Is More than a Paycheck

You can't go on LinkedIn, read a newspaper, or attend a trade show without the future of work coming up. Workers are lazy, great resignation, quiet quitting, work from home—all of these storylines paint a picture of a workforce that isn't willing, isn't skilled, and isn't interested in work.

Guess what? Not everybody sees it that way.

Why is a job important? This was a question that came up throughout the day. The answer had nothing to do with pay, benefits, or industry. It was something else.

A job gives people dignity and the feeling that they can contribute to something bigger than themselves. A job gives people a sense of agency, especially for individuals who may be returning from an environment that was designed to strip them of any. And a job ultimately gives you freedom.

A former death row inmate spoke briefly of his experience behind the wall. He wasn't allowed the opportunity to work, but he was given a privilege he said allowed him to focus his attention on something different, even though it was for just a few hours a week. The job was to clean the toilets on their block. I will never forget the pride in his voice as he talked about the opportunity to perform a job that so many would look down on. It wasn't about the task—it was about what the job gave him that made it so meaningful.

The value of work kept coming up in every conversation. A job is dignity and freedom. When our ability to work has always been assumed and never questioned, that's something we're likely to forget.

2. Investment in Job Training Must Start Earlier

We call it "corrections," but we aren't doing a great job at correcting anything. If we're serious about ensuring people return from prison and transition into work, and if we're serious about rehabilitation and reducing recidivism, then we must act accordingly. We must actually provide the opportunity to find meaningful employment. Alternatively, if the goal is to create a system that yields the worst possible outcomes, where you aren't able to get identification, you aren't able to get transportation, you aren't able to even apply for certain jobs, and you're not given the same learning opportunities—then our current system is designed perfectly.

We have to start preparing people behind the wall. Today, nearly two million Americans are in prison on any given day, and three in four of America's inmates receive no job training while incarcerated.

It's a failure. A failure for these individuals. A failure for our communities. A failure for our businesses. A failure for our workforce.

A topic that came up often in my conversations was it's not just about being able to work but having options in the work you choose. Often the blocker of choice is discriminatory interview practices by companies. Some companies automatically reject anyone who has served time, subjecting these people to a life sentence of jobs they can't fill. Former inmates often lack the basic credentials they need to apply for many jobs. Their options are limited because they never got the chance to attain the credentials while they were incarcerated. Not only because prisons make access to job training scarce or difficult, but also because even when they do, they are still censoring access to information by banning thousands of books. This routine book banning far surpasses the controversial bans on books by schools and libraries.

We must do better.

3. Systems Take Away Faces

Today there is a constant effort in this country to take away the faces of people returning from prison. It is imperative that we recognize no one should forever be defined by their worst mistake. Our current system reduces them to stereotypes that have long-lasting effects on the identity of people trying to transition back into a community.

An estimated 98.9 percent of people behind the wall will eventually be out. These people will need to be able to take the appropriate action to transition and get on their feet quickly and easily. They will need to know things like how to open a bank account, how to get a driver's license, and how to apply for a job.

As a speaker at the conference pointed out, "You can't just give them a Medicaid card and say good luck. You have to give them a Medicaid card and then show them how to use it."

You can say the same for a job. We can't just give them a job. We have to also then show them how to do it.

Today, we have a lot of work to do.

We have the highest rates of incarceration in the world. The U.S. population is equivalent to 4.25 percent of the world's population, yet a shocking 23 percent of the world's incarcerated are here in America. In this country, one in thirty-two Americans are in prison, on parole, or in a reentry program.

I believe it starts with connecting as a community. Government, nonprofits, and the private sector must work together better. Our shortcomings are not because of a lack of resources, but rather a lack of will. When we are willing to work together, we see amazing results. The current national average for reentry job placement is just 37 percent. Guess what the success rate is for the work of the New Jersey Reentry Corporation? It's 92 percent.

Our workforce is only strong if everyone can compete. It can no longer be about them. It's time we made it about us.

SECOND CHANCES

A 2017 Harvard study of the employment impacts of incarceration found, "Through the effects of criminal stigma or eroded human capital during incarceration, serving time in prison has itself been found to reduce employment by as much as a third, and hourly wages by ten to twenty percent."[20]

Once released from prison, the prospects aren't great for formerly incarcerated Americans. Within three years of release, two out of three former prisoners are rearrested, and more than 50 percent are incarcerated again.[21]

What percentage of previously incarcerated individuals are currently without jobs? In a 2021 report from the Bureau of Justice Statistics (BJS), it might be around 60 percent.[22] The report claims that out of 50,000 people released from federal prisons in 2010, one in three didn't find any work during the four years after their release. It went on to find that even those that found work were clearly not being afforded the tools to succeed or advance, given the velocity and frequency with which they switched jobs. Those in the study held 3.4 jobs over the four-year period.

Strict parole terms, limited support from social welfare programs, and a difficult job market are pushing previously incarcerated individuals, who are often part of a low-income, predominantly minority group, into less appealing jobs. However, some businesses are benefiting from this situation. They take advantage of the desperation of job seekers with criminal records, knowing that these individuals have fewer opportunities to negotiate for improvements in employment conditions, such as better wages, benefits, and protections. This exploitation leads to overall lower wages and worse working conditions, especially in low-wage frontline environments like hospitality, manufacturing, and warehouse work.

The effects of incarceration go beyond the low earnings and high joblessness faced by released prisoners, and its impact varies among racial groups. This difference is particularly evident in the disparities seen in imprisonment rates. Blacks are imprisoned five to eight times more often than whites, while the rate for Hispanics is twice as high as for whites. These statistics highlight the unequal and racially skewed nature of incarceration.

The labor market treats formerly incarcerated job seekers differently depending on if they are Black or white. Whites with criminal records often have better job connections than Blacks and Hispanics. Additionally, Blacks with contacts outside of prison are hesitant to vouch for them in employment settings, worried they might not be dependable. This combination of discrimination and networking influences job prospects after prison, echoing broader patterns of racial inequality seen in impoverished areas and low-paying job markets. Incarceration seems especially linked with the underlying poverty in minority communities. This connection between incarceration and poverty represents a unique, intensified disadvantage, impacting minorities, especially Blacks, more than whites.

Those who did find employment after release had lower

wages. In the first few months, formerly incarcerated people were earning just 53 percent of the median U.S. worker's wage. And after four years of seeking and obtaining irregular employment, the study population was making less than eighty-four cents for every dollar of the U.S. median wage.

Additional studies show that those returning from federal prison after serving a sentence of less than a year had a harder time finding and maintaining employment post release. While it is unknown why this is the case, it could be assumed then that a quick fix would be to avoid short-term sentences altogether—especially given its negative impact on our communities and economy.[23]

Most of the jobs for returning individuals are in low-wage jobs, including construction, manufacturing, and restaurants. These are industries with few protections for workers and declining unions, resulting in less support and a higher likelihood the worker will be taken advantage of.

OPENING AND CLOSING DOORS

He who opens a school door closes a prison.

—Victor Hugo, author of *The Memoirs of Victor Hugo*

The quote is easy to agree with at first glance.

Hugo's famous quote suggests investing in education and providing opportunities for learning empowers individuals and diverts them from paths that may lead to crime or incarceration. It suggests that by opening doors to education, society can cultivate understanding, skills, and moral values that might prevent people from engaging in behaviors that would lead them to prison. It suggests that education is a vital tool in societal development and crime prevention. By the way, nearly 75 percent of states have more prisons and jails than colleges.[24] The worst is Wyoming, with four colleges and 28 prisons and jails. That is a 600 percent difference between colleges and incarceration facilities.

WE ARE STRONGER WHEN EVERY WORKER HAS A SHOT
Each of us is more than the worst thing we've done.

—Bryan Stevenson, author of *Just Mercy*

We've got 4 percent of the planet's population in the U.S., but nearly 25 percent of the planet's imprisoned. That can't be OK.

In his book *Generation of Sociopaths: How the Baby Boomers Betrayed America,* Bruce Gibney says this about the rise of incarceration in America: "Many of its charges could have been saved by the schools the Boomers failed, by social programs the Boomers let decay, or by the exercise of empathetic clemency instead of automatic punishments that appealed to the boomers' crudest Old Testament instincts. Instead, boomer policy created a conveyor belt that leads from school detention to its lifetime equivalent."[25]

The cost of making a mistake in America can be devastating. In the U.S., 70 percent of criminal sanctions involve incarceration. Compare that to countries like Germany, where the number sits at just 6 percent and criminal actions are more likely to result in a fine, community service, or job training.[26] Job training! Think about that one.

We have a problem with forgiveness.

Today, 65 million people "need not apply" for all kinds of jobs because of their record. You don't even have to be convicted to feel the impact. On average, only 49 percent of arrests lead to a conviction, but many are left with a record that's used against them forever.[27]

We can fix this.

We can start with policies that include more development opportunities for inmates, dismantling discrimination by employers in their recruiting and selection process, investing more in frontline workforce training to ensure those with less formal education can compete, and volunteering in our community to inject fresh voices and knowledge into the prison industrial complex in hopes of building something fairer. Also, we can vote.

The tremendous talent and skills of the millions of currently or formerly incarcerated individuals are sitting on the sidelines in our communities. Everybody is suffering from this failure.

We are stronger when every worker has a shot.

We must be willing to forgive.

Choosing not to act will continue to yield poor outcomes. But are we willing to act?

CHAPTER 12

Unwilling on Poverty

Poverty is the mother of crime.

—MARCUS AURELIUS

Tina was a licensed home nurse and worked with several patients across Miami.

After catching COVID while caring for patients, she woke up one morning and found herself coughing, sneezing, and with a high fever. She decided to call her manager and let him know she needed to miss work for a few days.

She told him there was no way she could work. She asked for some time to get better and let him know that even if she came to work, it would be unsafe for patients, and she didn't feel she could even perform her work. He told her, "If you don't show up for work tomorrow, don't come back."

The next day she woke up even sicker and still feeling weak. She decided not to go to work. She was fired. And a few weeks later she was evicted from her apartment for missing rent.

WE HAVE A POVERTY NATION

Today, 42 million Americans live in poverty, including 11 million children—one-seventh of the country's kids.[1]

In their book *Tightrope*, the authors Nicholas Kristof and Sheryl WuDunn raise a question about the grave nature of poverty in America:

> Why did the United Nations official in charge of extreme poverty visit not only Mozambique and Mauritania in Africa, but also Alabama? And why did he warn that the U.S. now has the lowest rate of social mobility in the rich world and that, "the American dream is rapidly becoming the American illusion"?[2]

Today, more than 38 million people living in the U.S. can't afford basic necessities. The numbers are startling:

- Over 108 million Americans are surviving on $55,000 a year or less in wages.[3]
- Extreme poverty—living on $2 a day or less—has doubled since 1996.[4]
- 7.4 million families live in poverty.
- One in eighteen people live in deep poverty.
- Thirteen million children live in poverty; two million of them may live in extreme poverty.[5]

We haven't made much progress when it comes to poverty. Since the 1970s, the rate of poverty in America hasn't changed much:

- 1970: 12.6 percent
- 1990: 13.5 percent

- 2010: 15.1 percent
- 2022: 11.6 percent[6]

We should consider what poverty means for our workforce. Poverty is fear. It's the low-wage worker who's clocked in but can't help but be clocked out mentally as they consider the challenges they face at the end of their shift. It is the unending concern that makes your heart race as you consider all that can go wrong instead of all that is going right.

We need to talk about the levels of deep poverty in America. As if poverty couldn't get worse, we have a formal term for the level of poverty that is most extreme. Deep poverty, according to the U.S. Census Bureau, is defined as living in a household with a total cash income below 50 percent of the poverty threshold. This would mean less than $10,289 a year for a family of one parent and two children.

Let that sink in for a second.

Can you imagine living on $10,289 as a family! That's $197 per week. Yet 18.2 million of the 37.9 million people living in poverty are living in deep poverty. This means 48 percent of all people in poverty are living on or below half the line used to define being in poverty. And it's worse for children. We permit the same levels of deep poverty for children. Almost half (47 percent) of all children living in poverty live in deep poverty.

In his book *The Working Poor*, David Shipler says, "Poverty is like a bleeding wound. It weakens the defenses. It lowers resistance. It attracts predators."[7]

We must ask ourselves why. Why in the richest country in the world can we not solve a problem that hurts our families, communities, and economy?

Why are we unwilling?

IT'S EXTREMELY EXPENSIVE TO BE POOR

Predatory fees are crushing Americans and disproportionately impacting workers with low wages.

Every year we pay over $11 billion in overdraft fees, $1.6 billion in check-cashing fees, and up to $9.8 billion in payday loan fees.[8] That's over $61 million in fees, collected mostly from low-income Americans each day.

Financial systems that prey on low-wage workers create dangerous cycles of poverty that are nearly impossible for workers to get out of. Even if they work multiple jobs, long hours, and save, the slightest error or unexpected expense can cause them to fall into a terrible situation. This is important for employers to consider, given the effects that living on this type of edge can have on mental health and job performance. This is especially true for workers in customer-facing industries like hospitality and restaurants, who are encouraged to smile for the guest. It's even worse if you work in an environment that puts you in character—think Disney World.

When we think about poverty, we need to consider the details. Being in poverty means being cold and without electricity, stuck and without transportation, roaming and without a home, or hungry and without food. According to the World Food Programme of the United Nations, as many as 783 million people worldwide faced hunger in 2022. A separate report by the U.S Department of Agriculture found 44.2 million people in America had difficulty finding food for people in their household.[9]

Another term thrown around is a concept called "moderate working poverty." In this scenario, an individual lives on $3.20 per day. It makes up 402 million global citizens, or 12.2 percent of all employment. If you do the math of $3.20 per day multiplied by thirty days in a month, you get $96 a month.[10] Putting that in perspective, if that $96 a month has to be shared by four persons, that's $24 per person per month, or less than $1 per day.

But that's not the worst. As of 2021, 6.9 percent of total global workers live in "extreme working poverty," earning less than $1.90 per day.[11]

Speaking of Disney World . . .

THE MOST MAGICAL PLACE ON EARTH

Growing up in Florida and having family in Orlando means I was there often. This meant frequent trips to theme parks.

I recently was able to take my daughter to Disney World for the first time. My wife and I made the pilgrimage. Driving from the airport to the "Most Magical Place on Earth" meant we had to navigate International Drive, known to locals as I-Drive.

Driving down this long stretch of road was like its own amusement park. Both sides of the road are famously packed with every food option imaginable: McDonald's, Cracker Barrel, Outback, Pizza Hut, The Cheesecake Factory, and on and on. Franchise restaurants, chain stores, but no real small businesses—the view of a monopoly is abundantly clear on this stretch.

We eventually made it to our hotel. We checked in. We rode the monorail. We went to the Magic Kingdom. We went through the process of having our wristbands scanned for the first time. I got through first and stood watching as my wife and daughter were being helped by a manager. Standing a few yards from me was a Disney employee holding a small smiley face sign—but he wasn't smiling. I couldn't help it. I took a few steps over and asked, "How's it going, man?"

He responded, "The world is burning. But welcome to Disney!"

LOOK BACK, BUT DON'T STARE

The test of our progress is not whether we add more to the abundance of those who have much; it is whether we provide enough for those who have too little.

—President Franklin Delano Roosevelt, Second Inaugural Address

Being poor means being unprotected. In *Automating Inequality*, Virginia Eubanks says:

> If homelessness is inevitable—like a disease of a natural disaster—then it is perfectly reasonable to use triage-oriented solutions that prioritize unhoused people for a chance at limited housing resources. But if homelessness is a human tragedy created by policy decisions and professional middle-class apathy, coordinated entry allows us to distance ourselves from the human impacts of our choice to not act decisively. As a system of moral valuation, coordinated entry is a machine for producing rationalization, for helping us convince ourselves that only the most deserving people are getting help. Those judged "too risky" are coded for criminalization. Those who fall through the cracks face prisons, institutions, or death.[12]

Over the years I have become good friends with the leaders at Covenant House of New Jersey. Covenant House is a national nonprofit that offers shelter and services to young people experiencing homelessness. They have shared some startling numbers with me about their youths:

- 15 percent of their kids have experienced sex work trafficking.
- 25 percent of their kids have traded sex just to get through the night.

Covenant House sponsors an annual Sleep Out event to raise money for their programs. I have learned a tremendous amount from my experience at these events. I have also learned a lot from Jim White, the executive director. In November 2019, I joined Covenant House and nearly two hundred others to sleep out in Newark, New Jersey, to raise awareness and put an end to youth homelessness. It was the Friday before Thanksgiving. After the long night sleeping out, I woke up and listened to Jim as he talked about the message they share with young people. He talked about how they advise young people to "look back, but don't stare" as they consider moving forward with their lives. He talked about the "fear of not-enoughness" they experience as they reenter the workforce and go on job and school interviews.

He also pointed out that these young people are not homeless. They're simply "experiencing homelessness." An important point. He said that the least interesting thing about their kids is that they were homeless.

This is the mindset we need if we are going to fight to end homelessness in our communities.

If we are willing.

POVERTY IS ANTI-FAMILY

Poverty places a tremendous strain on families.

Today, a quarter of all children in America are being raised in a single-parent household. That's more than three times the global average. Additionally, most of these households are headed by women. One-fifth of them are considered low-income. They're receiving government benefits and aren't in the labor force.[13]

More than 1.1 million children in public school are homeless.[14] These children are living in motels, shelters, transitional housing, doubled-up with family, or on the street. Children constitute nearly a third of those living in poverty in the United States. In the mightiest nation on Earth, around 115,000 children find themselves without a home on any given night.[15]

I can only imagine the stress on parents who are trying to raise a child while poor—the challenge of juggling multiple jobs, the stress of day-to-day existence, and the responsibility of parenting. And being homeless means you do it all in public.

Those who talk about the deterioration of skills in workers should read carefully what I'm about to say. If you use words like "unskilled" and complain that workers don't show up on time or that your Gen Z workers aren't "made like they used to be," pay attention. The skills most companies expect from workers—the ones they claim are deficient—aren't academic. They're soft skills, like communication, discipline, loyalty, time management. These skills aren't learned in the classroom. They're learned at home. And when you're homeless or living in deep poverty with a parent that may not be around much, you're going miss out on those critical lessons.

Due to challenges within many families, the soft skills that should be taught in the family are now being outsourced to schools. And I would argue many schools have outsourced these to the employer.

We hear about studies of the negative effect of screen time on young people or, inversely, the positive impact on language for young children. Some research points to a word gap for children from the lowest income families, saying they hear far fewer words compared to children raised in affluent homes. By age four, the gap is 30 million words.[16]

As I always tell HR "leaders" who whine about so-called skills gaps, "It's not a skills gap, it's an opportunity gap."

Are we willing to do the work to change it?

CHILD POVERTY

Want to know how this future of work thing is working? Look at child poverty rates.

The expansion of the Child Tax Credit—an effort to help children/families in poverty—brought child poverty rates to a historical low in 2021.

Here is some data around child poverty rates:

- In 2020, before the expanded Child Tax Credit: 9.7 percent.
- In 2021, with the expanded Child Tax Credit: 5.2 percent (a historic low).
- In 2022, after the Child Tax Credit expired: 12.4 percent.

In 2022, child poverty in the U.S. more than doubled after support for the continuation of portions of President Joe Biden's Build Back Better program failed.[17] Thanks to opposition from a variety of elected officials, ranging from senators Joe Manchin and J. D. Vance to the entire GOP. They were convinced that the Child Tax Credit resulted in fraud and families using the money to buy drugs.[18]

Manchin claimed some of his constituents complained of knowing individuals that used the support—as much as $300 per child per month—on crack instead of supporting their children.

While there is much agreement that fraud exists in the overall program, it's important to note that providing folks with access to more dollars is proven to have an impact on poverty. While we shouldn't write blank checks and allow for fraud to take place, we should learn and iterate.

We need to break cycles of poverty that have been going on for too long. It is a cycle that is bad for kids, bad for parents, bad for workers, bad for business, bad for our society. The solution remains the same. We need to stop raising kids in poverty. And, how we do this is by giving families with kids more money.

It is unacceptable that in the richest country in the world any child experiences a night being homeless or in poverty.

BEING POOR IS A FULL-TIME JOB

It is a cruel jest to say to a bootless man that he ought to lift himself up by his bootstraps.

—Martin Luther King, Jr.

Today, a third of all Americans live without much economic security.[19]

A common belief is that if you're poor, it's because you're just lazy.

We tell people, "Pull yourself up by your own bootstraps," meaning figure it out on your own. But it's actually physically impossible to pull yourself up that way. The expression reflects an empathy gap that is only widening in America. It looks down on the people left in the struggle. It's a demand, a false symbol of strength, masking a disdain for those left behind.

The empathy gap grows, and with it, a misunderstanding of the struggle. Not all are given boots; not all are given the chance. The fight remains. It's a battle against a growing divide, against the very soul of a nation that once understood what it meant to strive together. It's a call to remember the forgotten and to recognize the struggle is ours, not theirs alone.

Poverty affects us all. It's not simply not having enough money. It's not having enough choice and being taken advantage of because of it. The workers who come to work while poor are invisible. Sit in a restaurant and watch how guests continue a conversation without even a simple thank you when the busser takes away a dish, or how they walk through the opened hotel door without even a thank you. Being invisible takes a toll.

Many workers wonder about the trade-offs they have to make if they take a job. In 61 percent of poor families, there's only one wage earner. This is a huge handicap when the work is low wage. Many workers must consider how taking on low-wage work affects their eligibility for income-based government support, such as Medicaid and SNAP benefits. In some cases going to work leaves them and their family worse off.

Here we confront a truth often overlooked: Too many workers live and work while on the brink of poverty or submerged in it, yet they don't fit the preconceived notion of what it means to "look poor." Consider this: 1 percent of Americans will endure at least one year below the poverty line between the ages of twenty and sixty-five. Two-thirds of those will reach for some form of public assistance, whether it's TANF, General Assistance, Supplemental Security Income, Housing Assistance, SNAP, or Medicaid.[20] Despite how shocking the numbers, we turn away, often treating poverty as a disease that affects only a small, lazy minority. This is not just inaccurate; it's a failure to recognize a struggle that affects us all.

No longer is having a job a guarantee that you'll avoid poverty's grasp. It has in turn created more work for the person it consumes—being poor is a full-time job.

Poor workers are stuck.

If you are willing to work then you shouldn't be poor. Period.

RIPPLE EFFECT

We need to attack poverty in America. Poverty is a factor that greatly contributes to early death from a variety of causes:

- 106,000 die annually from drug overdoses.
- 104,000 die from alcohol abuse.
- 49,000 die from suicide.

To put this in perspective: In eighteen years of war in Afghanistan and Iraq, total casualties numbered 7,000, compared to 259,000 deaths in one year from drugs, alcohol, and suicide.[21]

That's one of every thirty-seven deaths.

We need to attack poverty, the real enemy of achievement.

LOCATION, LOCATION, LOCATION

In many ways today, your earning potential is dependent more on where you live than on the experience on your résumé.

In *The New Geography of Jobs,* Italian economist Enrico Moretti shared that a typical man in affluent Fairfax, Virginia, would live fifteen years longer than a typical man in Baltimore, Maryland. Just sixty miles away.[22]

SHOPLIFTING

The poor know little of the motives which stimulate the higher ranks to action—pride, honour, and ambition. In general it is only hunger which can spur and goad them into labour.

—Joseph Townsend, author of *A Dissertation on the Poor Laws,* 1786

The news stories about shoplifting and retail theft always sound something like this: Thieves storm a CVS store, grab items off the shelves, and walk out. Police nowhere to be found.

Retail crimes is up 35 percent over the five-year average from 2017 to 2022. But here's a list of the most stolen items as reported by retailers: footwear, beauty and cosmetic products, power tools, laundry detergent, and Legos.

Something to look nice for work. Something to keep you clean for work. Something to use at work. Something to put on your feet to get to work. Something to clean your clothes with after work. And something for your kids.

Giant Food, a grocery store chain in D.C. and several Mid-Atlantic states, was reported to have to make changes in order to avoid shutting down. Among their decisions was to remove certain items from the shelves to deter theft. They were Tide, Colgate, and Advil.[23]

Gotta love the future of work.

FIXING HOMELESSNESS

As of 2023, 150 million people across the globe experience home-lessness. According to the United Nations, 1.6 billion worldwide reside in poor housing. Those experiencing homelessness have a life expectancy that is eight to thirteen years shorter than those who don't.

In 2018, the New Leaf Project, the University of British Columbia, and the charity Foundations for Social Change conducted a study to better understand how emergency services and social programs help prevent severe homelessness. They arranged a one-time payment of $7,500 to individuals that had experienced homelessness for two years or less.[24]

They found that when people received cash they spent it on rent, personal savings, clothing, transportation, and food. They didn't increase their spending on alcohol or drugs.

Lack of money is the primary cause of homelessness.

RIGHT VS. LEFT

We haven't talked politics much so far.

A Cato Institute survey in 2019 tried to assess our attitudes on wealth and welfare. They talked to liberals and conservatives. Here's what people say when asked how you accumulate wealth in America.

Liberals say it is:

- Family connections (48 percent)
- Inheritance (40 percent)
- Getting lucky (31 percent)

Conservatives say it is:

- Hard work (62 percent)
- Ambition (47 percent)
- Self-discipline (45 percent)
- Risk-taking (36 percent)[25]

HOARDING BY ELITES

Seventy-five percent of money spent on poverty research would be better spent if it were just given to poor people.

—Mollie Orshansky, American economist

Walk into a Starbucks in Midtown Manhattan and watch as everyday professionals drink lattes and eat their breakfast sandwiches while conducting a meeting about their weekend getaway to Montauk—just feet away from the utterly destitute on the sidewalk outside.

Many elites claim they're doing everything they can.

Unfortunately, the higher you go in today's economy, the easier it is to make a pile of money without taking any personal financial risk. And the lower you go, the bigger the risks and the smaller the rewards.

Here's the playbook for inaction:

1. **Enable the elites**: First, permit the privileged few to amass a resource, whether it's money or land, cornering it as their own.
2. **Deny and dismiss**: Next, act as though this concentration of wealth is natural, inevitable, or simply look the other way. Make it seem as though there's no alternative.

3. **Half-hearted solutions**: Try to resolve the societal issues from hoarding, but do so only with the limited resources that remain, never challenging the root cause.
4. **Inevitable failure**: Of course, these efforts fail. They fail to reduce poverty. They fail to create affordable housing. The problems persist because the true issue goes unaddressed.
5. **Resign to injustice:** Finally, shrug shoulders and say, "We tried. This is all we can do." Accept the failure as though there was no other option, no other path.

This playbook isn't new. It's a cycle, a trap that perpetuates inequality, keeping the many at a disadvantage while the few thrive. But recognizing the pattern is the first step toward challenging it, toward building a society that truly values justice and opportunity for all.

This is how the system has been built. Not by accident. On purpose.

REWARD POINTS

Inequality takes.

Here's a rundown from economist Robert Reich, Secretary of Labor in the Clinton administration, of fifteen takeaways you should know about how inequality works and how it affects our community:

1. **The wealthiest 0.1 percent:** This tiny fraction of American households holds as much wealth as the bottom 90 percent, a concentration that has doubled since the 1980s.
2. **Capitalism for whom:** America doesn't need to choose

between capitalism and socialism. We already have socialism—for the elite, while subjecting most Americans to harsh capitalism.

3. **The widening income gap:** Since 1980, the top 1 percent of Americans have more than doubled their share of total household income, leaving the bottom 90 percent stagnant.

4. **CEO pay skyrockets**: CEOs now earn 300 times as much as their typical worker, up from a 20-to-1 ratio in the 1960s.

5. **Money in politics**: In 2016, just 0.01 percent of Americans contributed 40 percent of all campaign donations, a significant increase from 15 percent in 1980.

6. **Wall Street vs. Main Street:** In 2018, Wall Street bonuses alone outpaced the annual income of all full-time minimum-wage workers in the U.S.

7. **The broken safety net:** Millions still lack health insurance, one in five children live in poverty, and millions can't afford basic needs like housing and food.

8. **Inequality in executive suites:** The McDonald's CEO who had an inappropriate relationship with an employee was permitted to receive a $42 million severance package in 2019, demonstrating how skewed compensation can be.

9. **Corporate vs. union lobbying:** American unions spend $48 million on lobbying, while corporate America spends a staggering $3 billion.

10. **The real measure of competitiveness:** Productivity is the backbone of competitiveness, but America is hamstrung by failing education, decaying infrastructure, and high healthcare costs.

11. **Globalization and standard of living:** Jobs go where corporations get the best returns, often at the cost of American workers' living standards.
12. **Unsustainable coping mechanisms:** Americans work longer hours and accumulate more debt to keep up with living costs, but these are Band-Aid solutions.
13. **Inherited inequality:** Your chances in life increasingly depend on the socioeconomic status of the family you're born into.
14. **Part-time America:** One in five Americans now works part-time, and 80 percent live paycheck to paycheck, signaling a shift in employment benefits and job security.
15. **The billionaire playbook:** Monopolies, insider trading, political pay-offs, and inheritance are the four main avenues to immense wealth in America.[26]

WE CAN END POVERTY

Poverty anywhere is a threat to prosperity everywhere.

But poverty can be good for business. Otherwise, why haven't we made as much progress as we're capable of?

We can end poverty, but some simply don't want to. A study on the cost to end poverty found it would cost $177 billion—less than 1 percent of GDP.[27] Unfortunately, too many organizations and individuals benefit too much from the cycle of poverty.

WE'RE ALL CITIZENS

Just because we're employers or employees doesn't mean we stop being citizens. It's our responsibility to care for each other.

We're stuck in a system that motivates us to think fast and cheap. It's how we prefer to consume in America. But somebody has to pay for it, and too often that somebody is the frontline American worker. Poverty wages lower prices. Relentless supervision and control facilitate fast service. The working class and working poor—and now even the working homeless—are bearing the costs of our entertainment and experiences.

In *Poverty, by America* Matthew Desmond writes:

> In 2020, Americans bought 310k new powerboats, spent $100b on pets, and over $550b on leisure travel. Our cars are bigger than everyone else's in the world — our homes are too. More than 1 in 8 American families own property besides their primary residence, including second homes and timeshares.[28]

As I said earlier, the higher you go in today's economy, the easier it is to make a pile of money without taking any personal financial risk. The lower you go, the bigger the risks and the smaller the rewards.

When I caught up with Jim White from Covenant House after the Sleep Out, I asked him how he gets others to care and consider the feelings and challenges that young people experience when being homeless. He said, "You have to name the pain." It is critical before moving forward.

We have to name the pain. It doesn't just scar the afflicted; it also scars those who do the inflicting.

We live in a society that's divided by many things: money, education, where we live, our race, our gender, our background, and our beliefs.

Are we willing to fight for each other? Are we willing to care and work to create a community where everyone has a shot?

Are you willing?

PART III

A WAY FORWARD

CHAPTER 13

The Frontline Formula: R.A.I.S.E.

Ending the book here is what happens all too often in books covering the challenges of the future of work.

We can't just talk about the problem. We should talk about what we can do.

We should be bold. We should be courageous. We should act.

A FUTURE OF WORK WORTH WORKING FOR

We've talked about the reality of work. Now it's time to look forward.

My hope was to share the challenges that face our frontline workers in this "future of work" moment. The problems are so big, but all our data, research, and experience show us that what we're doing is too little.

We are misaligned at work. With only 15 percent of global workers excited to go to work, we are doing too little.

We are failing at education. With $400 billion in student loan debt, we are doing too little.

We are deficient in training. With 80 percent of workers

receiving no job training in the last five years, we are doing too little.

We are under-resourced in human resources. With only 11 percent of companies offering year-round training opportunities, we are doing too little.

We are allowing too many people to be vulnerable when it comes to wages. With one in two Americans living a $400 unexpected expense away from poverty, we are doing too little.

We are retreating when it comes to the impacts of technology. With only 1 percent of workforce training being available mobile-first, we are doing too little.

We have a government with blinders on to its impacts on policy. With the U.S. ranked second to last in investment in workforce training programs, we are doing too little.

We have a mass incarceration system that is unforgiving for too many. With three in four inmates receiving no education or training opportunities while behind the wall, we are doing too little.

We are unwilling to end poverty. With the number of those living on $2 a day or less doubling since 1996, we are doing too little.

LOOKING FORWARD

Now it's time to look forward. We need a framework that can help us to create a future of work that's worth working for. It won't just result in more connected, engaged, prepared, dedicated, resilient workers. It will be good for business. It will drive growth. It will result in better service scores. It will drive more sales.

The framework needs to focus on how we create a high-performance workforce. The answer is it starts with your people. All of your people. A worker may not perform at the level they're capable of for a variety of reasons. They may not understand your expectations, they may not have clarity on their role, or they may not be motivated. The framework and suggestions to follow don't solve every challenge we have raised. But this book is about getting started. It's about moving toward creating a future of work where workers are able to be more respected, be more appreciated, and compete.

The suggestions ahead are also intended not just to be in the control of senior leadership. They are actions that can be taken by frontline managers and those who are elbow-to-elbow with our front line.

There is a way forward.

KNOWLEDGE, SKILL, AND MOTIVATION

Nobody leaps off the couch and becomes an Olympic anything.

—Joe Baker, author of *The Tyranny of Talent: How It Compels and Limits Athletic Achievement . . . and Why You Should Ignore It*, high-performance sports coach, professor at York University in our conversation on the *Bring It In* podcast

We're talking about performance.

There's a formula for building a high-performance workforce. I have observed this over decades on the front line with organizations across the globe. A high-performing workforce that is educated, engaged, excited, and enthusiastic is a result of an organization's ability to develop the knowledge, skills, and motivations of their workers. This is where we should start when thinking about performance:

(KNOWLEDGE + SKILL) X MOTIVATION = PERFORMANCE

Knowledge

What you know. A strong knowledge base is established by an organization's ability to transfer knowledge to the worker.

Skill

Ability to execute. A strong skill base is established by an organization's ability to teach a worker how to apply the knowledge they have acquired, while building upon the pre-existing skill foundation of the worker.

Motivation

Willingness to act. A strong motivational base is established by an organization's ability to create connection and inspire their workers.

Performance

The outcome of this formula will determine the level of performance of your workforce.

TAKING ACTION

Today, companies fall into five different categories depending on their stage of growth and culture.

	KNOWLEDGE	SKILL	MOTIVATION	MODE OF WORKER	ACTION STEP
1	Low	Low	Low	Disconnected	Invest
2	Low	Low	High	Beginner	Teach
3	High	Low	High	Learning	Model
4	High	High	Low	Disengaged	Encourage
5	High	High	High	Performance	Support

Over the last several decades, countless well-researched studies have identified the characteristics of consistently high-performing businesses. All the studies are in agreement. Consistently high-performing organizations have:

- Workers who are engaged and excited, instead of disconnected and deflated.
- A culture of constant learning and improvement, instead of compliance and stagnation.
- Leaders who coach and develop, instead of control and manage.

How do we create an environment where the formula yields high-performance outcomes? Let's pause and consider an organization that figured it out.

MONDRAGON

Founded in 1950s Spain, Mondragon Corporation is a network of ninety-five worker co-ops operating under a principle of democratic decision-making. The structure makes every worker an equal stakeholder, challenging traditional capitalism. The highest-paid executive earns only six times more than the lowest-paid employee. Workers become member-owners after a probation period and have a say in major company decisions.

The co-ops support each other financially and redistribute workers to save jobs during tough times. During the pandemic, many Mondragon workers voluntarily took pay cuts or reduced hours. Firing a worker is rare and requires a vote by the worker-owners.

The corporation employs about 80,000 people, with 76

percent of manufacturing workers also being owners. It has a diverse portfolio, from manufacturing bikes to consulting services, and generated over 11 billion euros in 2021. It also has a strong international presence, including subsidiaries in China, Germany, and Mexico.

If a large company like JPMorgan Chase adopted Mondragon's six-to-one pay ratio and democratic structure, its CEO Jamie Dimon would earn significantly less than the $34.5 million he earned in 2022 and workers would have a say in decision-making.

It's worth looking at.

R.A.I.S.E. EVERY WORKER

You have to equip them to take ownership of their own actions, behaviors, and development.

—Coach Margueritte Aozasa, head women's soccer coach at UCLA, two-time NCAA national champion in our conversation on the *Bring It In* podcast

It's time to raise every worker.

The word *raise* has a variety of meanings. It can refer to "raising a glass" in celebration or acknowledgement. It can refer to "raising a brick" by exerting effort to move or lift something up. It can refer to "raising funds" by convincing others to participate financially in your cause. It can refer to "raising a child" by nurturing and educating. It can refer to "raising the volume" by turning the knob on a radio so you can hear better. It can refer to "raising your hand" and asking for your voice to be recognized. But it can mean something more. It can mean to take action and initiate something. The word comes from the Old Norse word *reisa*, which means "to set in motion."

It's time to raise our workers.

If we're serious about creating a world where every worker,

from frontline to full-time, can compete and feel connected at work, we must stop raising up owners, we must stop raising up profits, and we must stop raising up corporate executive pay while forgetting about frontline workers. We must stop raising the bar and making it more difficult to survive in America. Instead, we must raise our workers.

We need to move on from a world of work that is all about extraction—extraction of labor, extraction of time, extraction of skills—and move toward a world of investment.

Let's begin.

CHAPTER 14

R.A.I.S.E.

R—Remove Barriers

Gate A12 at Detroit International Airport was packed.

It was 7 p.m. on a Thursday. Everybody in the lounge began to stand up. My flight to Newark was about to board. Then Carla took the microphone and made an announcement.

"What up, everybody?! We are just waiting on a few more things here, and then we will begin boarding United flight 7642 for Newark. My name is Carla. How many people here are planning on going to Newark? Raise your hands."

Carla didn't look like the normal gate agent. She was wearing an orange vest like the ones the people working on the tarmac wore. She also had noise-canceling headphones around her neck. It felt like she was taking control of the announcements for fun. It looked that way too. She was smiling from ear to ear. Happy.

"So, I know we are a bit delayed here, but we are going to get all you with your hands up on your way there shortly."

Still smiling.

"I like to play a little game with everybody. Who has the

most miles? So, let's do this. If you have a thousand miles raise your hands."

This went on for several minutes until one guy, standing at the front of the line (of course), raised his hand to over three million miles flown. He looked a little embarrassed by that.

Everybody was still waiting. Carla kept the energy up. And then she announced to a clapping audience that we were ready to board.

She was still smiling.

As I approached with my boarding pass, she greeted me as I scanned the pass. I paused and told her what she did was awesome. She replied, "My friend lets me come up here and do this for the last flight. This is the best part of my shift. Seeing people."

And then, she smiled.

IT WON'T HAPPEN ON ITS OWN

A high-performing workforce won't just happen on its own. It takes work.

The work must start by breaking down barriers that too often hold workers back. All corners of our community must work to ensure all workers have access to quality learning, coaching, and training opportunities to unlock their full potential.

The workforce is only strong if everyone can compete. Here's how we can do it.

1. Help Workers Upskill

Offer upskilling and cross-skilling opportunities to every worker for every role.

Employers need to continue to invest in developing that agile workforce, a workforce that's adaptive, that has access to training, that has access to continue to get that recurring educational training, so that they are prepared to make that kind of transformation and leap into the future.

—Guy Snodgrass, TOPGUN graduate and instructor, author of *TOPGUN's TOP 10: Leadership Lessons from the Cockpit,* speechwriter for the secretary of defense in our conversation on the *Bring It In* podcast

The ceiling is too low for too many in our workforce.

The problem is that the ceiling has been purposefully placed there by human resources teams and corporate leadership. The reality is it doesn't make any sense. This is the design that has resulted in record low employee engagement numbers, shaky employee retention stats, and challenges finding workers.

A good place to start is getting rid of the ceiling. There's no reason that training and development opportunities are available to leadership and managers within an organization, yet the same opportunities are restricted from the rest. The result is a weaker workforce and a failure to develop the next wave of high performers. It would be as if a Big League baseball organization had no coaches to develop players in their minor league system— and no line of sight into their performance.

If companies want to be serious about becoming high-performance organizations, they must ensure all workers can access upskilling and cross-skilling training. This should be offered both digitally and in live instruction.

2. Help Workers Reskill

Create and deploy reskilling opportunities for workers in

roles at risk of automation.

Today, many jobs are at risk of having at least some part of their functions automated or displaced by the impacts of automation or artificial intelligence.

Companies should be preparing for this now. They should be working to ensure that existing workers in frontline roles affected by these technologies are being prepared for their next role within the organization. And they need to be doing it today.

Those buying robots to flip burgers or make guacamole should be reporting on how they're reinvesting the savings and increased revenue from these investments back into their workforce to prepare them for the next job.

Show us how your investments are creating not just better returns and increased profits but more jobs and better outcomes for your front line.

3. Recognize Nontraditional Experience and Skills

Recognize work experience and skills acquired from nontraditional learning programs.

A major blocker to opportunities for workers starts with their application for a job. Too many blockers are in the way of workers being able to show the full breadth of their skills prior to an employment decision.

Additionally, too many organizations have offloaded hiring and critical elements of the interview process to technologies. We don't know if those algorithms have a positive or negative impact on candidates whose résumés and work experience don't fit neatly into a specific box. Workforce technology still doesn't provide effective ways to capture the necessary data in the screening process and determine if someone is actually qualified for the job.And let's be honest. Companies aren't that good at hiring to begin with. The data doesn't support that our workforce is filled with managers expert at identifying the right worker for the right job.

A history of one of the highest-stakes job interview processes is one we can look to for some perspective. It's a job interview process that is so high stakes it could make or break a professional sports franchise! I spent the early part of my career working in the sports performance industry, and every February would bring me to Indianapolis, Indiana, for the NFL Combine. The NFL Combine is the testing ground for the evaluation, grading, and assessment for the most elite talent rising out of college with the intention of working as a professional football player in the National Football League. The entire professional football operation invests millions of dollars in scouting, evaluation, interviewing, and testing to ensure that the decision of who to select and pay millions of dollars in signing bonuses will be a positive contribution to their team. With tremendous resources and MIT-level analytics going into the decision-making processes, you would assume that these folks know how to assess, interview, and select, right? But that's not true. Research into evaluating outcomes of NFL Draft selections finds that only 9 percent of the variance in the number of games the selection played in the NFL is predicted by draft number. So much for the effectiveness of franchises in identifying and picking talent efficiently.

Another major challenge of interview processes isn't necessarily the steps or the assessments or the silly-ass questions that interviewers ask to stump candidates. It's that these systems start from a position that the candidate is already a finished product. This often leaves out the reality that candidates, or draft selections, can still grow and develop within the right environment.

Organizations need to open up their hiring process to in order to give all workers a shot—and especially to let more diverse candidates apply. This includes everything from removing the requirement of "checking the box" for those with a criminal record to removing questions about background demographics that aren't direct indicators of the potential of a candidate.

This idea of open hiring is one that is already employed by some companies. An example would be a restaurant that has a sign-up clipboard. People put down their name and the restaurant hires the next person on the list, regardless of background or résumé. A major challenge today for workers is how well they signal or represent their skills to an employer. Research shows that 71.6 percent of résumés miscommunicate skills acquired from prior work experience.[1]

Another approach is a skills-based hiring model. In this approach, a candidate could put their skills on display by either completing an assessment or working a few shifts.[2] It is definitely not by just letting some AI algorithm on Indeed screen out a candidate because they're lacking a specific diploma or certificate. The skills-based approach may take more work by the employer, but it's more effective for accurately understanding baselines for a worker. If you're betting on skills rather than diplomas, you're five times more likely to predict job performance.[3] And experience? It's only half as reliable as skills when it comes to predicting how well someone will do on the job.

On the flip side, workers who feel underutilized are a whopping ten times more likely to be job hunting.[4] A skills-first approach isn't just about getting the best people; it's also about keeping them, especially when employee retention is tougher than ever.

Ditching that degree requirement doesn't just benefit you; it opens doors for tons of overlooked talent.[5] We're talking about leveling the playing field and breaking down barriers. This is a game-changer for diversity. Black and Latino individuals, who are less likely to hold degrees compared to non-Hispanic whites and Asian Americans, can finally get access to better-paying jobs. If you're serious about shrinking inequality and boosting diversity, a skills-first model is the way to go!

Which leads us into our next point: How to create a world where owning what you learn isn't just good for the worker but for the business?

4. Invest in Credentialing Your Workers

Invest in a digital credentialing system that allows every worker to acquire skills that are portable beyond your organization.

A sad reality for most workers is that they don't own what they learn.

Unlike workers who may have a college degree, the majority of American workers don't have a pretty diploma they can hang on a wall and mention on their LinkedIn page. Only one in three American workers has a four-year degree. This means workers lack a true means to show who they are and where they have been. Most workers can't show their skills. How can companies make the right decisions about offering them a position? You can help. Start with your current workforce by investing in technology and systems that ensure your existing workers have a formal credential they can take with them to their next job.

In a recent conversation with a major international nightclub owner about investing in this type of approach for his frontline workers (servers, bartenders, etc.), he responded by saying, "Why would I want this? Then they'll just take it and go somewhere else." This shortsighted view only hurts the entire community. The reality is that a worker's ability to stack their credentials and skills for easy sharing is good for businesses, reducing interview costs and accelerating onboarding time. It allows the organizations to identify new talent more easily, as well as assess their own.

The benefits of this may not be immediately obvious to you in your organization. However, I would argue that a well-defined curriculum with certificate levels would allow you to make better internal advancement and investment decisions. The certifications will have an outsized effect on the worker as they navigate to their next job. And imagine a worker who moves on from your company being able to walk into their next interview and promote the skills and learnings they have learned from you. These informal credentials are often more valuable for frontline workers when compared to the formal credentials that so many argue don't prepare workers for work anyway.

Do it for your people. Do it for your community. Somebody has to lead here.

5. Create Workplace Mentoring

Create a workplace mentorship program designed to promote racial equity, where experienced employees share advice, feedback, and coaching with new employees.

Whether you mean to or not, you're inevitably turning organizations one of two ways: towards equity or inequity.

—Chequan Lewis, president at Crunch Fitness in our conversation on the

Bring It In podcast

The 2019 Workforce Learning Report by LinkedIn reported that 94 percent of employees would stay longer if the company invested in their learning.[6] This sentiment comes across time and time again when workers are asked about what is most important to them.

Beyond formal learning programs, organizations should work to remove blockers of access to the institutional knowledge that exists within an organization. Often where you sit in an organization determines what informal learning you get access to when it comes to meetings, after-hours events, and personal conversations. And since where you sit in an organization is so heavily impacted by your race, socioeconomic background, and gender, we need to create more informal mentorship opportunities that directly target and afford this corner of your workforce with opportunities. Access to the wisdom of experienced employees is especially important for new workers.

Leaders dismantle discrimination.

TEAR DOWN BARRIERS

Frontline workers are:

- Stretched
- Traumatized
- Discriminated
- Marginalized

And they are:

- Capable
- Skilled

- Open
- Willing

High-performing organizations that want to unlock the full capability of their workforce should actively participate in tearing down barriers that block their people from advancement.

We will all be better for it.

CHAPTER 15

R. **A**. I. S. E.

A–Adopt a Continuous Approach to Developing People

It was a packed Zoom call.

We had all the big dogs from the learning team on the call: Director of Learning and Development, Director of Instructional Design, Chief Learning Officer, and then a bunch of other titles that sounded straight out of higher learning.

The call was to talk about strategy and how this major grocery retailer handles its training and development programming. It was going well. As my colleague Bri took the team through our capabilities at 1Huddle, I was doing a bit of multitasking by running through the LinkedIn profiles of each of the call attendees.

They all had a lot of LinkedIn Learning certificates and random skills, but what jumped out at me was how not a single one of the attendees had any formal credentials in learning design or pedagogical design. This wasn't a surprise, but it triggered me to ask a very specific set of follow-up questions. I wanted to understand how qualified and sophisticated the group was when it came to the science of designing learning development models.

After listening to them talk about how they print manuals and are PowerPoint rockstars, I couldn't take it anymore. Failing to even raise my hand, I jumped in.

"How do you know your training is working?"

Crickets. You know how Zoom makes awkward silence even more awkward? This group was staring around the boxes, hoping someone would jump in. I decided to clarify my question.

"What I mean is, I'm certain your goal isn't simply to dump information on your people in a single event. You're well aware most learning is just forgotten. So, given all the ways that you deploy training, what metrics or measures are you using to ensure learning is happening?"

Finally, I got someone with a pulse who seemed to be nodding in understanding—their Chief Learning Officer. He unmuted himself and said, "We make all our training mandatory so if you don't complete it then you don't get paid."

Not exactly a scientific approach.

LEARNING IS A PROCESS

We have to keep training. We have to keep educating. I don't care whether it's on the assembly line or whether it's in a classroom, but we've got to think about that once we get our employees trained. They have to continue that training.

—Dr. Donna Shalala, former congresswoman, health and human services secretary, university president and Presidential Medal of Freedom recipient in our conversation on the *Bring It In* podcast

By the year 2100, the worldwide number of people aged eighty and over will increase from 125 million to 944 million.

That's a seven-fold increase.

It's possible that the first people to live to 150 are already in a crib somewhere. Over the course of their longer working lives, they will need to learn more, learn faster, and learn continuously.

The new reality of work is creating challenges for workers. The functions and skills demands of their jobs are changing faster than they can manage. It isn't their fault. The speed of change is happening so fast that the real problem is the employer's inability to quickly modify and deploy new training and development programming to help workers transition. Many employers don't even know how the jobs are really changing. This is coupled with embarrassingly small budgets for training.

We know that failure to continuously develop people results in disengaged, underperforming workers and a high risk of churn. The data is clear, yet organizations consistently make the wrong choice. They choose to invest valuable resources into costly reactions to the problem instead of solving it. Organizations that complain about the costs associated with employee development should take a look at how much they're spending on things like recruiters and job boards. Today, companies spend $200 billion a year on recruiters as talent middlemen. Imagine if we took that $200 billion and instead invested it into our workers.[1]

In today's workforce, workers must be able to recall both knowledge and skills automatically, reliably, and quickly while under pressure and as they are busy performing other tasks. It's virtually impossible to become proficient at this level without continuous development. Too many organizations look at employee training and development as a one-and-done event.

It disrespects all that we know about human development, which is that we need to continuously practice. You don't work out once and then choose to never work out again and expect to be in good shape. You don't just eat well one day and then choose to never eat well again and expect to be healthy. Continuous development reinforces basic skills that are required to learn advanced skills. It protects against forgetting and it improves transfer to new skills.

To create a high-performance workforce we must ensure the development of our workers is continuous, not one-and-done. We need to ensure it's rooted in the science of learning, not our hunches on how we think learning works.

1. Offer Training Year-Round

Offer training and development programs fifty-two weeks a year to every worker.

We have to stop thinking about buying talent and focus on building talent we already have.

—Michelle Weise, author of *Life Long Learning: Preparing for Jobs that Don't Even Exist Yet* and future of education and workforce strategist in our conversation on the *Bring It In* podcast

Remember what we said about forgetting?

Research on the science of learning shows a worker will forget 70 percent of what they learn within three days and as much as 87 percent of what they learn within thirty days. The reality of weak retention means that workforce training can't be a one-and-done event. Companies are either unaware of this or unwilling to solve for it, which is why the majority of their learning opportunities aren't offered year-round to their workers. I would claim that they are outright negligent if they don't offer the same opportunities to the worker who enters through the service entrance as they do to the person sitting in the C-suite.

Ineffective training results in a variety of losses for an organization:

- Inconsistent execution
- Poor service
- Missed sales
- Low morale
- High employee turnover
- Slow, low, or no growth

The way an organization deploys their training and development offerings matter. These events can be designed well or badly. High-performance environments design them well. They invest in demanding activities that are proven to result in skill acquisition, retention, and transfer. And they provide repetition—workers receive continuous training.

Organizations must develop and invest in programs that are offered year-round for their workers, not just on Day 1.

Some points to consider when investing in a continuous development model:

- **Engineer it into the daily flow of work.** This allows workers to easily access the content throughout their workday, not just by a thirty-minute training module they can only access on a desktop.
- **Be flexible**. Allowing workers to access the learning any time, anywhere.

- **Blend learning.** Offer training from multiple angles with a variety of classroom and digital experiences.

The best work environments have exceptional leadership that understands their main priority is to develop all their people. Not just the few.

2. Base Your Training on the Science of Learning

Ensure your learning and development approach is based on the latest findings on cognitive psychology and the science of learning.

Learning takes practice.

—Justin Reich, associate professor at MIT and author of *Failure to Disrupt: Why Technology Alone Can't Transform Education* in our conversation on the *Bring It In* podcast

Herman Ebbinghaus was a famous German psychologist whose groundbreaking work in the study of memory uncovered a concept called the "forgetting curve." This research looked at the propensity for individuals to rapidly forget material they're introduced to in a learning environment. Ebbinghaus found that very specific learning mechanics must be present if learning is to be more robust, stickier, and lasting.

Unfortunately, much of Ebbinghaus's findings, as well as the work of countless cognitive behavior psychologists and learning scientists since, aren't widely adopted. Many learning or training leaders aren't even aware of this research. Organizations are therefore operating with instincts about learning that are misplaced, incomplete, and flat-out wrong. They're more rooted in superstition than science.

If an organization wants to create high-performing workers, then the approach to learning and development must be rooted in the latest science of learning. Five aspects of learning must be considered if your programming is to be up to the challenge of preparing today's workers.

RETRIEVAL

We know intuitively about the learning process that we, in order to learn something effectively, try something out, we get it wrong, we get feedback on what went wrong, and then we try it again. And although we know it intuitively, our school systems, our educational systems, are set up in exactly the opposite direction.

—Joshua Eyler, director of faculty development at University of Mississippi and author of *How Humans Learn: The Science and Stories behind Effective College Teaching* in our conversation on the *Bring It In* podcast

Retrieval practice is where we start.

With retrieval, you try to recall from memory something you've learned in the past. This can take many forms—a pop quiz, a multiple-choice test, flash cards—and is often referred to as "the testing effect." The act of retrieval is proven to strengthen memory, making information more retrievable (easy to remember) at a future date.

What can you learn from taking a simple test? Well, every time a memory is brought to mind, it's reconstructed and reinforced. When you take a quiz, you're not checking your memory; you're enhancing it.

Why retrieval works: Instead of putting more stuff into our brains, retrieval practice helps us take knowledge out of our brains and put it to use. That's what cements memory.

Retrieval is superior to other learning methods for several

reasons, but the primary one is that it challenges the brain by requiring more cognitive effort. Retrieval practice embraces a model of learning from failure, which is a powerful ally of learning because of our brain's natural motivation to find and construct knowledge from errors.

The opposite of retrieval includes shallow learning practices like cramming and rereading. Cramming and rereading feel good because they create a feeling of fluency and actually knowing. But we all know this feeling is short-lived and gives you a false impression that you will actually remember the material at a future date. Experts warn over and over that you should avoid the trap of "feel-good learning."

If you cover a hundred facts and a worker retains 60 percent without using retrieval, they'll remember sixty facts. However, if you teach ninety facts and a worker remembers 80 percent using retrieval, they end up retaining seventy-two facts. So, by teaching a bit less but employing effective memory techniques, your workers will actually remember more.

The practice of retrieval can feel difficult. Most organizations don't adopt the retrieval practice approach because they fear failure and the uncomfortableness that comes along with it. However, to be successful you must embrace risk. Your people can't grow if they live in fear of being wrong.

John Glover, a research professor of education at the Teachers College at Ball State University, said, "The question is not so much whether tests enhance memory—the data overwhelmingly indicates they do."

How to apply it: Low-stakes tests in the form of quick-burst trivia games with various question formats (multiple choice and short answer).

INTERLEAVING

Learning that is easy is like writing in the sand; here today, gone tomorrow.

—Patrice Bain, author of *Powerful Teaching: Unleash the Science of Learning*, educator, and speaker in our conversation on the *Bring It In* podcast

There is almost nothing you can master in a single exposure.

Interleaving is a learning technique that involves mixing together different topics or forms of practice in order to facilitate learning. By practicing jumping back and forth between different topics, you ultimately strengthen your understanding of the concepts and promote learning agility.

Interleaved practice is the opposite of "blocked practice," where you focus on one topic at a time. Think about how you learned U.S. history back in middle school. You probably went in a very specific timeline, starting with the American Revolution and ending with WWII. This format is a low-intensity learning approach when compared to interleaving content.

Mixing content up through interleaving produces poorer accuracy and speed during the learning event, but compared to blocked practice, it leads to significantly greater accuracy and speed on later testing sessions. Interleaving forces the brain to work harder to put content in the proper order. This increase in effort is believed to have a direct impact on the storage strength of the learning.

Why interleaving works: If learners spread out their study of a topic, returning to it periodically over time, they remember it better. One of the reasons is the increase in challenge that is introduced. Interleaving is a great example of a desirable difficulty. When you mix topics up, it forces the brain to discriminate and exert more effort. Hundreds of studies show that this healthy struggle results in stronger, longer-lasting retention. Yes, individuals will experience minor episodes of failure and some degree of frustration with interleaving, but research clearly shows the learning gains far outweigh the short-term setbacks.

How to apply it: Use a fast authoring tool to auto-create content that mixes and matches material across various content areas. This will effectively interleave your most important content for maximum retention.

PREDICTION

Prediction and retrieval actually worked very well together because prediction is something at the beginning of the learning journey and retrieval then is something that you would be able to do after with your learner.

—Jim Lang, author of *Small Teaching: Everyday Lessons from the Science of Learning*, speaker, and workshop leader for teachers and writers in our conversation on the *Bring It In* podcast

Mistakes are opportunities for learning.

Research proves that guessing the answer on a question where you have no chance of getting it right is a powerful learning exercise. This process is often referred to as "generative learning" because it challenges the learner to generate an answer by predicting—in other words, taking a stab at it.

A popular learning myth is that you must know the information before you're tested. Mountains of research point out we have that process backward. A test isn't a measurement tool. Its effect is to alter what we remember and change how we subsequently organize knowledge in our minds. Testing in this manner is actually studying of a different and more powerful kind.

Why prediction works: In the book *Make It Stick: The*

Science of Successful Learning by Dr. Henry Roediger III, Peter Brown, and Mark McDaniel, the authors say, "Unsuccessful attempts to solve a problem encourages a deep processing of the answer when it is later supplied, creating fertile ground for its encoding, in a way that simply reading, hearing, or watching the answer cannot."[2]

Research finds when we come up against things for which we earlier made incorrect predictions, our brain is stimulated to avoid repeating the error. The brain sends a signal of recognition almost immediately—in just a tenth of a second—after seeing the object that first foiled us, in an effort to avoid repeating the error. Failure is just information. It's a signal to try something else and another chance to learn. Learning greatly hinges on the surprise of getting things wrong.

Unsuccessful retrieval attempts are remarkably more effective than spending the same time studying the answers to be recalled later. When you're forced to make a prediction or respond to a question you don't have the answer to yet, your brain sparks and grows.

How to apply it: Introduce new concepts by creating a game and deploying it to your people ahead of additional instruction or use it as a more effective replacement for classroom or live instruction.

PLAY

First thing is you gotta have fun.

—Chef Nick Wallace, *Chopped* Season 34 winner, Top Chef contestant, named 2020's best chef of Mississippi, executive chef, founder of Nick Wallace Culinary in our conversation on the *Bring It In* podcast

A bored learner is a poor learner—and prone to distractions. Making sure the training environment sustains the brain's interest in the challenge is critical to effective activity design. This is where play can be a powerful addition to your learning approach.

Play has some real benefits beyond just fun. When playing, you're more likely to try out new strategies and approaches without threatening your physical or emotional well-being. You're safe precisely because you're *just playing*. When playing, you're constantly stretching yourself and have to deal with not always winning. Playing is always on the edge between success and failure.

Why play works: When talking with Benedict Carey, the author of *How We Learn: The Surprising Truth About Where, When, and Why It Happens,* he told me, "Without play our learning is hindered and we are unable to function at our highest levels."[3]

Play is vastly underrated for learning. When you're playing games, you're engaged in a learning process where the brain is making sense of itself through simulation and testing. Play activity is actually helping sculpt the brain.

Play is engaging. Play is just fun. People are willing to invest more time and interest when playing games because they experience genuine interest, excitement, and fun. They can sometimes be learning without even realizing it.

When training games are designed well, workers will ultimately build stronger connections to content that will aid later retrieval.

Brian Sutton-Smith, in *The Ambiguity of Play,* says, "It gives brains a workout. It is cognitively challenging. It requires attention. It sharpens senses. It both demands and inspires mental dexterity and flexibility. It thrives on complexity, uncertainty, and possibility. That makes play just about the perfect preparation for life in the 21st century."[4]

How to apply it: Create a competition and introduce leaderboards around your most important topics. Research proves games get workers to competency 45 percent faster than traditional learning methods.

SPACING

Good practice is no matter how hard it is to change something you're not used to doing, to keep doing it in small portions until you have that and then develop the next skill and then the next goal.
—Dara Torres, 12x Olympic medalist swimmer, author of *Age Is Just a Number*, speaker, and entrepreneur in our conversation on the *Bring It In* podcast

The spacing effect means that long-term memory is enhanced when learning events are spaced apart in time rather than massed in immediate succession.

With spaced repetition, you repeat the same piece of information over varying intervals of time. It's the reason companies space advertising out over the course of a show. They know the spacing effect will lead to better stickiness long term.

Why spacing works: K. Anders Ericsson, PhD, whose research uncovered the concept of the 10,000 hour rule that Malcolm Gladwell eventually took and bastardized to sell a bunch of books, has talked at length on the power of spacing to create stickier learning. In *Make It Stick: The Science of Successful Learning*, the authors Roediger, McDaniel, and Brown say, "Spaced practice, which allows some forgetting to occur between sessions, strengthens both the learning and the cues and routes for fast retrieval."[5]

Repetitions spaced out over time make it harder and lead to greater retention of information in the long run than the same number of repetitions close together in time. The reason has to do with the way spacing impacts the forgetting process. Spacing learning intervals introduces forgetting, which in turn results in stronger retention as the material is reintroduced and forces the brain to retrieve and restructure what it has learned.

Varying the time intervals when spacing also plays a role. The more time that has passed, the more difficulty you will have when it comes to retrieving the information. Naturally, a few days after we learn something, forgetting begins to set in. That's why retrieval is so powerful—it interrupts the forgetting process.

How to apply it: Build a year-round training calendar and spread content across the schedule.

Now let's talk about how we measure success.

3. Measure Knowledge Retention
Measure knowledge retention data.
To know and not to do, is in fact, not to know.

—Maya Angelou

A group of researchers approached new graduates after their commencement at MIT and Harvard. The graduates in engineering were still in their caps and gowns when researchers approached with a challenge. They offered each student a light bulb, a battery, and a length of wire and challenged them to get them to work making something.[6] You might think a new graduate in engineering from an elite school would have some ideas. They couldn't do it.

When you analyze what happens with ineffective training and development programs, you find that most workers are in environments where they acquire shallow knowledge. They may remember the material but their understanding is limited—and that's in the best-case scenarios. In most scenarios, the learning methods, such as cramming to pass a compliance or online test, is like filling a leaky bucket. You pour a lot in but it quickly spills out.

The data supports this. The widely used Learning Pyramid model shows individuals retain 5 percent of what they learn in a lecture, 10 percent from reading, 20 percent from audiovisual sources, 30 percent from demonstration, 50 percent from group discussion, 75 percent in practice, and 90 percent from teaching others.

Organizations need to be relentless at measuring the effectiveness of their teaching and coaching methods.

People leaders should be measuring knowledge retention and current proficiency levels on core knowledge on a quarterly basis, at a minimum. Once that approach is established, organizations should use this intelligence to inform the ongoing and additional training they are deploying as part of their continuous development program. It can't just be one and done.

We need to constantly invest in a cycle of reinforcement and reintroduction.

4. Lifelong Learning
Provide every worker with a lifelong learning account.
Workers today fall into three categories:

- **Incumbent workers**: workers currently employed
- **New entrant workers**: workers new to the workforce
- **Displaced and underemployed workers**: workers who are out of work or employed below their skill level

Continuous development models need to ensure every worker is not only afforded the opportunity to learn but that they have some choice in what they learn and how they learn it.

Incumbent workers need to raise their skill levels to meet the demands of new technologies in the workforce. New entrant workers need better pathways from school to work. And underemployed and displaced workers need personal, mental, and financial support.

Each of these categories of workers have their own unique challenges and opportunities for continuous development. Each of these categories have different economic challenges they face at home. Each of these categories has different realities when it comes to transportation.

Lifelong learning accounts aren't new, but they haven't been widely adopted. Think of them like a health savings account. An organization contributes to a learning account the worker can then use for a variety of pre-approved learning and development opportunities. It's a way to afford workers the opportunity to decide how to invest their learning benefit, instead of just offering limited opportunities in the form of paying for a college degree only at select programs. The more structured approach might sound good but may not be the best route for many workers. The program might not match their career pathway, or it's logistically difficult for them to access due to transportation issues or overloaded work schedules, or it has additional costs that aren't covered, like childcare and textbooks. The learning account offers much more flexibility.

Workers struggle to access the many on and off ramps for learning and pathways necessary to succeed. Only 36 percent of 18- to 24-year-old college-attending workers felt they had the skills and knowledge to be successful in their careers after graduation.[7] We must ensure, as leaders, that every worker has the opportunity to level themselves up.

Isn't that what leaders do?

5. Diversity, Equity, Inclusion Year-Round

Offer diversity, equity, and inclusion programming fifty-two weeks a year.

In an internal memo in 2020, Starbucks aimed to have 30 percent of its corporate roles and 40 percent of its retail and manufacturing positions filled by people of color by 2025. However, their 2022 internal demographics report indicates they were far from meeting the goal, with less than half the positions in the company having met diversity targets.

Notably, the numbers for Black representation were especially concerning. Between 2020 and 2022, there was virtually no change in the percentage of Black baristas and shift supervisors. Store manager roles saw less than a 1 percent increase in Black representation, and at the regional VP level, only a 1-point gain was reported.[8]

Offering diversity, equity, and inclusion programming has become all the rage in the last few years. Some companies have hired executives to lead the charge. Some companies have added the responsibility to the human resources team. Some have brought in keynote speakers. Whether these programs work or not isn't the question we should be asking. Instead, we should acknowledge that many organizations, like Starbucks, are struggling to create a workforce where all workers feel accepted and represented.

What do we need to do? More.

We should hire new executives. We should challenge the human resources team to do more. We should hire more keynote speakers. We should do it all. Then, we should optimize and make sure offerings and programs aren't just lip service. The DEI programs that are believed to have the best outcomes are intentional, fully supported, and consistent.

We have to get to work here. Make it continuous and make it for everyone. We have too much ground to make up.

BETTER EVERY DAY

Failure should be a part of everything you do.

—John O'Sullivan, author of *Every Moment Matters: How the World's Best Coaches Inspire Their Athletes and Build Championship Teams*, and founder of the Changing the Game Project in our conversation on the *Bring It In* podcast

Your reaction to failure is going to create the ultimate outcome.

—Coach Kirk Everist, two-time U.S. Olympian, five-time national champion, head men's water polo coach at the University of California, Berkeley, in our conversation on the *Bring It In* podcast

High-performing workforces create environments where every worker can get better every day. Failing to offer opportunities to every worker and effective learning events is a recipe for an organization to underperform.

Contrary to popular belief, not all practice is effective. A lot of managerial assumptions about learning are actually based on myths, biases, and superstitions. Re-reading material, for example, generates a false sense of understanding and retention. Cramming only creates an illusion of mastery.

A few questions for you to pause and consider:

- What is your learning philosophy?
- How would you describe your teaching style?
- How do you measure success?
- How many hours of training does an average employee receive per year? How about a frontline worker?
- How do you acquire and act on employee feedback on

your approach to training?

- How much struggle is present in your learning approach?

When it comes to learning, the easier path is not always the most effective. Instead of avoiding failure, we should actively engage with it. This approach has major ramifications, not just for innovation but also for education. Currently, our educational system is designed to furnish students with a set body of knowledge, rewarding them for correct application and penalizing them for mistakes. However, this is a limited view of the learning process. True learning occurs not just through success but also through failure. Failing helps us acquire new skills, stretch our limits, and foster creativity. After all, innovation doesn't come from simply rehashing known information, no matter how advanced.

As we consider our frontline workers, we should also be aware of the challenges they face as they try to learn. We know that a brain on excessive stress is a brain in crisis mode, while a brain with a complete lack of stress is a brain that is on vacation. Neither of these are good for mental performance. The best learner is the worker who's paid a fair wage and has the security of knowing that missing a paycheck will not result in them being evicted. And our businesses would perform better if it was true. Yet, too many workers on our front lines don't have that reality.

We must ensure that how we design work considers it all.

CHAPTER 16

R.A.I.S.E.

I—Invest in Technology to Meet Workers Where They Are

I grab a seat at the bar. In my opinion, the bar is always the best spot when I just want a small bite to eat while getting some work in. The outdoor pool area is packed, and servers are hustling around serving lunch to families enjoying their vacation and couples just hanging out and enjoying their first cocktail of the afternoon.

It's a big bar, and before I could even get my laptop opened, I was greeted by Michelle, asking if I'd like to see the lunch menu. I put in an order and asked for a ranch water—my go-to drink of tequila, soda water, and lime. A must when I'm on the West Coast.

Given my occupation, I love to observe service action. Every bar has its own energy, and it's most often directly impacted by the alpha bartender. This is the person who's running point and making sure that the whole operation is smooth, from servers racing to pick up for tables to the barback's efficiency at restocking the well to ensuring the other bartenders are keeping their heads on a swivel and seeing everything they are supposed to.

Some small talk with Michelle ensues. I ask, "How long have you been a bartender?" She says, "Just one month."

Pretty surprising given the speed at which she operates and how smooth and comfortable she looks behind the bar.

"Where did you work before?"

"Oh, I've worked here for six years. But I used to be on the fifth floor."

She went on to tell me how she used to work in housekeeping. And after years in the grueling job, with unpredictable hours, heavy lifting, uncomfortable guest interactions, and of course, low pay, she began to explore opportunities in other roles on the property. She very much likes the security of the hotel brand.

I asked, "How did you go from housekeeping to bartender?"

She reached into her pocket and pulled out her phone. Turned it to me, opened an app, and said, "Every employee here gets 1Huddle. It isn't just for training. It lets me explore games on different career paths here. I just so happened to win all the bartending games and really found myself interested in making a switch."

"When did you play the games?" I asked.

"Normally before my shift I can get a few games in because I have two buses that I have to take to get to work. That's a lot of downtime and I just started using it in the mornings, then in the evenings. Kind of made it really easy."

"What's the best part?"

"It lets me do it on my terms."

Michelle noticed a guest on the other side of the bar about to sit down. She flashed a smile. "I'll be right back."

And off she went.

BETTER INFRASTRUCTURE

We need better infrastructure.

I used to have a coach who would say, "You can't fire a cannon out of a canoe."

High-performance organizations need a strong foundation to reach their goals. Just as strong national infrastructure requires roads, bridges, tunnels, and airports, the same underlying needs are true of our workforce. We need roads that are accessible to all, bridges that connect us, tunnels that help us move faster, and airports that are reliable. The same is true for work.

What does your employee development infrastructure look like?

For too many workers, their journey through work is like driving down a road full of potholes. Smooth in certain spots, but largely an accident waiting to happen.

To raise every worker to the level they are capable of, we must invest in technology that meets workers where they are. We need workforce infrastructure that is accessible, connects us quickly, and is reliable.

It requires action.

1. Mobile Accessible

Make every part of your training and development programming mobile accessible.

For a long time, there's been this huge pushback that online learning is always inferior to learning face to face, which is simply not true.

—Dr. Barbara Oakley, author of *Uncommon Sense Teaching: Practical Insights in Brain Science to Help Students Learn*, engineer, professor at Oakland University, and former Army captain in our conversation on the *Bring It In* podcast

Out of the seven billion people on earth, six billion have mobile phones. That's more than have access to toilets.[1]

Unfortunately, today only 1 percent of workforce training and development tools are available mobile-first. This failure to invest in technology that meets workers where they are is a major miss for employee development. I'm pretty sure most companies have taken the time to ensure all of their customer-facing apps and information are available and optimized for mobile.

Why not for your workers?

Your entire training and development technology stack should be accessible to support the entire employee lifecycle. This includes:

- **Recruiting**: pre-learning and role-specific education
- **Onboarding**: initial learning
- **Engagement**: ongoing job-specific communication and development
- **Development**: ongoing upskilling, reskilling, cross-skilling
- **Compliance**: regulatory or mandated training

The best organizations know that taking into account the full employee lifecycle sets the stage for a worker to have a long-term career with a brand. A broken model will yield low performance outcomes.

2. Allow Complete Training Access

Allow every worker in your organization to access your complete training and development technology stack.

The future of work looks like developing systems or culture within a system within that culture that could take someone with the least and develop into the most.

—Chef Brandon Chrostowski, James Beard-nominated chef, restaurateur, sommelier, fromager, politician, and founder, president, and CEO of Edwins Leadership & Restaurant Institute, in our conversation on the *Bring It In* podcast

A company that doesn't work to unlock the full spectrum of talent across every worker in its workforce is weaker for it.

We have a real digital divide today that doesn't just impact people at home—it impacts them at work. I don't expect organizations to make sure all workers have reliable internet at home. I do expect them to be purposeful and ensure they invest in technology that considers the demographics and realities of their whole workforce.

Whether you're the one serving a table of four or sitting in the corner office, you should treat your employees as your #1 customer. The reality is that the customer experience can never exceed the employee experience. Unfortunately, today leadership gives the minimum to managers, who then turn around and give the minimum to frontline employees, who then turn around and give the minimum to the customer. The best organizations know that happy employees ensure happy customers. And happy customers ensure happy shareholders.

Great people-development technology must be:

- Progress-oriented
- Trustworthy
- Easy to work with

- Fit into the flow of work
- Engaging and cool to use
- Individualized

This one is simple. Just make everything available to every worker.

Told you it was simple.

3. Budget for Updated Training Technology

Create a budget to update existing training and development technology every year.

The University of Pennsylvania conducted a study on the effectiveness of MOOCs (massive open online courses).

These courses have become very popular. The study looked specifically at 1 million students enrolled in MOOC classes using the Coursera platform. The researchers reported: "MOOC's have relatively few active users, user 'engagement' falls off dramatically—especially after the first 1-2 weeks of a course—and few users persist to the end."

They went on to find that barely 50 percent of the students who signed up viewed even a single lecture; the course completion rates were only between 2 and 14 percent. Worse was who actually joined in the online class: 80 percent already had a college degree, meaning that even in an open consumer setting these types of courses do not make it to the majority of consumers that are lacking skill credentials.[2]

These outdated technologies are no longer effective at meeting workers with the right information at the right moment in time. That the majority of corporate e-learning follows the MOOC model and that the majority of MOOC courses don't even gain engagement in an academic setting where students are the ones paying for learning should be additional proof that companies need to be more aggressive at upgrading their technology stack if they want it to yield the type of skill enhancements they expect.

The concept of an online course that is made up of just long-form videos and tests (which often result in workers just guessing until they pass) is ineffective, inaccessible, and too often comprised of content that is outdated. Organizations need to create a budget with the specific intention of updating the library of content they offer for training and development.

You should ask some important questions before investing in new learning technology.

- What assumptions about employees is this technology built upon?
- Who will benefit most from this approach?
- Who will this approach hurt most?
- How will it affect our culture?
- What new skills does this technology require?
- What jobs and tasks will this technology displace?
- How will this technology change the way employees work together?
- What unintended consequences might this technology entail?
- Who will take full responsibility for the launch, implementation, and ongoing maintenance of the technology?

Putting the specific technology platform aside for a moment, remember that the platform means even less if the content available is outdated, incomplete, or irrelevant.

4. Give Workers Training Flexibility

Give workers the flexibility to train and upskill anytime, anywhere.

The restaurants who have survived are the businesses that have taken care of their workers.

—Chef Ken Hom, Michelin Star-winning chef, author, TV host, cookware producer, restaurant consultant, and ambassador for Action Against Hunger in our conversation on the *Bring It In* podcast

I had a conversation with a CEO recently about workers being paid to do training off the clock. She argued that allowing workers to do training whenever they wanted created an "unnecessary liability" to the business. This is because current wage and hour laws, which vary greatly by state, were written in a time before they could have predicted a worker would be trying to upskill or acquire new skills while on a mobile device. This additional time, especially if done before or after a shift, could be seen as working time and trigger the expectation that the employer should treat this as time worked.

Let's put aside that she considers upskilling workers as "unnecessary." I responded with an idea that I thought of all on my own. I asked her, "What if you just pay them for training?"

A few groans and redirections later, I had my answer. She wasn't willing to pay for it.

We have the technological ability to let workers access learning and development opportunities wherever they may be, whenever they want. We should offer workers incentives and compensation for completing required training. We should invest in ways that allow workers the flexibility to decide when and where they get better.

5. Use Game-Based Technologies

Meeting workers where they are means not just geographically but also generationally.

Use game-based technologies or simulations to boost engagement, knowledge retention, and performance outcomes.

The only learning which significantly influences behavior is self-discovered, self-appropriated learning. Such self-discovered learning, truth that has been appropriated or assimilated in experience, cannot be directly communicated to another.

—Carl Rogers, American psychologist

Today, research shows that gamers are all around us. The average millennial will have spent over 10,000 hours on a game platform before they turn twenty-one. Even if you don't stay up late playing *Halo*, you understand gaming mechanics, ranging from frequent flyer mile programs to fantasy sports.

As Brian Sutton-Smith, author of *The Ambiguity of Play*, writes:

> Play is an incredibly effective way to boost performance, yet it's often overlooked. While adults focus on goal-oriented tasks, play thrives in its lack of objectives. Far from trivial, play engages our brains in ways that are mentally challenging, it requires focus, hones our senses, and encourages cognitive agility and adaptability. Given its affinity for complexity, uncertainty, and endless possibilities, play is practically tailor-made for equipping us for life in this unpredictable 21st century.[3]

FIVE REASONS GAMES WORK

Your benefit in terms of your ability to remember something (or recall) is inversely related to how difficult it was to retrieve.

—Scott Young, author of *Ultralearning: Master Hard Skills, Outsmart the Competition, and Accelerate Your Career*, entrepreneur, and programmer in our conversation on the *Bring It In* podcast

Games as learning and training tools work incredibly well. Here's why:

1. **Games enhance learning agility.** A well-designed video game gets a player to try new things. When you fail, a good game will encourage you to reset and play again—maybe with different tactics, strategy, or tools. And when you finally figure it out, you put it into memory and move on to the next level.

2. **Games provide a sense of autonomy.** Workers need to feel they have meaningful choices. The Zeigarnik Effect helps to better understand how games are a powerful tool for learning. This is the belief that people are more apt to remember tasks they've started but haven't finished. When we begin a task without completing it, it seems to stick in our minds, creating a sense of internal tension and ongoing preoccupation. This is because our brains are wired to seek closure. Finishing the task not only brings relief from this tension but also delivers a sense of happiness.

3. **Games allow us to feel a connection to** others. They are a highly effective way to create community through the presence of leaderboards, social profiles, and in-game chat.

4. **Gamers are grinders.** In video games, grinding means doing the same thing over and over again to slowly

progress toward some goal. When you fail, you just re-load and try again.

5. **Games enhance a growth mindset.** The best games teach us to default to a mindset where we believe in possibilities and opportunities.

The best workplaces and best games have a lot in common: they teach you to fail. They challenge you. They increase difficulty in response to your progression. They give you feedback to let you know how to get better. And they get you to try new things. All are great for workers today.[4]

When learning and development programs employ simulations and game mechanics, they fulfill the goal of meeting workers where they are, with how they want to learn, and how they have grown up learning.

And when it's done right, learning becomes the outcome, not the journey.

1 PERCENT BETTER

In 2019, *The Irish Times* named the sports star of the year. It wasn't an athlete. It was a shoe.

In 2019, the Nike Vaporfly was responsible for a staggering thirty-one of the thirty-six podium positions in the six World Marathon Majors. All the runners wore Nike Vaporflys.

The saga of Nike's Vaporfly shoe is nothing short of extraordinary. In 2016, Kenyan marathon sensation Eliud Kipchoge put an under-the-radar prototype to the test—a prototype that would later make waves as the Nike Zoom Vaporfly Elite. A year later, in 2017, Nike raised the bar by introducing a revolutionary carbon fiber plate technology, which claimed to improve running economy by a whopping 4 percent. That translates into cutting down running times by 2.5 to 3 percent. For once, the buzz surrounding a product was backed by hard numbers.

Innovation in the running shoe game is as old as the industry itself. Long before Nike became a multi-sport giant, it was a scrappy venture aimed at delivering high-performance footwear to runners keen on shaving off those crucial seconds. In 1971, co-founder Bill Bowerman made waves by creating a shoe sole using a waffle maker, pouring urethane to form a unique shape. Over the decades, every shoe company worked tirelessly to make the next big leap in technology, sometimes even courting controversy.

The New York Times, armed with data from public race reports and shoe company records, found in 2019 that Vaporfly-wearing runners ran 3 to 4 percent faster than peers in other shoes, and over 1 percent faster than those wearing the next-best racing shoe. What's the secret sauce? A feather-light midsole with incredible energy return, and an embedded carbon fiber plate that propels the runner forward. In plain language, the carbon fiber plate keeps your toes straight, conserving energy, and improving your running economy by approximately 1 percent.[5]

Coaches across the sport even hold the belief that the margin of victory in elite marathon running is so small that if you fail to wear Vaporflys you are basically guaranteeing failure. It's a testament to the impact technology can have in sports. Since their launch, Vaporflys have dominated the marathon world, at one point claiming the fastest men's and women's marathon times ever.

Kipchoge went on to break more records by becoming the first person to run a marathon in under two hours while wearing the Vaporflys. Nike called him "the essence of progress." His epic performance forever redefined what it means to run. So, if you're aiming for the fastest times, it's clear: Vaporfly is the quickest shoe money can buy.

The Nike experiment is a case study in the law of marginal gains. The law of marginal gains comes from the idea that if you break down a big goal to small parts and improve just a little on each small part, you can have a huge improvement when you put all the parts back together.

It's hard to make everything 1 percent better. Know why? Because the results can't be noticed when you make the changes. It may take months or even years to see the changes and tens of millions or hundreds of millions of dollars. We aren't sure what Nike spent—they won't reveal it.

It's not easy to invest in infrastructure. Employing the concept of marginal gains and improving 1 percent at a time is what we should strive for. A strong infrastructure for all our people is a critical key to not just a high-performing worker but a high-performing workforce system. No one person or sector knows everything there is to know.

Things change. Events change. People change. When you think about it, the world of work is all about change. It's our responsibility as leaders to work tirelessly, every day, and make sure the people that give us their all at work get all we have as leaders.

CHAPTER 17

R.A.I.S.E.

S–Support Community Workforce Programs and Education Partners

In November 2022, exactly one week before Thanksgiving, hundreds of executives from across the state took part in the Executive Edition of Covenant House New Jersey's Annual Sleep Out.

For the fourth time in four years, I was one of them.

The idea is to raise funds in support of the organization, which provides critical immediate shelter for kids aged eighteen to twenty-one, and for executives to experience, by sleeping out on the streets for just one night, what 4.2 million American kids experience every night.

We weren't exactly out on the streets, but that doesn't mean it was easy. We spent the night wrapped in sleeping bags, huddled in the private parking lot behind Covenant House's Newark Crisis Center, under the protective watch of two cops stationed nearby.

It was an uncomfortable night for everyone. First-timers were easy to spot.

As a returning sleeper, I'm savvier than I used to be after doing this for four years in a row. And I've had a lot of help along the way.

During my first Sleep Out, a couple of the kids took pity on me, and showed me how to set up and angle the cardboard box I'd been given against the wind. Each Sleep Out since, I've gotten a little bit better at it. Better at picking out my place in the parking lot, about how many layers I wear, and managing my discomfort.

But what always surprises me, despite the police presence and the other participants nearby, is how isolating the experience feels.

In the dark, in the cold, you sleep in fits. The city sounds different when you're lying on the concrete. You're more alert to your surroundings: the people passing by, every car that starts near you, every sleeping bag that jostles beside you. You imagine that every time you hear a glass bottle break, it's behind you or just around the corner.

I feel vulnerable in a way that, frankly, I'm not accustomed to. Every year, that's the hardest thing to prepare for.

But at the beginning of each Sleep Out, I try to keep in mind something I've heard Jim White, Executive Director of Covenant House New Jersey, say, more times than I can count, to the kids who pass through the shelter.

"You can look back on this time," he'll tell them, "but don't stare."

There's an element to those words that puts a lot of things in focus.

The Sleep Out, the more I think about it, is itself an exercise in not staring.

As participants, we're encouraged to raise $5,000 if we can but discouraged from making that our aim. We're encouraged to empathize with homeless youth, but not to believe that our empathy can grant us special knowledge—as if one night in a parking lot could ever count as insight into what it's like not to have a home.

It's easy to focus on trees at the expense of the forest, especially if one of those trees can be held up as evidence of a good deed done, a goal achieved, or a milestone reached. This might be true, especially in the corporate world, and especially in the fourth quarter.

This time, before the Sleep Out, I had spent most of October traveling, attending conferences, meeting customers, and schmoozing investors—first in New York, then in Miami, Detroit, Los Angeles, and finally, Las Vegas. It was a blur.

There was some irony in that. After all those many days on the road, I had come home not to wake in my own bed but to wake up half-in and half-out of a cardboard box. Still, looking back now, what strikes me is how nice it felt to be back in Newark, to wake up not far from the office, the company, and the life I have built here—and how relieved I was to go back to that life.

The guilt that comes with that relief is complicated. Learning later that we managed to raise over $1.4 million for Covenant House doesn't make it go away. But, as Jim says, best not to stare.

I always like watching Jim make the rounds in the morning, as the Sleep Out ends. Each morning after feels fresh and cold. Jim is a welcome presence, patting backs and checking up on the rows of disheveled executives, still in their sleeping bags.

I pass him as I head out. He asks, as he always does, how the night went.

"Crappy as usual," I say.

"You're welcome" is always his response.

It's one I'm always grateful for.

THE VALUE OF COMMUNITY

It's time we started acting like a community.

Sometimes words lose meaning.

A community requires sacrifice, selflessness, and sharing. We must realize that to create a high-performing workforce, where every worker can compete and every organization can unlock the full skills and abilities of all their workers, we must start acting like a community.

Charles Vogl, in his book *The Art of Community,* defined a community as "a group of individuals who share a mutual concern for one another's welfare."[1] Making our workforce ecosystem work requires participation from more than just private sector companies. It requires workforce programs, nonprofits, workforce development boards, and education providers all coming together—as a community. They all have a role.

According to Gallup, only 14 percent of CEOs believe colleges are preparing people for work.[2] Expenditures on higher education in the U.S. are the highest percentage in the world, at 2.6 percent of GDP.[3] And, every year since 1983, the demand for college-educated workers has grown by 3 percent, but the supply has only grown by 2 percent.

We have discussed how our education system has problems. Our workforce development programs also have their own challenges—outcomes and job placements have struggled to show lasting results for workers. Maybe this isn't so surprising, given the ridiculously small amount of money we invest in these programs. But these programs are critical resources for so many people. We can't afford for them to struggle.

We need to be talking about how we move forward. It starts with strong support for community workforce programs and education partners. This isn't just a call to action for private sector companies. It's a call for collaboration among all parties. Just as private sector companies should take action on the recommendations I suggest below, nonprofits, schools, universities, workforce programs, and other education partners must not just talk together but take action together.

It's what leaders do.

1. Create Ongoing Relationships

Create ongoing relationships with a local high school, college, or university to share business learnings, insights, advice, and education.

A critical first step is to have an active, open line of communication between those hiring workers and those trying to connect workers.

In today's workforce, employers are the primary consumer of training and education programs for workers. Being in this position means that their insights and perspectives on the skills and tasks being performed have to be communicated and well understood by those preparing workers for work. Today's workforce education system struggles with being connected to the jobs and careers that are in demand.

A popular play for workforce development programs and nonprofits is to invest in government-accredited training providers and for-profit technical schools. The training is challenging, expensive, and often results in workers who may have completed a certification but may not be better connected to work. We can't place the blame solely on workforce development boards. As a member of the City of Newark Workforce Development Board, I know that one of the biggest challenges is the absence of participation from the local business community.

Companies need to get more actively engaged in their communities. As consumers of skills, they need to share their learnings and perspective on the demands and profile of the work they are hiring for. We should be aware that teaching the skills necessary for success in the workplace is in fact something that the employer is best suited for. Job training programs outside of those funded or supported by employers will always have an extreme amount of waste. For the worker, time spent sitting there may mean learning things that may not apply.

Companies must get involved and share insights with their community. Let your community know what you know.

Time to step up.

2. Volunteer or Teach

Volunteer or teach at least one class every semester at a local high school or college.

Business leaders need to get more involved in their community to share best practices. Teaching is one way communicate.

There are two benefits of volunteering or teaching at your local high school or college. First is the impact on the students and the faculty. When you invest the time to share learnings in a manner that allows both students and teachers to better understand what the workforce expects, you create more opportunities for better alignment and a smooth on-ramp of new job candidates into the workforce.

Second is the impact on your company. Companies aren't in the business of higher education. When a private sector company creates an in-house "academy" or "university," they're not working within their strengths. Teaching is a real opportunity for your company to learn from academia to better modify and enhance the way you package and deliver learning.

Win-win.

3. Join a Workforce Development Board

Get active in your community by supporting your workforce policy groups.

Today, 93 percent of CEOs say they believe we have an issue of underinvestment in workforce development, but only 61 percent have taken any action to fix it.[4]

I have an idea. Why don't you get involved?

Joining the local workforce development board is a tremendous opportunity to learn, share, and inspire action. Our current workforce development boards struggle with how to handle their charge while dealing with a variety of realities today:

- The impact of rising economic inequality.
- The variety of programs offered by government agencies (many overlap or conflict with each other, making it harder to know where to start).
- Educating and engaging incumbent workers with the right skills.
- Educating and engaging new entrant workers with the right skills.
- Understanding new technologies.
- Evaluating and recommending the right career and technical certifications for varying sectors.
- Communicating and understanding the hiring needs of local companies.

We need a labor market system that helps workers, employers, and educators. Too often our leaders in community programs are flying blind. They're thirsty for inputs from the local business community.

4. Hire Local

Want to help? Hire local.

Talent is everywhere; hunger is everywhere; thirst is everywhere, but the access and opportunity is not.

—Arshay Cooper, author of *A Most Beautiful Thing* and a member of the first all-Black rowing team in our conversation on the *Bring It In* podcast

Hire candidates from a local high school, college, or university.

High school, college, and university students who are local deserve an opportunity first.

Build a home field advantage.

5. Support Community Efforts

Measure the time spent sharing best practices with a community program or nonprofit committed to improving learning pathways for young or vulnerable people.

Some of the hardest working people in a community are those working in nonprofits and community programs.

Companies need to invest more time here by sharing and supporting the nonprofits and organizations servicing workers or potential workers in your community:

- Reentry programs
- Homeless shelters
- After-school programs
- Job-training programs

These programs provide a valuable service to a communi-ty. They often work with displaced and out-of-work individuals trying to find their on-ramp to return to work.

STRAIGHTENING THE QUESTION MARK

We must move from not knowing where to start to starting. And let's start in our community.

If our current workforce system, from schools to nonprofits, continues in the direction it's headed, then we should expect more racial and economic segregation, less social mobility, growing political polarization, and more struggles for workers as they transition into and out of work.[5]

These failures are often absorbed by those with the fewest opportunities. We must begin the work of redesigning our work-force system to be better connected, better funded, and better able to offer opportunities for all.

You have your checklist:

1. Volunteer for a nonprofit.
2. Join the workforce board.
3. Offer to teach at a high school or college.
4. Hire from the local community.
5. Spend time with programs supporting vulnerable workers.

We have too much confusion around our current system. We have too many unknowns caused by a lack of commu-nication and participation between companies and the community. It's time we straighten the question mark into an exclamation point. We must turn this critical community connection into a strength of our workforce and a strength for work in the years ahead.

We can do it!

CHAPTER 18

R.A.I.S.**E**.

E—Elevate Managers to Coaches

Casa Mono is a Michelin-starred restaurant in New York City. It's small, and its kitchen is even smaller. It's basically just big enough to fit the chef and two line cooks while they cook for an entire restaurant that seats more than you'd think it could.

I sit and watch as the three chefs in the kitchen navigate a space about as big as the aisle on an airplane. Moving economically to complete their tasks. Heads down and focused. Not saying much yet communicating through a chef's look or a slight touch to the elbow. It was like watching a ballet. Clean and fast—and together.

Each look or touch from the head chef was one of reinforcement, validation, or suggestion. But it was also something else. To let the other chefs know he is there, he sees them, and he appreciates them.

TALKING COACHING AT A CONFERENCE

The National Restaurant Association Show is massive.

It's held in Chicago every year. In 2023 I attended and had conversations with operators across the restaurant industry. Some were good conversations; some made me shake my head.

I wanted to understand their perspective on investing in coaching development for their frontline managers. Here are the best quotes:

- "Coaching? A good manager should just know what to do—that's why we hire 'em."
- "We don't need our managers to think, we just need them to do the job."
- "There are good restaurants and bad ones—we can't really do much to change that."
- "They don't make them like they used to."

Guess you could say the same for leaders. I believe the world needs better leaders, and frontline workers are thirsty for leaders that invest in them like a coach.

It's unanimous. Talk to frontline workers and they'll tell you they want to feel a sense of belonging, they want to feel empowered with the right tools and technology, and they want great leaders to support them. But only one in three managers, the ones who deliver to the front line, agree that they had opportunities to learn and grow in the last year.[1]

A Gallup study asked workers what would increase their engagement at work. It wasn't pay, it wasn't benefits, it wasn't a foosball table in the corner. It was the presence of a very specific type of manager called a *coach*. Team members who rate their coaches as effective at helping them reach their career goals are 27 percent more likely to be effective at achieving them. They're more engaged not only in their long-term objectives but also in their current role, reporting a 31 percent higher level of motivation to perform.[2]

The best organizations do everything possible to make sure the skills of every worker are seen, developed, and utilized the right way. It starts with coaches, but we have a coaching gap today. In most companies, coaches do only 54 percent of the necessary coaching activities. Instead, they're spending an outsized percentage of their time on tasks ranging from administration, individual contributor functions, or traditional command and control management behaviors. When they are coaching their team members, 45 percent of coaches are falling short of the standard that a coaches exemplifies when unlocking the discretionary effort of their people that is needed to hit performance goals.[3]

Coaches know that if a worker isn't doing their job well, the most likely reason is they haven't been taught how. So, they teach 'em. Coaches know how to design effective practice.

Fredo Taylor, in *The Principles of Scientific Management*, wrote that "if there is one best, most productive, way of doing things, then workers should have no choice but to work this way, however mind-numbing and soul-destroying it might be." Mindsets like this have created the role of manager in today's workforce.[4]

The term *manager* is an archaic term describing a role that, by definition, limits growth and performance. A manager oversees the management of tasks and the management of people to complete those tasks. They spend their time focusing on standard operating procedures, processes, hierarchy, and order.

These methods aren't working anymore.

The English utilitarian philosopher Jeremy Bentham (1748–1832) was interested in the role of power. He believed power needs to be visible and unverifiable if it is going to be taken seriously. In his important writing on prison reform he used the metaphor of the *panopticon*—a circular prison with cells arranged around a central well, from which prisoners could at all times be observed but couldn't see who was observing them. Control was literally built into the design. The prisoners are blind to when and if they were being watched. The panopticon plays out in today's prison blocks, where a guard can sit in a tower or elevated desk and see every inmate—but the inmates may not be able to see them.

The panopticon can also be seen in the workplace. In grocery stores, for example, managers may sit at elevated counters or look down on the store from above. These control mechanisms were designed in, just like the role of managers.[5] In a factory, a manager atop their perch may observe the specific tasks being performed by their workers. They can use their observations to break down the job functions into smaller, simpler tasks that can be done by workers with less training and skill. But all too often this vantage point isn't used to catch workers doing things right but instead to catch them in the wrong—looking for those goofing off, stealing, cutting corners.

This is the way work was built. This is what efficiency experts and management "scientists" like Fredo Taylor were thinking when they created the role of the manager. We must move beyond this to create a more connected and empowered workforce that has the potential to come to work every day with all of their skills on display.

Today, it is clear that while the best managers are leaders, the best leaders are coaches. Their differences are often visible in how they view the people they work with every day. Managers have employees. Leaders have followers. Coaches have partners.

I believe the world needs better coaches.

C.O.A.C.H.

One thing I have realized is that to fully develop competitive drive, players need coaches to be demanding of them. In turn, players must be demanding of themselves. They must consistently play on their edge. Most, however, train at a comfortable level.

—Anson Dorrance, 22x national champion head women's soccer coach for the University of North Carolina

If our goal is to create a high-performance environment for our workforce to succeed, then we can't do it with ordinary managers. We need extraordinary coaches. We need coaches who perpetuate growth, drive performance in a healthy way, and at times even introduce healthy discomfort into the process to challenge their people to achieve.

A great coach does five things consistently well, which we can remember by the acronym C.O.A.C.H.

C—Creates the Right Environment

If you want to have a championship culture, you're going to have some conflict.

—Coach Muffet McGraw, 2x national champion head women's basketball coach for Notre Dame University, in our conversation on the *Bring It In* podcast

The belief that you can do better is a key prerequisite to doing better.

—Alex Hutchinson, author of *Endure: Mind, Body, and the Curiously Elastic Limits of Human Performance*, two-time Canadian Olympic runner, and Cambridge PhD, in our conversation on the *Bring It In* podcast

The best organizations work every day to create an atmosphere that prepares their people to handle the adversity they'll face in the course of the job.

The work environment should have the dual goal of getting your workforce to exhibit their best performance given their current skill level, and consistently improving their current level of performance. The best environments do this. The rest don't.

Hall of Fame football coach Tom Landry said, "A coach is someone who tells you what you don't want to hear, who has you see what you don't want to see, so you can be who you have always known you could be."

Consider this model as a way to understand if your working environment is yielding the right results:

- **Low Frequency/Low Challenge**. This approach results in low impact on the team. In this approach, a coach fails to create enough frequency of practice or difficulty and is largely using practice to check a box.
- **High Frequency/Low Challenge.** This approach results in a superficial impact on the team. In this approach, a coach ensures the necessary frequency of practice events but due to a lack of difficulty, the practice results in shallow learning that doesn't transfer beyond a practice environment and into a real workplace setting.
- **Low Frequency/High Challenge.** This approach results in a negative impact on the team. In this approach, a coach ensures the necessary difficulty in practice but is infrequent in their coaching routine.
- **High Frequency/High Challenge.** This approach results in a high impact on the team. In this approach, a coach

ensures the necessary frequency of practice and difficulty in order to ensure behaviors have a high likelihood of transferring into skill.

	LOW CHALLENGE (By a Coach)	HIGH CHALLENGE (By a Coach)
HIGH FREQUENCY (Training/Practice Events)	Superficial Impact	High Impact
LOW FREQUENCY (Training/Practice Events)	Low Impact	Negative Impact

Workers must be able to recall both knowledge and skills automatically, reliably, and quickly while they are busy doing and perceiving other things. This reality is a byproduct of a coach creating the right environment for their workforce.

O—Obsesses About Effort

When you're in the present moment of something and you're totally engrossed in that moment, you're operating at your highest performance level . . . when you set a goal and you attach yourself to this moment and this achievement, you put yourself at war with the process of achieving it, and that's kind of a caveat.

—Tom Sterner, bestselling author of *The Practicing Mind* and CEO of The Practicing Mind Institute in our conversation on the *Bring It In* podcast

Building upon a foundation of a healthy environment, the best coaches then take the next step. They challenge their people by focusing on effort.

We live in a world where we overemphasize outcomes. Sales numbers, customer service scores, transactions, tasks, activities—these all may be important business metrics, but a coach knows that focusing only on outcomes is a recipe for failure.

A challenge in our workforce today is that workers may reach a plateau, where they stop choosing to improve. In some cases, it's because they feel management's goals aren't achievable. The best coaches reframe success and center it on effort over outcomes. This means taking the time to ensure that goals are not simply connected to a metric that's an outcome of specific behaviors (e.g., sales, number of support tickets resolved, customer service rating). Instead, focusing on the smaller behaviors that affect the outcome is a coaching strategy that keeps the focus on the elements of a process you can control. An example would be focusing on sending a certain number of sales emails, not the number of responses.

The best ice skaters fall down more during their practice sessions than ice skaters who aren't quite as good. They challenge themselves more, which means they fail more on the way to achieving outstanding performance. Elite coaches always try to introduce new challenge points to stretch the effort of their people, instead of centering all their attention on the outcome.

A—Always Believes—and Shows It

Thirty years of this sport has definitely turned into being adaptable, being creative, changing your approach, and admitting that you don't have all the answers and searching more.

—Jeff Graba, head women's gymnastics coach at Auburn University, 2x SEC Coach of the Year, and coach for US Olympic gold medal-winning gymnast Suni Lee in our conversation on the *Bring It In* podcast

The best coaches don't just believe in their workers, they show it.

Research shows the human mind absorbs negativity five to seven times more easily than it absorbs positivity. When something is said out loud (versus just keeping it to yourself) it can affect you ten to twelve times more than if you stayed silent. This means that when a coach speaks a negative out loud, or inspires workers to do the same, it can have a seventy-times impact.

We live in a world where social media and news platforms overwhelm us with negativity and bad news. The best coaches know that their workers come to work daily thirsty for positive leadership that believes in them and displays it.

C—Corrects Feedback

Positive feedback has a stronger role than negative feedback.
—Tom Vanderbilt, author of *Beginners: The Joy and Transformative Power of Lifelong Learning* in our conversation on the *Bring It In* podcast

Steve Kerr, the former chief learning officer of Goldman Sachs and a leader on leadership development, says that practicing without feedback is like bowling through a curtain that hangs down to knee level. You can work on technique all you like, but if you can't see the effects, then you won't get any better, and you'll stop caring.[6]

Our goal every day is to make our worst day better than everybody else's best day.
—Tommy Moffitt, director of football strength and conditioning, Texas A&M University, three-time national champion in our conversation on the *Bring It In* podcast

Coaching style has a major effect on employee motivation.

- **Low Support/Low Challenge.** The coach provides a low level of challenge to the worker's current skill level without providing support and care. This approach results in a worker who rejects the coach.

- **Low Support/High Challenge.** The coach provides a high level of challenge to the worker's current skill level in an attempt to stretch them in a positive direction while providing limited to no support and care. This approach results in a defiant worker.
- **High Support/Low Challenge.** The coach provides a low level of challenge to the worker's current skill level while providing a high level of support and care. This approach results in a fragile worker.
- **High Support/High Challenge.** The coach provides a high level of challenge to the worker's current skill level in an attempt to stretch them in a positive direction while providing the appropriate level of support and care. This approach results in a motivated worker.

	LOW CHALLENGE (By a Coach)	HIGH CHALLENGE (By a Coach)
HIGH SUPPORT	Fragile	Motivated
LOW SUPPORT	Rejecting	Defiant

H–Hard. Makes It Hard

We all quit before we should. We are wired to do less, not more.

—Joe De Sena, founder and CEO of Spartan Race, author and podcast host of *Spartan Up!*, and host of CNBC's *No Retreat: Business Bootcamp in* our conversation on the *Bring It In* podcast

The best coaches aren't afraid to make it hard.

Not hard in a senseless way. Hard in a way that enhances the performance of the worker. I bring this one up last because a coach has to earn the right to challenge their people by properly executing their other functions first.

Challenge in the learning process isn't normally enjoyable. However, the best coaches know that challenge and creating a culture where people learn from their errors is critical to long-term development.

The opposite can be devastating, not just to a culture but to the performance of a brand. Bad managers who avoid difficulty often believe in the myth of errorless learning. They live in fear that failure is like poison. Believing in "no-risk learning" defeats the most powerful principle of learning: making mistakes teaches the most powerful lessons. Science shows that effortful learning changes the brain, building new connections and capability.[7]

If we want to fulfill our potential as individuals and organizations, we must redefine failure. To be successful in the long run, you must embrace risk. You can't grow if you live in fear of being wrong. You must show that mistakes are normal and even valuable. This will help shift employees away from deflecting blame, rationalizing mistakes, or seeking to hide mistakes (not just from their coaches but from themselves). You can't get to great unless you are willing to fail.

The best coaches know that it isn't about succeeding all the time, but about playing on the edge between success and failure. Hard practice isn't usually enjoyable. And yes, if an appropriate level of challenge is created during training and coaching events, then some degree of short-term failure should occur, allowing an opportunity for growth.

FROM MANAGERS TO COACHES

A teacher affects eternity. He can never tell when his influence stops.
—Henry Brooks Adams, American historian (1838–1918)

Now let's talk about some immediate actions you can take in your organization to elevate managers into coaches.

1. Define Coaching

Design a coaching development model that clearly defines what it means to be a coach.

A coach is a social worker, a teacher, a parent, a big brother, a security guard. So many jobs rolled into one.

—Kent Babb, sportswriter for *The Washington Post* and acclaimed author of *Across the River: Life, Death, and Football in an American City* in our conversation on the *Bring It In* podcast

They were called the team of shame in the 1996 Summer Olympics in Atlanta, Georgia. Across all events, the United Kingdom won only one gold medal. They finished thirty-sixth in the Olympic medal table, below North Korea, Algeria, and Kazakhstan. That's pretty bad.

The UK Olympic Committee then hired Chelsea Warr to help them fix the problem. Her approach would go on to create a massive turnaround of the program. A much different UK showed up to Rio in the 2016 Olympics. They won twenty-seven gold medals—twenty-six more than in Atlanta two decades prior. This was good enough for second in the medal table. And, looking closer, the United Kingdom teams won more gold medals in Rio than in the last six Olympics from 1976 to 1996 combined.

How did they do it?

Their success was more about talent development than talent acquisition. From 2012 to 2018, only ten of the UK's 141 medals were won by those identified by national talent recruitment campaigns; 131 medals were won by those already in the system. That means 93 percent of all medals came as a byproduct of improved performance by the individuals already in the program. The effect was the same for the Paralympics games, where forty-seven out of 100 of the UK's medals were won by those from recruitment campaigns. This means 90 percent of medals won were by those already in the system.

At a time when the natural move is to clean house, let go of all your players, and start over, the UK did things differently. Their Olympic success at Rio owed far more to getting more out of those already in the system than recruiting new athletes into it.

Chelsea Warr was asked how she did it. She responded that they chose to invest in their coaches. She went on to say that if they did it all over again, she would have tripled her investment in coaching because they are the closest person to the performer who can influence the outcome.[8]

The best organizations choose to invest in the people closest to their people. This may mean investing in the frontline leadership that affects your frontline workers. You must take the time to define a coaching development model so that the best leaders know exactly what it means to be a coach.

You can't just wake up and say you have a coaching model. You need to define it.

Several challenges face organizations here:

- Employing too many leaders who are unwilling to give up or unlearn what they know.
- Failing to identify weak coaches.
- Not providing adequate resources to coaches.
- Lack of understanding on how to improve.

The cost of a bad leader in your organization can be disastrous, resulting in millions of dollars in lost revenue, negative service scores, high turnover, one-star Glassdoor reviews, and so on. Organizations know this, but many still either fail to address the challenge or invest in inadequate resources or people to bring about change.

Daniel Goleman, author of *Emotional Intelligence,* said, "Many leaders told us they don't have the time in this high-pressure economy for the slow and tedious work of teaching people and helping them grow."[9]

Maybe we should tie coaching to something that will motivate coaches to make the time?

2. Link Compensation

Create compensation and bonus plans that are directly linked to employee retention and satisfaction.

I started my career in sales. It was hard. It was tough. But I was always compensated in a manner connected to my performance.

Too many organizations don't create an environment where their leaders have skin in the game for the outcomes they are expected to achieve. But before I talk about why I believe organizations should restructure the compensation models of their leaders to connect them to performance outcomes, let's talk about the ultimate goal of the role of a frontline leader, training manager, or human resources representative.

The best leaders are responsible for the discretionary effort of their people. Discretionary effort is the additional output produced by an individual because of the coaching effect. It's that little bit extra the worker may be willing to give but often holds back. Bad managers can't tap into it. It's a reserve beyond their reach, resulting in workers holding back skills and effort from the organization. A good coach develops and inspires people to do their best work, getting more discretionary effort from them and ultimately elevating performance.

How do you create an environment where your leaders have some skin in the game and focus relentlessly on obtaining the best performance from your people? Well, one way *not* to do it is by designing compensation plans that fail to incentivize a manager for the coaching responsibilities you expect from them.

It's not usual to track coaching inputs. The reasons range from a lack of belief that a coach affects the performance of the team to not knowing what to measure because the organization doesn't understand which activities lead to the greatest impact on performance. However, there are some good metrics to consider to create a performance element to compensation that better connects those responsible for teaching, motivating, and developing their workforce to the outcomes:

- **Speed of onboarding**. Conduct a test for all new candidates on a specific target date after hire (e.g., Day 90) to understand how well onboarding was performed.
- **Knowledge checks.** Conduct a benchmark assessment of all employees on an ongoing basis (e.g., Day 90, 180, 365) to understand current knowledge strengths and gaps.
- **Employee churn.** Review the percentage of workers that churn.
- **Employee reviews.** Review what former employees are saying about specific leadership on platforms like Glassdoor after they move on.

Some organizations use metrics like sales performance, customer service scores, Net Promoter scores, Yelp reviews, and other feedback from clients to drive performance bonuses. These lagging indicators are corrupted by a variety of organizational elements that oftentimes shouldn't be attributed to the front-line leader. These metrics, if they are captured in the correct manner, can be used for a performance bonus, but shouldn't be a core part of a leader's compensation.

The more skin in the game the better. If your organization is structured in a manner that places all of the professionals responsible for employee learning and development into human resources, tie this group's compensation to revenue and customer service performance.

3. Meet with Workers

Conduct routine 1:1 meetings with every worker, focusing on personal, positional, and professional development.

For coaches—love is not a commodity, it's a capacity.
—Jerry Lynch, sports psychologist and author of *The Competitive Buddha*

Dr. Jerry Lynch knows what it takes to be a great coach.

He has delivered coaching and mentorship to teams that are responsible for over 144 championships, including coaches like Phil Jackson, Steve Kerr, and Anson Dorrance. In a conversation on what makes the best coaches he told me, "So many who call themselves coaches operate out of fear—the fear of losing control over those they lead."

Coaching is a complex combination of skills. One of the most important is the ability to communicate with your people. A coach must have a robust knowledge base, but knowledge isn't enough. A coach must be able to effectively transfer what they know to those they coach. It is also true that the better you know something, the more difficult it becomes to teach it. And no matter how inspiring, accurate, or effective your message, if no one is receiving it, you aren't communicating.

The best leaders conduct 1:1 meetings with their team because they know that they are only effective if they have the ability to:

- Challenge behavior, not accommodate it.
- Unpack complex tasks while avoiding their own expert blind spots.
- Be relentless at pursuing and investing in new tools to make their people better.
- Realize that knowledge isn't static.
- Act less as owners of all knowledge and more as a guide.
- Develop underachieving talent.

Additionally, these 1:1 meetings don't start and stop with a selfish focus on what the worker is doing right and wrong in their current role. It must go beyond their role. Great leaders ensure that they make space to discuss personal and professional aspects of development, not just those related to their current position. Here are some examples:

- **Personal development.** A discussion around what is affecting them before and after work. This includes life goals, personal aspirations, family, friends, mental health, etc.
- **Professional development.** A discussion around how they are developing and progressing toward their career

goals and an assessment around how they are navigating their career pathway.

- **Positional development.** A discussion around performance related to their current job, such as sales performance and activity history.

Even the ancient Spartans had coaches. It is said that one of the strengths of the Spartan system was the function of pairing each boy in training with a mentor other than their own father. They believed that a mentor would be more likely to share feedback, advice, and insights that a father would not.

Coaches are direct. They invest time. They talk.

4. Coach the Coaches

Make leadership and development content and programming available to frontline leaders.

A leader unfortunately thinks it's about sending information down the chain to be a great leader. But you've got to bring the information up the chain.

—Martin Rooney, author of *Coach to Coach*
in our conversation on the *Bring It In* podcast

Coaches don't create followers, they create coaches.

High-performing organizations know this. They ensure a major element of their people development culture is a pathway to develop their frontline leaders. However, research continues to confirm that organizations aren't spending enough time on coaching their coaches. According to recent findings by McKinsey, "Across industries, frontline managers spend 30 to 60 percent of their time on administrative work and meetings, and 10 to 50 percent on nonmanagerial tasks (traveling, participating in training, taking breaks, conducting special projects, or undertaking direct customer service or sales themselves). They spend only 10 to 40 percent actually managing frontline employees by, for example, coaching them directly."[10]

The report goes on to share that even when managers spend time on coaching, they aren't really coaching their front line. Instead, they're spending time employing command and control tactics like auditing, ensuring compliance, or performing tasks. They even found at certain companies, managers spent just 4 to 10 percent of their time, or ten minutes a day, on coaching. This would equate to just one hour of coaching time per month.

To unlock a team's abilities, a manager at any level must spend a significant amount of time helping the team understand the company's direction and its implications for team members and enhancing performance through coaching. Too few companies are focusing on our frontline workforce today. The best organizations need to invest the time, systems, and resources to develop their frontline leadership.

In the best organizations, frontline leaders spend a substantial portion of their time helping the team understand the company's direction.

In the best organizations, frontline leaders spend a substantial portion of their time coaching. These organizations give leaders the autonomy to make choices and act on immediate coaching and development opportunities. The revenue and growth impact as it pertains to sales, service, and employee retention are considerable.

It's easy for organizations, especially human resources and learning and development, to just invest in limited-event coaching and learning opportunities. These programs must be as continuous and ongoing as all other development initiatives.

Nothing elevates performance more than coaching. We need more organizations investing time to develop the skills of front-line leaders.

5. Discuss the Bigger Picture

Engineer discussions on the impacts of poverty, gender discrimination, racial discrimination, forced labor, and mass incarceration into your people development program.

You can be a great coach, but if you're a poor communicator, you're going to fail in life, in love, in business, in sports.

—Nancy Lieberman, basketball Hall of Famer, Olympian, former NBA coach, and WNBA player in our conversation on the *Bring It In* podcast

Just calling yourself a coach isn't enough.

The limitations in the effectiveness of coaching strategies trace back to the Industrial Revolution, when the focus moved to compartmentalized, highly specialized tasks that were repetitive and easy to monitor. Instead of crafting an entire shoe, for instance, each worker would consistently hammer a nail into a specific spot, optimizing for both speed and quality. Workers had little understanding of the bigger picture. Organizations invested in managers to act as supervisors to ensure these specific tasks were performed on time and correctly. The same strategy is still used by companies with large frontline workforces, from restaurants to retail, in an attempt to offer a consistent "customer experience" across all locations.

This strategy has made the customer the focus—and has developed training programs that focus narrowly on these outcomes. The programs avoid meaningful discussion with workers around the economic and societal elements that may be affecting them not just at work, but at home as well, before they clock in and after they clock out.

We live in a pluralistic society. People of different races, colors, social classes, and religions work together in a society but maintain different traditions and beliefs. These differences make us stronger. We must talk about them.

Coaches must fight for all of their people. This means making the space for meaningful discussions around:

- Impacts of poverty and inequality
- Gender discrimination
- Racial discrimination
- Forced labor
- Mass incarceration

These social issues aren't affecting just a few workers—they affect the majority. Avoiding the hard discussion, hiding from it, and failing to educate yourself on it are fundamental failures of leadership. And a missed opportunity to build a stronger relationship and connection with your people.

The problem in the workforce isn't a talent shortage. It's not lazy workers. It's not a lack of skills. It's not millennials. It's bad managers.

It is time for leaders at every level to look in the mirror and ask themselves whether they are an obstacle to growth or a catalyst for it.

KNOW WHY YOU COACH

Rules without relationships equal rebellion.

—John Mosley, coach from Netflix's *Last Chance U: Basketball*, head men's basketball coach at East Los Angeles College, named one of the Top 50 Most Impactful JUCO coaches in our conversation on the *Bring It In* podcast

Character is when words and action match.

—Melissa Kutcher, 2019 NCAA Coach of the Year and head women's gymnastics coach at the University of Denver, 25x in the NCAA Regionals in our conversation on the *Bring It In* podcast

I used to coach high school football in Hialeah, Florida.

One day we were having a pretty rough practice. I used to coach the wide receivers, and on this particular day, early in my coaching career, everything was going wrong. I yelled at them about focus. I threatened them with fear of what would happen if we lost. I punished them with hundreds of push-ups.

Our head coach observed me having a hard day. After practice, he pulled me aside and asked me a question I still remember to this day.

"How should it feel to be coached by you?"

I would go on to learn that managers who are transactional and degrade, monitor, and control their workers fail to build meaningful relationships. Coaches are different. The right ones mentor, invest, develop, promote, teach, and ultimately build strong relationships.

We need more coaches.

Organizations go wild buying new technology, changing systems, hiring new staff, bringing on consultants, and more. In reality, organizations should just stop. Everything they're spending money on that they think is going to lift performance should be cut from the budget. They should buy nothing else until they fully understand the effectiveness of their coaches.

Companies either boost or bust performance dependent on

the way that they coach, every day. They should start here.

Whakapapa is a Māori word meaning genealogy. In the larger sense, it encourages you to "be a good ancestor and plant trees you will never see." The best leaders are the coaches who do the planting. There is no secret sauce. This is hard work. The Māori know that the message they pass on will continue beyond the moment. They know that developing another person is character work, something bigger than yourself.

Everybody thinks there is a secret here. There is no secret. It takes what it takes.

THE FUTURE OF WORK SCORECARD

Everybody is responsible for the future of work, and I'm not sure that everybody's been invited yet.

—Shadae McDaniel, senior vice president, programs and strategic initiatives at All Stars Project of New Jersey in our conversation on the *Bring It In* podcast

For more than a decade I have worked with hundreds of global organizations and tens of millions of workers. My experiences and observations led me to create this scorecard, which has been used by brands to help identify gaps in their approach to their workforce, as well as serve as a plan of action.

Like any self-assessment, sometimes it's tough to step on the scale and be honest about your performance. But since you've gotten this far, I'm confident you'll take this next step.

I challenge you to take a crack at this by looking at the questions through the lens of either

- Your personal coaching approach.
- Your organization's approach.

Answer the questions yes or no. The more yes answers you have, the closer you are to creating a workplace that helps your workers achieve their potential.

THE FUTURE OF WORK SCORECARD: R.A.I.S.E.

Let's put in some work. The Future of Work Scorecard is a tool for individuals and organizations to use to assess their current performance when it comes to creating an environment that unlocks the full potentia of their workforce.

Go through the twenty-five questions below and give yourself a score for each question based on your current execution of the listed behavior:

- Yes: 0 points
- Sometimes: 0.5 points
- No: 1.0 point

	R–REMOVE BARRIERS	SCORE
1	Do you provide access and support for every worker in your organization to upskill and cross-skill for any role?	
2	Are you proactively creating and deploying reskilling for workers who are in roles at risk of automation?	
3	When hiring new employees, do you recognize work experience and skills acquired from nontraditional learning programs (e.g., apprenticeships, military service, technical schools)?	
4	Have you invested in a digital credentialing system that allows every worker to acquire skills that are portable beyond your organization?	

		SCORE
5	Do you have a workplace mentorship program that is designed to promote racial equity where experienced employees share advice, feedback, and coaching with new employees?	
A—ADOPT A CONTINUOUS APPROACH TO DEVELOPING PEOPLE		**SCORE**
6	Do you have a continuous 52-weeks-a-year training program?	
7	Is your learning and development methodology informed by the latest findings on cognitive psychology and the science of learning?	
8	Do you measure knowledge retention data on a quarterly basis (at a minimum) to inform what should be reinforced or reintroduced?	
9	Do you provide every worker with an annual Lifelong Learning Account (LiLA) that they can use for personal or professional enrichment on their own terms?	
10	Is your organization's diversity, equity, and inclusion programming fifty-two weeks a year?	
I—INVEST IN TECHNOLOGY TO MEET WORKERS WHERE THEY ARE		**SCORE**
11	Is every part of your learning and development programming mobile accessible?	
12	Is your training and development technology stack available for every worker in your organization, regardless of role?	
13	Do you have a budget dedicated to updating existing learning and development technologies every twelve months?	
14	Do you give your workers the flexibility to train and upskill anytime, anywhere, rather than limiting training time to being solely on the clock?	
15	Do you use game-based technology or online simulations as a method to ensure strong engagement, knowledge retention, and performance outcomes?	

	S—SUPPORT COMMUNITY WORKFORCE PROGRAMS AND EDUCATION PARTNERS	SCORE
16	Do you have an existing relationship with a local high school, two-year college, or four-year college where you share business learning, insights, advice, and education at least once every twelve months?	
17	Do you volunteer or teach at least one class every semester at a local high school or college?	
18	Do you participate in quarterly workforce development board meetings as a member of the board or as an observer?	
19	Have you hired a candidate in the last twelve months for a paid internship, part-time, or full-time role from an existing relationship with a local high school or two- or four-year college?	
20	Do you measure the time spent sharing best practices with a community program or nonprofit committed to improving learning pathways for young or vulnerable people?	
	E—ELEVATE MANAGERS INTO COACHES	SCORE
21	Do you have a coaching development model that clearly defines what it means to be a coach versus a manager?	
22	Do managers have compensation or bonuses directly linked to employee retention and satisfaction?	
23	Do you have 1:1s with every member of your team on a monthly basis that focuses on personal, positional, and professional development?	
24	Do your frontline managers have access to the same leadership and development content and programming that you do?	
25	Does your employee development programming include specific discussions on the impacts of poverty, gender discrimination, racial discrimination, forced labor, and mass incarceration?	

TOTAL POINTS ____ / 25

SUMMARY

Nice work. The results of your Future of Work Scorecard can be used to start the process of creating an action plan to close your individual or organization's talent gaps.

Now, if you want to go a step further and run through our more detailed version of the Future of Work Scorecard, you can do so by scanning the QR code below.

Bonus: participants who complete the advanced scorecard below will unlock a free resource to assist in getting your action plan underway.

Epilogue

I know what I am asking is impossible. But in our time,
as in every time, the impossible is the least that one can demand.

—JAMES BALDWIN, *THE FIRE NEXT TIME*

The future of work isn't about work. It's about people.

Shouldn't an employer be responsible for more than just a wage for a worker? In a civilized society this would be true.

Unfortunately, today work is something to be endured. You get bossed around, you aren't valued, your pay is low, your hours are long, and at any moment, you might get put out on the street like the trash. This approach, and the way we treat our frontline workers, makes work less safe and secure for all of us.

We have too many workers that go to work at a company, but not for the company—robbed of not just the security a full-time position provides but also of the dignity to be treated with the same respect as other workers.

We have too many workers that toil in exhausting low-wage work that provides real value to our communities. Yet their paycheck, for everything from home care to cleaning to delivery jobs, seems not to respect their work as much as others.

We have too many workers receiving the minimum investment

in their development by their employer. At the same time they are robbed of any respect, their CEO sits on stage at a conference and complains about lazy and unskilled workers.

As we march forward into the next chapter of the evolution of work, how we think about work is vital.

We have a choice.

Will we finally put people at the center of work? Will we acknowledge that our businesses and communities are most productive and profitable when we consider our colleagues not as resources or labor, but as people?

My message has not been one saying that we have to raise wages. Even though I think we should. My message has not been one in support of unions. Even though I think we should. My message has not been one lobbying that tipping is bad for workers. Even though I think it is. My real message is that if organizations want to fix problems, they must start by investing more in their people and not just talking about it.

I have found that how much an organization believes in a cause is put on display only though what they are willing to risk for it. What they are willing to say out loud or from their LinkedIn feed or by how they allocate resources and sponsorship or what technology they invest in.

A FINAL STORY

I was watching the seaweed blanket the beach in Jamaica.

Two workers dressed in matching green jumpsuits were on cleanup duty.

One had a shovel and was scooping up the seaweed, while the other had a shovel and was digging holes in the sand to bury the seaweed. When they finished in a few hours, they walked back down the beach and covered up the seaweed graves.

It was hard work. Demanding. The green jumpsuits were clearly dark green with sweat.

The next morning my family and I headed for the beach to give it one more look before leaving for the airport. The beach is again covered with seaweed. And there are the two men. Both in their green jumpsuits and with their shovels. Again, doing the work.

There is no end to work. We might fear robots and AI and other disruptive things, but life has a way of finding more work.

The more important questions to consider are, will the work be something worth doing? Who are we doing the work for? Why do we work?

These questions are critical for leaders to answer. Show people respect. Give them a fair wage. Make work something worth working for. It's not about if the work is hard or dirty or challenging or dangerous.

Respect.

The problem with writing this book wasn't starting; it was stopping. It felt like every day something new would happen that would have expanded one of these chapters. I have so much more to say, but this is where I must end. The amount of research and conversations that I couldn't fit into this book would have made it feel like a second job for you just to read. I wanted to give you the numbers. I wanted to share some stories. I wanted to be real with you.

Work was built. This is the way we built it. Now it's on you to go change it. Now, back to work.

Endnotes

CHAPTER 1

1   James Suzman, *Work: A Deep History, from the Stone Age to the Age of Robots* (New York, NY: Penguin Books, 2022).

2   Michael Yates, *Work Work Work: Labor, Alienation, and Class Struggle* (New York, NY: Monthly Review Press, 2022).

3   Amelia Horgan, *Lost in Work: Escaping Capitalism* (London, UK: Pluto Press, 2021).

4   David Graeber, *Bullshit Jobs: A Theory* (New York, NY: Simon & Schuster, 2018).

5   Andy Stern, *Raising the Floor: How a Universal Basic Income Can Renew Our Economy and Rebuild the American Dream* (New York, NY: PublicAffairs, 2016).

6   Graeber, *Bullshit Jobs.*

7   Matthew Taylor, *Do We Have to Work?* (London, UK: Thames, and Hudson, 2021).

8   Suzman, *Work: A Deep History.*

9   Stern, *Raising the Floor.*

10 Farah Stockman, *American Made: What Happens to People When Work Disappears* (New York, NY: Random House, 2021).

11 Lawrence Mishel, "Growing inequalities, reflecting growing employer power, have generated a productivity–pay gap since 1979," *Economic Policy Institute,* September 2, 2021; https://www.epi.org/ blog/growing-inequalities-reflecting-growing-employer-power-have-generated-a-productivity-pay-gap-since-1979-productivity-has-grown-3-5-times-as-much-as-pay-for-the-typical-worker/

12   Jamie McCallum, *Essential: How the Pandemic Transformed the Long Fight for Worker Justice* (New York, NY: Basic Books, 2022).

13   Matthew Desmond, *Poverty, by America* (New York, NY: Penguin Random House, 2023).

14   Suzman, *Work: A Deep History.*

15   [Enrico Moretti, *The New Geography of Jobs* (New York, NY: Harper Business, 2013).

16   Moretti, *The New Geography of Jobs.*

17   Moretti, *The New Geography of Jobs.*

18   Moretti, *The New Geography of Jobs.*

19   Adie Tomer and Joseph Kane, "To Protect Frontline Workers During and After Covid-19, We Must Define Who They Are," *Brookings*, June 10, 2020, http://www.brookings.edu/research/to-protect-frontline-workers-during-and-after-covid-19-we-must-define-who-they-are/.

20   Michael Yates, *Work, Work, Work: Labor, Alienation and Class Struggle* (New York, NY: Monthly Review Press, 2022).

21   Hye Jin Rho, Shawn Fremstad, and Hayley Brown, "A Basic Demographic Profile of Workers in Frontline Industries," *Center for Economic and Policy Research*, April 7, 2020, http://www.cepr.net/a-basic-demographic-profile-of-workers-in-frontline-industries/.

22   Jim Clifton, *It's the Manager: Moving from Boss to Coach* (Washington, D.C.: Gallup Press, 2019).

23   Clifton, *It's the Manager.*

24   Gallup, Employee Engagement Strategies: Fixing the World's $8.8 Trillion Problem, https://www.gallup.com/workplace/393497/world-trillion-workplace-problem.aspx

25   Gallup, State of the Global Workplace, https://www.gallup.com/workplace/349484/state-of-the-global-workplace.aspx#:~:text=Worldwide%2C%2044%25%20of%20employees%20said,likely%20due%20to%20othe%20pandemic.

26   Dylan Croll, "Gen Z are the most disgruntled workers and that's a problem for employers," *Yahoo! Finance*, July 2, 2023. https://finance.yahoo.com/news/gen-z-are-the-most-disgruntled-workers-and-thats-a-problem-for-employers-150517925.html?guccounter=2]

27   Clifton, *It's the Manager.*

28   Nicholas Kristof and Sheryl WuDunn, *Tightrope: Americans Reaching for Hope* (New York, NY: Vintage, 2020).

CHAPTER 2

1   Oliver Burkeman, *Four Thousand Weeks: Time Management for Mortals* (New York, NY: Farrar, Straus and Giroux, 2021).

2   Graeber, *Bullshit Jobs*.

3   Daniel Cable, *Alive at Work: The Neuroscience of Helping Your People Love What They Do* (Cambridge, MA: Harvard Business Review Press, 2019).

4   Robert Waldinger, MD and Marc Schulz PhD, *The Good Life: Lessons from the World's Longest Scientific Study of Happiness* (New York, NY: Simon and Schuster, 2023).

5   US Bureau of Labor Statistics Reporting, https://www.bls.gov/cps/cpsaat11b.htm

6   Burkeman, *Four Thousand Weeks*.

7   Josephine Harvey, "Man Who Reported Crack In Roller Coaster Says He Received Concerning Response From Staff," *HuffPost*, July 4, 2023. https://www.huffpost.com/entry/carowinds-roller-coaster-shut-down_n_64a3fbb5e4b0035bc5c905c5

8   Yates, *Work Work Work*.

9   Daniel Susskind, *A World Without Work* (London, UK: Picador, 2021).

10   Jack Grove, "New Study Challenges Conventional Wisdom on Shortage of STEM Graduates," *Inside Higher Ed*, February 9, 2024. https://www.insidehighered.com/news/global/2024/02/09/few-stem-graduates-pursue-jobs-or-careers-related-fields

11   Susskind, *A World Without Work*.

12   Susskind, *A World Without Work*.

13   Graeber, *Bullshit Jobs*.

14   Davey Alba, "We must remake society in the coming age of AI: Obama," *Wired*, October 12, 2016, https://www.wired.com/2016/10/obama-aims-rewrite-social-contract-age-ai/

15   Gordon Lafer, *The Job Training Charade* (Ithaca, NY: Cornell University Press, 2004).

CHAPTER 3

1   Lonnie Golden, Irregular Work Scheduling and Its Consequences, April 9, 2015, Economic Policy Institute; https://www.epi.org/publication/irregular-work-scheduling-and-its-consequences/

2   Jamie McCallum, *Worked Over: How Round-the-Clock Work Is Killing the American Dream* (New York, NY: Basic Books, 2020).

3   Joseph Aoun, *Robot Proof: Higher Education in the Age of Artificial Intelligence* (Cambridge, MA: The MIT Press, 2018).

4   Michelle Weise, *Long Life Learning: Preparing for Jobs that Don't Even Exist Yet* (Hoboken, NJ: Wiley, 2020).

5   Elsie Gould, "Millions of Working People Don't Get Paid Time Off for Holiday or Vacation," *Economic Policy Institute*, September 1, 2015, http://www.epi.org/publication/millions-of-working-people-dont-get-paid-time-off-for-holidays-or-vacation/

6   Weise, *Long Life Learning*.

7   Graeber, *Bullshit Jobs*.

8   Graeber, *Bullshit Jobs*.

9   Jean Twenge, *iGen: Why Today's Super-Connected Kids Are Growing Up Less Rebellious, More Tolerant, Less Happy—and Completely Unprepared for Adulthood—and What that Means for the Rest of Us* (New York, NY: Atria Books, 2018).

10 Bruce Cannon Gibney, *A Generation of Sociopaths: How the Baby Boomers Betrayed America* (New York, NY: Hachette Books, 2017).

11 Aoun, *Robot Proof*.

12 Peter Cappelli, *Why Good People Can't Get Jobs: The Skills Gap and What Companies Can Do About It* (Philadelphia, PA: Wharton School Press, 2012).

13 Cappelli, *Why Good People Can't Get Jobs*.

14 Cappelli, *Why Good People Can't Get Jobs*.

15 Cappelli, *Why Good People Can't Get Jobs*.

16 Daniel Costa, "The H2B Temporary Foreign Worker Program: For Labor Shortages or Cheap, Temporary Labor?," *Economic Policy Institute*, January 19, 2016, http://www.epi.org/publication/h2b-temporary-foreign-worker-program-for-labor-shortages-or-cheap-temporary-labor/

17 Virginia Eubanks, *Automating Inequality: How High-Tech Tools Profile, Police, and Punish the Poor* (London, UK: Picador, 2019).

18 Cappelli, *Why Good People Can't Get Jobs*.

CHAPTER 4

1   Caleb Naysmith, "8.7 Million Americans Now Work Two Jobs To Make Ends Meet Despite Inflation Continuing To Cool," Yahoo Finance, January 30, 2024. https://finance.yahoo.com

2   Kristof and WuDunn, *Tightrope.*

3   Stern, *Raising the Floor.*

4   Chambers, E. G. & Foulon, Mark & Handfield-Jones, Helen & Hankin, Steven & Michaels, Edward. (1998). "The War for Talent." *The McKinsey Quarterly* 3. 44-57.

5   Joe Baker, *The Tyranny of Talent: How it compels and limits athletic achievement... and why you should ignore it* (3SD Publishing, 2022).

6   Dan Mangan and Lora Kolodny, "Elon Musk's $56 billion Tesla compensation voided by judge, shares slide," *CNBC,* January 30, 2024, https://www.cnbc.com/2024/01/30/tesla-shares-slide-after-judge-voids-elon-musks-56-billion-compensation.html

7   Jack Ewing, "Tesla Seeks to Revive Musk's $47 Billion Pay Deal After Judge Says No," *The New York Times,* April 17, 2024, https://www.nytimes.com/2024/04/17/business/tesla-elon-musk-pay.html

8   Kristof and WuDunn, *Tightrope.*

9   William Kerr, *The Gift of Global Talent: How Migration Shapes Business, Economy & Society* (Palo Alto, CA: Stanford University Press, 2018).

10 Robert Reich, *Beyond Outrage: What has gone wrong with our economy and our democracy, and how to fix it* (New York: Vintage Books, 2012).

11 Aoun, *Robot Proof.*

12 Suzman, *Work, A Deep History.*

13 Stern, *Raising the Floor.*

14 Stern, *Raising the Floor.*

15 Stern, *Raising the Floor.*

16 Reich, *Beyond Outrage.*

17 Yates, *Work Work Work.*

18 "Occupational Outlook Handbook," *US Bureau of Labor Statistics,* April 9, 2021, http://www.bls.gov/ooh/most-new-jobs.htm

19 William Bonvillian and Sanjay Sarma, *Workforce Education: A New Roadmap* (Cambridge, MA: The MIT Press, 2021).

20   Kerr, *The Gift of Global Talent.*

21   Aoun, *Robot Proof.*

22   David H. Autor, "Work of the Past, Work of the Future," *AEA Papers and Proceedings* 109 (2019): 1-32.

23   Bonvillian and Sarma, *Workforce Education.*

24   Edward Chisholm, *A Waiter in Paris: Adventures in the Dark Heart of the City* (New York, NY: Pegasus Books, 2022).

CHAPTER 5

1   Bryan Caplan, *The Case Against Education: Why the Education System is a Waste of Time and Money* (Princeton, NJ: Princeton University Press, 2019).

2   Jamie Merisotis, *America Needs Talent: Attracting, Educating & Deploying the 21st-Century Workforce* (New York, NY: Rosetta-Books, 2016).

3   Merisotis, *America Needs Talent.*

4   Bryan Caplan, *The Case Against Education.*

5   Greg Lukianoff, *The Coddling of the American Mind: How Good Intentions and Bad Ideas Are Setting Up a Generation for Failure* (New York, NY: Penguin Press, 2018).

6   Bonvillian and Sarma, *Workforce Education.*

7   Enrico Moretti, *The New Geography of Jobs* (New York, NY: Harper Business, 2013).

8   Bonvillian and Sarma, *Workforce Education.*

9   Caplan, *The Case Against Education.*

10   Kristof and WuDunn, *Tightrope*

11   Reich, *Beyond Outrage.*

12   Colleen Flaherty, "A Non-Tenure Track Profession," *Inside Higher Ed,* October 2018. https://www.insidehighered.com/news/2018/10/12/about-three-quarters-all-faculty-positions-are-tenure-track-according-new-aaup

13   Hara Estroff Marano, *A Nation of Wimps: The High Cost of Invasive Parenting* (New York, NY: Crown Archetype, 2008).

14   Jake Humphrey and Prof Damian Hughes, *High Performance: Lessons from the Best on Becoming Your Best* (Cornerstone, 2023).

15 Kate Rix, "How Much Recess Should Kids Get?," *US News*, October 14, 2022, https://www.usnews.com/education/k12/articles/how-much-recess-should-kids-get

16 Brian Sutton-Smith, *The Ambiguity of Play* (Cambridge, MA: Harvard University Press, 1998).

17 Kerr, *The Gift of Global Talent.*

18 Matthew Desmond, *Poverty, by America* (New York, NY: Penguin Random House, 2023).

19 Anthony Carnevale, Peter Schmidt, and Jeff Strohl, *The Merit Myth: How Our Colleges Favor the Rich and Divide America* (New York, NY: The New Press, 2020).

20 Kristof and WuDunn, *Tightrope.*

21 Carnevale, *The Merit Myth.*

22 Anthony P. Carnevale, Megan L. Fasules, Michael C. Quinn, Kathryn Peltier Campbell, "Born to Win, Schooled to Lose," *Georgetown University Center on Education and the Workforce*, 2019, https://cew.georgetown.edu/cew-reports/schooled2lose/

23 Aoun, *Robot Proof.*

24 Weise, *Long Life Learning.*

25 Caplan, *The Case Against Education.*

26 Peter Smith, *Free Range Learning in the Digital Age: The Emerging Revolution in College, Career, and Education* (New York, NY: SelectBooks, 2018).

27 Jamie McCallum, *Essential: How the Pandemic Transformed the Long Fight for Worker Justice* (New York, NY: Basic Books, 2022).

28 Carnevale, *The Merit Myth.*

29 Desmond, *Poverty, in America.*

30 Caplan, *The Case Against Education.*

31 Farah Stockman, *American Made: What Happens to People When Work Disappears* (New York, NY: Random House, 2021).

32 Caplan, *The Case Against Education.*

33 Weise, *Long Life Learning.*

34 Smith, *Free Range Learning in the Digital Age.*

35 Caplan, *The Case Against Education.*

36 Jake Bryant, Samvitha Ram, Doug Scott, and Claire Williams, "K–12 teachers are quitting. What would make them stay?," *McKinsey*

& *Company*, March 2, 2023, https://www.mckinsey.com/industries/education/our-insights/k-12-teachers-are-quitting-what-would-make-them-stay

37   Charlotte Lytton, "'The world is rapidly evolving': How Gen Z is rethinking the idea of college," *Business Insider*, September 5, 2023, https://www.businessinsider.com/gen-z-not-going-to-college-tuition-costs-higher-education-2023-9

38   Bruce Cannon Gibney, *A Generation of Sociopaths*.

39   Pooja K. Agarwal and Patrice M. Bain, *Powerful Teaching: Unleash the Science of Learning* (Hoboken, NJ: Jossey-Bass, 2019).

40   Jean Twenge, *iGen: Why Today's Super-Connected Kids Are Growing Up Less Rebellious, More Tolerant, Less Happy—and Completely Unprepared for Adulthood—and What that Means for the Rest of Us* (New York, NY: Atria Books, 2018).

41   Vanessa Solis and Elizabeth Heubeck, "Teachers: Calculate Your Tax-Deductible Expense," *Education Week*, April 3, 2024, https://www.edweek.org/teaching-learning/teachers-calculate-your-tax-deductible-expenses/2024/04

42   Kerr, *The Gift of Global Talent*.

CHAPTER 6

1   Executive Office of the President, Artificial Intelligence, Automation and the Economy, December 2016. https://obamawhitehouse.archives.gov/sites/whitehouse.gov/files/documents/Artificial-Intelligence-Automation-Economy.PDF

2   Michelle Weise, *Long Life Learning*.

3   Bonvillian and[Sarma, *Workforce Education*.

4   Carnevale, *The Merit Myth*.

5   Accenture 2014 College Graduate Employment Survey; www.accenture.com/CollegeGradSurvey.

6   Cappelli, *Why Good People Can't Get Jobs*.

7   Weise, *Long Life Learning*.

8   Weise, *Long Life Learning*.

9   Jim Clifton, *It's the Manager: Moving from Boss to Coach* (Washington, D.C.: Gallup Press, 2019).

10   David Fuller, Bryan Logan, Pollo Suarez, and Aneliya Valkova, "How Retailers Can Attract and Retain Frontline Talent," August 17, 2022. https://www.mckinsey.com/industries/retail/our-insights/

how-retailers-can-attract-and-retain-frontline-talent-amid-the-great-attrition

CHAPTER 7

1   Stern, *Raising the Floor.*

2   Taylor, *Do We Have to Work?*

3   Steve Glaveski, "Where Companies Go Wrong with Learning and Development," *Harvard Business Review*, October 2, 2019. https://hbr.org/2019/10/where-companies-go-wrong-with-learning-and-development

4   Nassim Taleb, *Skin in the Game: Hidden Asymmetries in Daily Life* (New York, NY: Random House, 2018).

5   Ruha Benjamin, *Race After Technology: Abolitionist Tools for the New Jim Code* (Cambridge, UK: Polity, 2019).

6   Bertrand, Marianne, and Sendhil Mullainathan. 2004. "Are Emily and Greg More Employable Than Lakisha and Jamal? A Field Experiment on Labor Market Discrimination." *American Economic Review* 94 (4): 991–1013. DOI: 10.1257/0002828042002561.

7   Horgan, *Lost in Work.*

8   Weise, *Long Life Learning.*

9   Society for Human Resources Employee Benefits Survey, https://www.shrm.org/topics-tools/research/employee-benefits-survey.

10 Dave Jamieson, "Medieval Times Broke The Law By Getting Union's TikTok Account Banned: Feds," HuffPost, August 22, 2023, https://www.huffpost.com/entry/medieval-times-labor-board-complaint-tiktok_n_64e4d74ce4b0947038519e1f

CHAPTER 8

1   Martha Ross, Nicole Bateman, and Alec Friedhoff, "A Closer Look at Low-Wage Workers Across the Country," *Brookings*, March 2020, https://www.brookings.edu/articles/low-wage-workforce/?keyword=low%20wage]

2   Kristof and WuDunn, *Tightrope.*

3   Nicholas D. Kristof and Sheryl Wudunn, "There Are Far Too Many 'Deaths of Despair' in the U.S. How Much Longer Will We Turn Our Backs on This Crisis? *Time*, January 16, 2020, https://time.com/5766180/tightrope-book-excerpt-working-class-america/

4   Lawrence Golden, "Flexibility and Overtime Among Hourly and Salaried Workers," *Economic Policy Institute*, September 30, 2014, http://www.epi.org/publication/flexibility-overtime-hourly-salaried-workers/.

5   McCallum, *Essential*.

6   Bureau of Labor Statistics, "Unemployment Rate Rises to Record High 14.7 Percent in April 2020," *Economics Daily*, May 13, 2020, http://www.bls.gov/opub/ted/2020/unemployment-rate-rises-to-record-high-14-point-7-percent-in-april-2020.htm?view_full.

7   Stern, *Raising the Floor*.

8   Bonvillian and Sarma, *Workforce Education*.

9   Stern, *Raising the Floor*.

10   Martin Ford, *Rise of the Robots: Technology and the Threat of a Jobless Future* (New York, NY: Basic Books, 2016).

11   Graeber, *Bullshit Jobs*.

12   Valerie Wilson and Janelle Jones, "Working Harder or Finding it Harder to Work," *Economic Policy Institute*, February 22, 2018, http://www.epi.org/publication/trends-in-work-hours-and-labor-market-disconnection/.

13   Weise, *Long Life Learning*.

14   Kristof and WuDunn, *Tightrope*.

15   Jamie McCallum, *Worked Over: How Round-the-Clock Work Is Killing the American Dream* (New York, NY: Basic Books, 2020).

16   Susskind, *A World Without Work*.

17   Gina Cummings, "The federal minimum wage hasn't risen in almost 13 years and US workers are paying the price," *CNN Business*, March 22, 2022, https://www.cnn.com/2022/03/22/perspectives/oxfam-federal-minimum-wage/index.html

18   Tami Luhby, "Biden continues to push $15 federal minimum wage," *CNN Politics*, February 17, 2021, https://www.cnn.com/2021/02/17/politics/15-dollar-minimum-wage-biden/index.html

19   Lauren Fox, Ryan Nobles, Manu Raju, and Phil Mattingly, "Senate parliamentarian rules against including minimum wage in Covid relief bill," *CNN Politics*, February 25, 2021, https://www.cnn.com/2021/02/25/politics/minimum-wage-covid-relief-senate-parliamentarian/index.html

20   Yates, *Work Work Work*.

21 Elise Gould and David Cooper, "Seven facts about tipped workers and the tipped minimum wage," Economic Policy Institute, May 31, 2018. https://www.epi.org/blog/seven-facts-about-tipped-workers-and-the-tipped-minimum-wage/

22 Rachel Kurzius, "Here's What Happened After Compass Coffee Eliminated Tips," *DCist*, October 4, 2021, https://dcist.com/story/21/10/04/heres-what-happened-after-compass-coffee-eliminated-tips/

23 Department of Labor: News Release, "U.S. Department of Labor Recovers $1.8m in Back Wages, Damages from New Jersey Supermarkets that Denied Overtime to 226 Workers," *U.S. Department of Labor*, https://www.dol.gov/newsroom/releases/whd/whd20230622

24 Department of Labor: News Release, "Department of Labor Recovers $505k for Mississippi Delta Farmworkers After Dozens of Employers Violated Workers' Rights, Assesses $341k in Penalties," *U.S. Department of Labor*, https://www.dol.gov/newsroom/releases/whd/whd20230628

25 Marianne Levine, "Behind the Minimum Wage Fight, a Sweeping Failure to Enforce the Law," *Politico*, February 18, 2018, http://www.politico.com/story/2018/02/18/minimum-wage-not-enforced-investigation-409644.

26 "Study: Wage Theft Runs Rampant During Recessions," *The Rutgers School of Management and Labor Relations*, September 3, 2020, https://smlr.rutgers.edu/news-events/news-releases/study-wage-theft-runs-rampant-during-recessions

27 Shipler, *The Working Poor.*

28 Josh Bivens and Jori Kandra, "CEO Pay Has Skyrocketed 1,460% Since 1978," Economic Policy Institute, October 4, 2022, https://www.epi.org/publication/ceo-pay-in-2021/

29 Stern, *Raising the Floor.*

30 Keith Payne, *The Broken Ladder: How Inequality Affects the Way We Think, Live, and Die* (New York, NY: Penguin Books, 2018).

31 Payne, *The Broken Ladder.*

32 Chuck Collins, "Updates: Billionaire Wealth, U.S. Job Losses and Pandemic Profiteers," Blogging Our Great Divide, Inequality.org, July 14, 2021, https://inequality.org/great-divide/updates-billionaire-pandemic/.

33 Todd Frankel and Douglas MacMillan, "IRS Records Show Wealthiest Americans, Including Bezos and Musk, Paid Little

in Income Taxes as Share of Wealth, Report Says," *Washington Post*, June 8, 2021, http://www.washingtonpost.com/business/2021/06/08/wealthy-irs-taxes/.

34 AFL-CIO Executive Paywatch, https://aflcio.org/executive-paywatch-0

35 "U.S. Cities with the largest affordable housing shortages," *United Way NCA*, July 20, 2022, https://unitedwaynca.org/blog/affordable-housing-shortages-across-america/

36 Organization for Economic Co-Operation and Development, https://data.oecd.org/benwage/working-hours-needed-to-exit-poverty.htm

37 Michael Lynn and Christopher Boone, "Have Minimum Wage Increases Hurt the Restaurant Industry? The Evidence Says No!", Cornell University eCommons, December 16, 2015, https://ecommons.cornell.edu/items/b00f2cc0-313e-4e49-88cd-1a4dbe52a8c2

38 Center on Budget and Policy Priorities, "Policy Basics: The Earned Income Tax Credit," Center on Budget and Policy Priorities, April 28, 2023, https://www.cbpp.org/research/policy-basics-the-earned-income-tax-credit

39 Moretti, *The New Geography of Jobs.*

40 Kristof and WuDunn, *Tightrope.*

41 Desmond, *Poverty, by America.*

42 Dinesh Puranam, Vrinda Kadiyali, and Vishal Narayan, "The Impact of Increase in Minimum Wages on Consumer Perceptions of Service: A Transformer Model of Online Restaurant Reviews," Inform PubsOnLine, April 25, 2021, https://pubsonline.informs.org/doi/10.1287/mksc.2021.1294

CHAPTER 9

1 Eric Bryanjolfsson, *The Second Machine Age: Work, Progress, and Prosperity in a Time of Brilliant Technologies* (New York NY: W.W. Norton, 2014).

2 Paul Daugherty, *Human+Machine: Reimagining Work in the Age of AI* (Cambridge, MA: Harvard Business Review Press, 2018).

3 Aoun, *Robot Proof.*

4 Daugherty, *Human+Machine.*

5 Kai-Fu Lee, AI Superpowers: China, Silicon Valley, and the New World Order (Boston, MA: Houghton Mifflin, 2018).

6   Suzman, *Work.*

7   Carl Benedikt Frey and Michael A. Osborne, " The Future of Em-
      ployment: How Susceptible are Jobs to Computerisation?" *Oxford
      Martin,* September 17, 2013, https://www.oxfordmartin.ox.ac.uk/
      downloads/academic/The_Future_of_Employment.pdf

8   Jacob Solis, "As more jobs are automated, Las Vegas set to be center
      stage for economic shifts," *The Nevada Independent,* September 29,
      2019, https://thenevadaindependent.com/article/as-more-jobs-are-
      automated-las-vegas-set-to-be-center-stage-for-economic-shifts

9   Pedro Solimano, "40% of Workers Will Need New Job Train-
      ing Due to AI: IBM," Emerge, August 18, 2023, https://decrypt.
      co/152914/40-of-workers-will-need-new-job-training-due-ai-ibm

10   Marina Fang, "Background Actors Sound Off On Alarming AI Fu-
      ture And What's At Stake In The Actors Strike," *HuffPost,* July 14,
      2023, https://www.huffpost.com/entry/sag-actors-strike-ai-back-
      ground-actors_n_64b1b07de4b0ad7b75f2f616

11   Danielle Wiener-Bronner, "AI drive-thrus may be good for
      business. But not for the rest of us," *CNN Business,* June 19, 2023,
      https://www.cnn.com/2023/06/17/business/ai-drive-thru/index.
      html

12   Eric Bryanjolfsson, *The Second Machine Age: Work, Progress, and
      Prosperity in a Time of Brilliant Technologies* (New York NY: W.W.
      Norton, 2014).

13   Amanda Russo, "Recession and Automation Changes Our Fu-
      ture of Work, But There are Jobs Coming, Report Says," *World
      Economic Forum,* October 20, 2020, https://www.weforum.org/
      press/2020/10/recession-and-automation-changes-our-future-of-
      work-but-there-are-jobs-coming-report-says-52c5162fce/

14   Nathan Rennolds, "The $500 million robot pizza startup you nev-
      er heard of has shut down, report says," *Business Insider,* June 3
      2023, https://www.businessinsider.com/robot-pizza-startup-zume-
      shutting-down-raised-500-million-softban-2023-6

15   Brian Heater, "DoorDash bought Chowbotics last year, now it's
      shutting down the salad robot startup," *TechCrunch,* July 11, 2022,
      https://techcrunch.com/2022/07/11/doordash-bought-chowbotics-
      last-year-now-its-shutting-down-the-salad-robot-startup/

16   Geoff Colvin, *Humans are Underrated: What High Achievers Know
      That Brilliant Machines Never Will* New York, NY: Portfolio, 2016).

17   Megan Brenan, "Women, Hourly Workers Less Satisfied With
      Some Job Aspects," *Gallup,* October 4, 2019, https://news.gallup.

com/poll/267206/women-hourly-workers-less-satisfied-job-aspects.aspx

18   Igor Bonifacic, "Amazon was responsible for more than half of all 'serious' US warehouse injuries last year, report finds," *Engadget*, April 12, 2023, https://www.engadget.com/amazon-was-responsible-for-more-than-half-of-all-serious-us-warehouse-injuries-last-year-report-finds-191753314.html#:~:text=Nearly%20two%20years%20after%20Jeff,in%20the%20US%20last%20year.

19   Bernie Sanders, *It's OK to Be Angry About Capitalism* (New York, NY: Crown, 2023).

20   Igor Bonifacic, "Amazon was responsible for more than half of all 'serious' US warehouse injuries last year, report finds," *Engadget*, April 12, 2023, https://www.engadget.com/amazon-was-responsible-for-more-than-half-of-all-serious-us-warehouse-injuries-last-year-report-finds-191753314.html#:~:text=Nearly%20two%20years%20after%20Jeff,in%20the%20US%20last%20year

21   Jason Del Rey, "Leaked Amazon memo warns the company is running out of people to hire," *Vox*, June 17, 2022. https://www.vox.com/recode/23170900/leaked-amazon-memo-warehouses-hiring-shortage

22   Martin Ford, *Rise of the Robots: Technology and the Threat of a Jobless Future* (New York, NY: Basic Books, 2016).

23   Sanders, *It's OK to Be Angry About Capitalism*.

24   Jordan Valinsky, "Trader Joe's says it's not adding self-checkout lines to its stores," *CNN Business*, August 17, 2023, https://www.cnn.com/2023/08/17/business/trader-joe-self-checkouts-cashier/index.html

25   Ruha Benjamin, *Race After Technology: Abolitionist Tools for the New Jim Code* (Cambridge, UK: Polity, 2019).

26   Benjamin, *Race After Technology*.

27   Benjamin, *Race After Technology*.

28   Adrian Daub, *What Tech Calls Thinking: An Inquiry into the Intellectual Bedrock of Silicon Valley* (New York, NY: FSG Originals, 2020).

29   "Uber fares allegedly linked to phone battery levels," The Brussels Times, April 8, 2023, https://www.brusselstimes.com/449143/uber-fares-allegedly-linked-to-phone-battery-levels

30   Dan Schawbel, *Back to Human: How Great Leaders Create Connection in the Age of Isolation* (Lebanon, IN: De Capo Lifelong Books, 2018).

31   Farah Stockman, *American Made.*

32   Executive Office of the President, Artificial Intelligence, Automation and the Economy, December 2016. https://obamawhitehouse.
archives.gov/sites/whitehouse.gov/files/documents/Artificial-Intelligence-Automation-Economy.PDF

CHAPTER 10

1   Alec Ross, *The Industries of the Future* (New York, NY: Simon and Schuster, 2017).

2   Moretti, *The New Geography of Jobs.*

3   Moretti, *The New Geography of Jobs.*

4   Jelisa Castrodale, "Diners Are Tipping Less Than They Did Before the Pandemic, Data Shows," *Food & Wine,* February 28, 2022, http://www.foodandwine.com/news/restaurant-tipping-rates-decline-pandemic

5   Desmond, *Poverty, by America.*

6   Hadi Elzayn et al. "Measuring and Mitigating Racial Disparities in Tax Audits," Stanford Institute for Economic Policy Research (SIEPR) working paper, January 2023. https://siepr.stanford.edu/
publications/working-paper/measuring-and-mitigating-racial-disparities-tax-audits

7   Kennedy, Patrick and Wheeler, Harrison, Neighborhood-Level Investment from the U.S. Opportunity Zone Program: Early Evidence (April 15, 2021). http://dx.doi.org/10.2139/ssrn.4024514

8   Larry McGrath, "CVS Health Presents Strategy for Revolutionizing Consumer Health Experience While Driving Profitable Growth," CVS Health, September 12, 2021, https://investors.cvshealth.com/
investors/newsroom/press-release-details/2021/CVS-Health-Presents-Strategy-for-Revolutionizing-Consumer-Health-Experience-While-Driving-Profitable-Growth/default.aspx

9   Ayana Archie, "CVS and Walgreens agree to pay $10 billion to settle lawsuits linked to opioid sales," *NPR,* December 13, 2022, https://www.npr.org/2022/12/13/1142416718/cvs-walgreens-opioid-crisis-settlement

10   WesleyLife, "20 Stats to Know about Hospice Care in the US," WesleyLife, July 24, 2014, https://www.wesleylife.org/blog/20-stats-to-know-about-hospice-care-in-the-us]

11   Treasury.gov, " Gifts to Reduce the Public Debt," TreasuryDirect, https://treasurydirect.gov/government/public-debt-reports/gifts/

12   Jonathan Cohn, "Boston May Have Cracked The Code On Universal Pre-K," *HuffPost*, July 8, 2023, https://www.huffpost.com/entry/boston-free-universal-pre-k_n_64a7f68be4b03d308d946c76

13   Karen D'Souza, "Universal pre-kindergarten helps women in the workforce, study suggests," *EdSource*, June 8, 2022, https://edsource.org/updates/universal-pre-kindergarten-helps-women-in-the-workforce-study-suggests

14   Jonathan Cohn, "Boston May Have Cracked The Code On Universal Pre-K," HuffPost, July 8, 2023, https://www.huffpost.com/entry/boston-free-universal-pre-k_n_64a7f68be4b03d308d946c76

15   Press release, Hinson Introduces Legislation to Expand Career Advancement Opportunities for Workers, April 1, 2022. https://hinson.house.gov/media/press-releases/hinson-introduces-legislation-expand-career-advancement-opportunities-workers

16   H.R.7365 - Flexibility for Workers Education Act, 117th Congress (2021-2022). https://www.congress.gov/bill/117th-congress/house-bill/7365?s=1&r=6

17   Senator Ted Budd, September 22, 2023; https://www.budd.senate.gov/2023/09/22/budd-introduces-bill-to-cut-red-tape-increase-worker-education-flexibility/

18   Kerr, *The Gift of Global Talent*.

19   Gordon Lafer, *The Job Training Charade* (Ithaca, NY: Cornell University Press, 2004).

20   Lafer, *The Job Training Charade*.

21   Andrew Yang, *The War on Normal People: The Truth About America's Disappearing Jobs and Why Universal Basic Income Is Our Future* (New York, NY: Hachette Books, 2019).

22   Andrew Yang, *The War on Normal People*.

23   Meredith Kolodner and Sarah Butrymowicz, "'Wasted money': How career training companies scoop up federal funds with little oversight," The Hechinger Report, February 25, 2023, https://hechingerreport.org/wasted-money-how-career-training-companies-scoop-up-federal-funds-with-little-oversight/

24   Kerr, *The Gift of Global Talent*.

25   Kerr, *The Gift of Global Talent*.

26   Tierney Sneed, "Why Justice Amy Coney Barrett wrote about babysitters in her student loan opinion," CNN Politics, June 30, 2023, https://www.cnn.com/2023/06/30/politics/amy-coney-barrett-student-loans-babysitter/index.html

27   Alexander Stremitzer, Benjamin M. Chen, and Kevin Tobia, "Would Humans Trust an A.I. Judge? More Easily Than You Think," Slate, February 28, 2023, https://slate.com/news-and-politics/2023/02/chatgpt-law-humans-trust-ai-judges.html

CHAPTER 11

1   Kristof and WuDunn, *Tightrope.*

2   Wendy Sawyer and Peter Wagner, "Mass Incarceration: The Whole Pie 2023," Prison Policy Initiative, March 14, 2023, https://www.prisonpolicy.org/reports/pie2023.html

3   Sawyer and Wagner, "Mass Incarceration: The Whole Pie 2023."

4   Kristof and WuDunn, *Tightrope.*

5   Sawyer and Wagner, "Mass Incarceration: The Whole Pie 2023."

6   Gibney, *A Generation of Sociopaths.*

7   Sawyer and Wagner, "Mass Incarceration: The Whole Pie 2023."

8   "Recidivism." National Institute of Justice, 2023. www.nij.ojp.gov

9   Sawyer and Wagner, "Mass Incarceration: The Whole Pie 2023."

10   Christpher Ingraham, "The U.S. has more jails than colleges. Here's a map of where those prisoners live," *The Washington Post,* January 6, 2015, https://www.washingtonpost.com/news/wonk/wp/2015/01/06/the-u-s-has-more-jails-than-colleges-heres-a-map-of-where-those-prisoners-live/

11   Desmond, *Poverty, by America.*

12   Gibney, *A Generation of Sociopaths.*

13   Valerie Bauman, "Incarceration vs. education: America spends more on its prison system than it does on public schools – and California is the worst," *Daily Mail,* https://www.dailymail.co.uk/news/article-6317783/Incarceration-vs-education-America-spends-prison-does-public-schools.html

14   Daliah Singer, "Inmates are using VR to learn real-world skills," *MIT Technology Review,* April 23, 2023, https://www.technologyreview.com/2023/04/26/1071412/inmates-vr-real-world-skills-incarcerated-instructions/

15   Robert Abare, "Poor job opportunities are a problem both in and out of prison," *Urban Institute,* August 31, 2018, https://www.urban.org/urban-wire/poor-job-opportunities-are-problem-both-and-out-prison

16   Wendy Sawyer and Peter Wagner, "Mass Incarceration: The Whole Pie 2023," *Prison Policy Initiative,* March 14, 2023, https://www.prisonpolicy.org/reports/pie2023.html

17   Jaime Lowe, "The Incarcerated Women Who Fight California's Wildfires," *New York Times,* August 31, 2017. https://www.nytimes.com/2017/08/31/magazine/the-incarcerated-women-who-fight-californias-wildfires.html

18   Jaime Lowe, "What Does California Owe Its Incarcerated," *The Atlantic,* July 27, 2021, Firefighters? https://www.theatlantic.com/politics/archive/2021/07/california-inmate-firefighters/619567/

19   NJRC Videos, "Annual Reentry Conference - Training For The Dignity Of Work," *NJRC Videos,* Apr 6, 2023, https://www.youtube.com/watch?v=l9BiyLN87zE

20   [Bruce Western and Catherine Sirois, "Racial Inequality in Employment and Earnings after Incarceration," *Harvard University,* February 2017, https://scholar.harvard.edu/files/brucewestern/files/racial_inequality_in_employment_and_earnings_after_incarceration.pdf

21   Liz Benecchi, "Recidivism Imprisons American Progress," *Harvard Political Review,* August 8, 2021, https://harvardpolitics.com/recidivism-american-progress/

22   Liz Benecchi, "Recidivism Imprisons American Progress," *Harvard Political Review,* August 8, 2021, https://harvardpolitics.com/recidivism-american-progress/

23   Keith Finlay and Michael Mueller-Smith, "Justice-involved Individuals in the Labor Market since the Great Recession," *U.S. Census Bureau,* September 2021, https://www.census.gov/content/dam/Census/library/working-papers/2021/econ/ADEP-WP-2021-04.pdf

24   "The US states with more places for incarceration than higher education," Studee, 2024, https://studee.com/discover/usa-prison-v-college/

25   Gibney, *A Generation of Sociopaths.*

26   Kristof and WuDunn, *Tightrope.*

27   Robert Abare, "Poor job opportunities are a problem both in and out of prison," Urban Institute, August 31, 2018, https://www.urban.org/urban-wire/poor-job-opportunities-are-problem-both-and-out-prison

CHAPTER 12

1   Areeba Haider, "The Basic Facts About Children in Poverty," The Center for American Progress, January 12, 2021, https://www.americanprogress.org/article/basic-facts-children-poverty/

2   Kristof and WuDunn, *Tightrope*.

3   Desmond, *Poverty, by America*.

4   McCallum, *Worked Over*.

5   Kristof and WuDunn, *Tightrope*.

6   Desmond, *Poverty, by America*.

7   Shipler, *The Working Poor*.

8   Adam Hardy, "Despite Reforms, Overdraft Fees Are Still Plaguing Low-Income Americans," Money, June 05, 2023, https://money.com/overdraft-nsf-fees-low-income-americans/

9   Matthew P. Rabbitt, Laura J. Hales, Michael P. Burke, Alisha Coleman-Jensen, "Household Food Security in the United States in 2022," Economic Research Service, October 2023, https://www.ers.usda.gov/webdocs/publications/107703/err-325.pdf?v=7814.4

10   Yates,Work Work Work.

11   "End Poverty in All Its Forms Everywhere," United Nations, https://unstats.un.org/sdgs/report/2022/goal-01/

12   Virginia Eubanks, *Automating Inequality: How High-Tech Tools Profile, Police, and Punish the Poor* (London, UK: Picador, 2019).

13   Jamie McCallum, *Worked Over: How Round-the-Clock Work Is Killing the American Dream* (New York, NY: Basic Books, 2020).

14   Desmond, *Poverty, by America*.

15   Kristof and WuDunn, *Tightrope*.

16   Dale Russakoff, *The Prize: Who's in Charge of America's Schools* (Boston, MA: Mariner Books, 2016).

17   The White House, "The Anti-Poverty and Income-Boosting Impacts of the Enhanced CTC," *The White House*, November 20, 2023, https://www.whitehouse.gov/cea/written-materials/2023/11/20/the-anti-poverty-and-income-boosting-impacts-of-the-enhanced-ctc/

18   Arthur Delaney, "Joe Manchin Said Constituent Complained Of 'Crackhead Daughter' Wasting Child Tax Credit," *Huff-Post*, Dec 21, 2021, https://www.huffpost.com/entry/joe-manchin-child-tax-credit-drugs_n_61c23de2e4b04b42ab65c2c8

19   Desmond, *Poverty, by America.*

20   Eubanks, *Automating Inequality.*

21   Kristof and WuDunn, *Tightrope.*

22   Moretti, *The New Geography of Jobs.*

23   Jaclyn Peiser, "A D.C. grocery store is removing Tide, Colgate and Advil to deter theft," *The Washington Post*, September 2, 2023, https://www.washingtonpost.com/business/2023/09/02/giant-food-grocery-store-theft/

24   Bridgette Watson, "A B.C. research project gave homeless people $7,500 each — the results were 'beautifully surprising'," *CBC*, October 07, 2020, https://www.cbc.ca/news/canada/british-columbia/new-leaf-project-results-1.5752714

25   Suzman, *Work: A Deep History.*

26   Robert Reich, *The System: Who Rigged It, How We Fix It.*

27   Desmond, *Poverty, by America.*

28   Desmond, *Poverty, by America.*

CHAPTER 13

1   Weise, *Long Life Learning.*

2   Rand Ghayad, "Why skills-first hiring is the solution to the global talent shortage," *World Economic Forum*, April 27, 2023, https://www.weforum.org/agenda/2023/04/growth-summit-2023-why-skills-first-hiring-is-the-solution-to-the-global-talent-shortage/

3   Hunter, John E., Hunter, Ronda F., "Validity and utility of alternative predictors of job performance,"APA Psych Net, https://psycnet.apa.org/record/1984-30168-001

4   "The Skills Advantage Report," LinkedIn, 2022, https://learning.linkedin.com/resources/future-of-skill-building

5   "Census Bureau Releases New Report on Bachelor's Degree Attainment," United States Census Bureau, February 22, 2021, https://www.census.gov/newsroom/press-releases/2021/bachelors-degree-attainment.html

6   Artem Chelovechkov, Rachel Lefkowitz, Benjamin Spar, and Amanda Van Nuys, "2019 Workplace Learning Report," LinkedIn Learning, 2019.

CHAPTER 14

1   Weise, *Long Life Learning*.

2   Peter C. Brown, Henry L. Roediger III, and Mark A. McDaniel, *Make It Stick: The Science of Successful Learning* (Belknap Press: An Imprint of Harvard University Press, 2014).

3   Benedict Carey, *How We Learn: The Surprising Truth About When, Where, and Why It Happens* (New York, NY: Random House, 2015).

4   Sutton-Smith, *The Ambiguity of Play*.

5   Brown, Roediger III, and McDaniel, *Make It Stick*.

6   Weise, *Long Life Learning*.

7   Weise, *Long Life Learning*.

8   Savannah Kuchar, "'The opportunities are gatekept': Coffee shops continue to fall short on diversity," *USA Today*, August 14, 2023, https://www.usatoday.com/story/news/investigations/2023/08/14/coffee-shop-employee-diversity-promises/70547157007/

CHAPTER 15

1   Alec Ross, *The Industries of the Future* (New York, NY: Simon and Schuster, 2017).

2   Martin Ford, *Rise of the Robots: Technology and the Threat of a Jobless Future* (New York, NY: Basic Books, 2016).

3   Brian Sutton-Smith, *The Ambiguity of Play*.

4   Jamie Madigan, *The Engagement Game: Why Your Workplace Culture Should Look More Like a Video Game* (Naperville, IL: Simple Truths, 2020).

5   Kevin Quealy and Josh Katz, "Nike's Fastest Shoes May Give Runners an Even Bigger Advantage Than We Thought," *New York Times*, December 13, 2019, https://www.nytimes.com/interactive/2019/12/13/upshot/nike-vaporfly-next-percent-shoe-estimates.html

CHAPTER 16

1   Charles Vogl, *The Art of Community: 7 Principles of Belonging* (Oakland, CA: Berrett-Koehler Publishers, 2016).

2   Brandon Busteed, "Higher Education's Work Preparation Paradox," *Gallup*, February 25, 2014, https://news.gallup.com/opinion/gallup/173249/higher-education-work-preparation-paradox.aspx

3   William Bonvillian and Sanjay Sarma, *Workforce Education: A New Roadmap* (Cambridge, MA: The MIT Press, 2021).

4   Weise, *Long Life Learning.*

5   McCallum, *Worked Over.*

CHAPTER 17

1   Gallup, State of the Global Workplace.

2   Bill Eckstrom and Sarah Wirth, *The Coaching Effect: What Great Leaders Do to Increase Sales, Enhance Performance, and Sustain Growth* (Austin, TX: Greenleaf Book Group Press, 2019).

3   Eckstrom and Wirth, *The Coaching Effect.*

4   Frederick Winslow Taylor, *The Principles of Scientific Management* (Mineola, NY: Dover Publications, 2017).

5   Yates, *Work, Work, Work.*

6   Geoff Colvin, *Talent is Overrated: What Really Separates World-Class Performers from Everybody Else* (New York, NY: Portfolio, 2010).

7   Peter C. Brown, Henry L. Roediger III, and Mark A. McDaniel, *Make It Stick.*

8   Jake Humphrey, *High Performance: Lessons from the Best on Becoming Your Best* (Cornerstone, 2023).

9   Daniel Goleman, "Leadership That Gets Results," *Harvard Business Review*, March-April 2000. https://hbr.org/2000/03/leadership-that-gets-results

10   Aaron De Smet, Monica Mcgurk, and Marc Vinson, "Unlocking the potential of frontline managers," McKinsey & Company, August 1, 2009, https://www.mckinsey.com/capabilities/people-and-organizational-performance/our-insights/unlocking-the-potential-of-frontline-managers

Podcast Guests in the Book

These guests on 1Huddle's *Bring It In* podcast, hosted by author Sam Caucci, were quoted throughout the book. Check out the full episodes at the links below.

Aozasa, Margueritte (p. 250): https://podcasts.apple.com/us/podcast/110-margueritte-aozasa-head-womens-soccer-coach-at/id1511770027?i=1000623336015

Babb, Kent (p. 318): https://podcasts.apple.com/us/podcast/76-kent-babb-sports-writer-for-the-washington-post/id1511770027?i=1000552013308

Bain, Patrice (p. 270): https://podcasts.apple.com/us/podcast/49-patrice-bain-author-of-powerful-teaching-unleash/id1511770027?i=1000529694582

Baker, Joe (p. 247): https://podcasts.apple.com/us/podcast/97-joe-baker-author-of-the-tyranny-of-talent-how/id1511770027?i=1000604153614

Bonvillian, William B. (p. 88): https://podcasts.apple.com/us/podcast/120-william-b-bonvillian-author-of-workforce/id1511770027?i=1000633599355

Brown, Dr. Jeff (p. 74): https://podcasts.apple.com/us/podcast/101-dr-jeff-brown-harvard-psychologist-psychologist/id1511770027?i=1000612643412

Chrostowski, Brandon (p. 286): https://podcasts.apple.com/us/podcast/104-brandon-chrostowski-james-beard-nominated-chef/id1511770027?i=1000615755778

Lafer, Gordon (p. 134): https://podcasts.apple.com/us/podcast/46-gordon-lafer-author-of-job-training-charade-fmr/id1511770027?i=1000527122261

Lang, Jim (p. 272): https://podcasts.apple.com/us/podcast/89-jim-lang-author-of-small-teaching-everyday/id1511770027?i=1000579201713

LeGrand, Eric (p. 96): https://podcasts.apple.com/us/podcast/19-eric-legrand-renowned-motivational-speaker-sports/id1511770027?i=1000501611084

Lewis, Chequan (p. 260): https://podcasts.apple.com/us/podcast/30-chequan-lewis-chief-equity-officer-at-pizza-hut/id1511770027?i=1000513448176

Lieberman, Nancy (p. 326): https://podcasts.apple.com/us/podcast/25-nancy-lieberman-basketball-hall-of-famer-olympian/id1511770027?i=1000509556658

Lythcott-Haims, Julie (p. 79): https://podcasts.apple.com/us/podcast/35-julie-lythcott-haims-former-dean-at-stanford-university/id1511770027?i=1000516289455

McDaniel, Shadae (p. 329): https://podcasts.apple.com/us/podcast/27-shadae-mcdaniel-vice-president-city-leader-at-all/id1511770027?i=1000511497826

McGraw, Muffet (p. 311): https://podcasts.apple.com/us/podcast/29-muffet-mcgraw-former-head-coach-notre-dame-womens/id1511770027?i=1000512701607

Moffitt, Tommy (p. 315): https://podcasts.apple.com/us/podcast/24-coach-tommy-moffitt-lsu-strength-conditioning-coach/id1511770027?i=1000508226739

Mosley, John (p. 327): https://podcasts.apple.com/us/podcast/73-john-osullivan-author-of-every-moment-matters-how/id1511770027?i=1000549072158

Oakley, Dr. Barbara (p. xx): https://podcasts.apple.com/us/podcast/81-barbara-oakley-author-of-uncommon-sense-teaching/id1511770027?i=1000558190378

O'Sullivan, John (p. 280): https://podcasts.apple.com/us/podcast/73-john-osullivan-author-of-every-moment-matters-how/id1511770027?i=1000549072158

Pahlka, Jennifer (p. 285): https://podcasts.apple.com/us/podcast/129-jennifer-pahlka-author-of-recoding-america-why/id1511770027?i=1000651555792

Quart, Alissa (p. 11): https://podcasts.apple.com/us/podcast/126-alissa-quart-author-of-bootstrapped-liberating/id1511770027?i=1000649076090

Reich, Justin (p. 266): https://podcasts.apple.com/us/podcast/92-justin-reich-associate-professor-at-mit-and-author/id1511770027?i=1000590896533

Rooney, Martin (p. 324): https://podcasts.apple.com/us/podcast/1-ufc-strength-coach-and-author-martin-rooney-on-his/id1511770027?i=1000473665128

Sarma, Sanjay (p. 211): https://podcasts.apple.com/us/podcast/98-sanjay-sarma-professor-at-mit-author-of-grasp/id1511770027?i=1000606510668

Shaefer, Luke (p. 200): https://podcasts.apple.com/us/podcast/65-luke-shaefer-author-of-%242-00-a-day-living-on/id1511770027?i=1000542953487

Shalala, Dr. Donna (p. 264): https://podcasts.apple.com/us/podcast/28-dr-donna-shalala-former-congresswoman-hhs-secretary/id1511770027?i=1000512417414

Smith, Talmon (p. 177): https://podcasts.apple.com/us/podcast/103-talmon-smith-economics-reporter-for-the-new-york/id1511770027?i=1000614022705

Snodgrass, Guy (p. 254): https://podcasts.apple.com/us/podcast/70-guy-snodgrass-topgun-graduate-instructor-author/id1511770027?i=1000546424304

Sterner, Tom (p. 313): https://podcasts.apple.com/us/podcast/38-tom-sterner-bestselling-author-of-the-practicing/id1511770027?i=1000518828276

Ton, Zeynep (p. 110): https://podcasts.apple.com/us/podcast/121-zeynep-ton-author-of-the-case-for-good-jobs/id1511770027?i=1000634780345

Torres, Dara (p. 275): https://podcasts.apple.com/us/podcast/77-dara-torres-12x-olympic-medalist-swimmer-author/id1511770027?i=1000553478194

Vanderbilt, Tom (p. 315): https://podcasts.apple.com/us/podcast/69-tom-vanderbilt-author-of-beginners-the/id1511770027?i=1000545926724

Vogl, Charles (p. 59): https://podcasts.apple.com/us/podcast/107-charles-vogl-author-of-the-international/id1511770027?i=1000618755547

Acknowledgments

I am appreciative of so many that have contributed their experiences or support to this work.

To my coaches and friends who have all made their own unique impact on this project: Soto, Bjorn, Delroy, Martin Rooney, Coach Mark Guandolo, Steve Smith, Michelle Harrolle, Pete Bommarito, Keith Shimon, John Cirilo, Bill Parisi, John Annillo, Jon Beason, Glenn Cook, Karthik Sridhar, Ron Bellamy, Vic Davanzo, Manny Gonzalez, Stephanie Quinones, Natalie Gonzalez, and Paul Sojo.

To so many that I have had the privilege to work alongside: Bri Hernandez, Roger Bernardino, Eddie Jimenez, Dana Safa, Vinnie Renz, Jaime Lara, Oliver Kaczor, Mike Paintner, and Jared Center, as well as hundreds of former team members, interns, and associates.

To an amazing team of software engineers and creatives that inspire me: Rakesh Raju, Dinesh Patil, and the entire 1Huddle team.

To my friends at Apulia in Hoboken, New Jersey, for allowing me to spend countless hours writing from their bar: Frank, Red, and the Apulia team.

To the investors and supporters that have believed: Ivan Marandola, Aziz Hashim, John Teza, Chip Meakam, Dan Borok, 500 Startups, Max Cantor, Slava Rubin, Dimitris Kouvaros, Dan Magy, Mat Focht, Dave Bagley, Andy Berndt, Hilary Slocum, Chris Mossa,

Jack Gibbons, Jeff Carcara, Scott Lawton, Jim Van Stone, Brandi Copeland, Tracy Curtis, Jarred Fajerski, Erica Farage, Mike Finkelstein, Gary Garcia, Mark Geddis, Jorge Gener, Ginger Gilard, Paul Goldstein, Matt Haller, Tonya Harris Cornileus, Scott Hendrickson, Bill Hanni, Jim Kadlecek, Bill Sutton, Don Katz, Justin Kavanaugh, Greg Kish, Kenny Koperda, Anson Kwan, Dorian Langlais, Steve Lantz, Helen Lao, Scott Lawton, Chequan Lewis, Brendan Long, Steve Madonna, Gary Magenta, Brian Martin, Sean O'Brien, Dan Martoe, Jim McGreevey, Dan Meth, Chris Moriarty, Michael Neuner, Brian Quinn, Chris Rodriguez, Hadley Rossitter, Steve Salis, Paul Epstein, Chris Salles, Brandon Sebald, Jason Singh, Jason Smylie, Andy Stern, Rob Sullivan, Scott Taylor, Eddie Tock, Adam Vogel, Seth Wainer, James Walker, James Webb, Jim White, Anthony Valleta, Hagop Giragossian, Jenny Lucas, Jeff Flowers, Bill Pugh, Seth Salzman, Kika Mela, and Roberto Mela.

To Naren and Myles with Amplify Publishing.

To the hundreds of people leaders across thousands of brands that I have had the privilege to work with. It is their energy and dedication that makes me hopeful.

To my family: Lisa Ramirez, Chris Ramirez, Bella Ramirez, Karen Williams, Gloria Bell, Bob Racik, Paul Thomas, and Lyudmila Simonova.

To my daughter Nicolette—I love being your Dad.

And to my wife, Jahmila. I love you.

So many more deserve to be thanked for their impact on myself and this work. However, I find that creating the complete list would still come at the chance of not being complete.

So to all of my family, friends, team, supporters, clients, partners, coaches, and teachers: thank-you.